RIPPLE
EFFECTS

RIPPLE
EFFECTS

discover the

miraculous motivating

power of a woman's

influence

Pam Tebow

TYNDALE
MOMENTUM®

The nonfiction imprint of
Tyndale House Publishers, Inc.

Visit Tyndale online at www.tyndale.com.

Visit Tyndale Momentum online at www.tyndalemomentum.com.

TYNDALE, *Tyndale Momentum*, and Tyndale's quill logo are registered trademarks of Tyndale House Publishers, Inc. The Tyndale Momentum logo is a trademark of Tyndale House Publishers, Inc. Tyndale Momentum is the nonfiction imprint of Tyndale House Publishers, Inc., Carol Stream, Illinois.

Ripple Effects: Discover the Miraculous Motivating Power of a Woman's Influence

Designed by Dean H. Renninger

Edited by Karin Stock Buursma

Published in association with the literary agency of The Fedd Agency, Inc., P.O. Box 341973, Austin, TX 78734.

For information about special discounts for bulk purchases, please contact Tyndale House Publishers at csresponse@tyndale.com, or call 1-800-323-9400.

Library of Congress Cataloging-in-Publication Data
Names: Tebow, Pam, author.
Title: Ripple effects : discover the miraculous motivating power of a woman's influence / Pam Tebow.
Description: Carol Stream, Illinois : Tyndale Momentum, [2019] | Includes bibliographical references.
Identifiers: LCCN 2018047466 | ISBN 9781496431318 (hc)
Subjects: LCSH: Christian women—Religious life. | Christian women—Conduct of life. | Influence (Psychology)—Religious aspects—Christianity.
Classification: LCC BV4527 .T4523 2019 | DDC 248.8/43—dc23 LC record available at https://lccn.loc.gov/2018047466

Printed in the United States of America

25   24   23   22   21   20   19
7   6   5   4   3   2   1

To my wonderful family—my husband, Bob;
our children, Christy, Katie, Robby, Peter, and Timmy;
their spouses; and our sweet grandchildren. You encouraged
me to write, supported my efforts, and provided my best
illustrations. I love you all more than words can express!

CONTENTS

MISSION

PASSION

FOREWORD

The only reason I'm here today is because Mom gave me a chance. Thirty-one years ago, when she was pregnant with me and really sick, a doctor told her I was a mass of fetal tissue. In fact, this doctor strongly recommended that Mom abort me, telling her that if she didn't, she would probably die. But Mom chose to trust God with her life and mine. While you know how that story ended, in this book you'll get to read about the details of what she went through in the process.

Not only did my mom give me a chance at life, but through her example she also gave me a chance to live my best. She cared for me and my four siblings through her love for Jesus. She engrafted the Word of God into our hearts by singing Bible verses to us. She loved us selflessly, even when life was hard. Mom was always encouraging, cheering for me from the sidelines, encouraging me after losses and humbling me after wins. The impact Mom had on me and my brothers and sisters is almost indescribable. No words can adequately express the depth of her love, the power of her example, the strength of her spirit, the beauty of her soul, and her commitment to God in words and in action.

From having the courage to be one of the first parents to homeschool their children, to moving her family with Dad to a mission field in the Philippines, far from the comforts of home, to living out her faith day in and day out as a wife and mother, Mom has shown me what it means to love God and serve others. She is truly one of my biggest heroes. I thank God for her every day.

In the pages that follow, you'll read story after story about how God showed up through Mom's willingness and her leaps, and sometimes tiny steps, of faith. You'll learn about the building blocks of becoming a woman of influence—like realizing the importance of prayer, studying the Bible, using words to uplift others instead of to complain or criticize, trusting God when nothing makes sense, finding strength in spaces of weakness, and above all else, cultivating a deep relationship with Jesus. I am confident that as you read this, you'll be encouraged that God can use you, no matter what season you're in, to affect those around you.

I am so proud of Mom. Seeing how her influence has grown over the years as she's reached countless women through the power of Jesus is awe-inspiring. I don't know God's complete plan for your life, but I do know that He has called you to live an extraordinary life. As Mom has taught us at home and will teach you in this book, it starts by living for Jesus. It starts by realizing life isn't about you. It's about making a difference that will last beyond your life on earth and throughout eternity. If you use whatever God has given you—your experiences, your talents, even just your willingness—and share it with others, you can truly leave ripple effects on this world that will have a lasting impact.

Tim Tebow

INTRODUCTION

When I picked up the phone, the caller introduced herself as a producer from *Good Morning America*. "We would love for you and your son to be our guests on the show," she said.

I was both stunned and honored. Never in a million years could I have envisioned this moment. Not when I was a young pastor's wife trying to make ends meet and keep up with all my responsibilities. Not when family and friends thought I was crazy for having so many kids and then homeschooling them before *homeschool* was a word. Not when I was an anonymous missionary in a place no one had heard of. Not when the baby in my womb and I were both expected to die.

It was 2012, and my youngest son, Timmy (known outside our family as Tim), was playing football for the New York Jets. His Heisman Trophy win in 2007 had pushed him into the national spotlight, and he had made a number of television appearances. But this was the first time I'd been asked to join him in a high-profile interview.

The two *Good Morning America* segments were filmed in Jacksonville, Florida, where I live. *GMA*'s whole production crew came to us. Our four older children and our grandchildren arrived for the second segment, since they were attending Timmy's football game in our hometown that weekend.

Anchor Robin Roberts is delightful and puts everyone at ease. She and Timmy seem to have a special rapport, and I was surprisingly relaxed as I sat beside Timmy on the set. Then Robin asked me about my well-documented pregnancy with my youngest son. In between questions and answers, I flashed back to my experiences of living on the southern Philippine island of Mindanao in the 1980s, when signs of civil war were rampant. While Timmy was joking with Robin about his siblings referring to him as "Timmy the Tumor," I remembered the not-so-funny details: I was told to abort my son because he was a "tumor," and I would likely die if I carried him. But I chose to trust God for my life and the life of the child we had prayed for by name. For most of my pregnancy, I was very sick and had no medical care, while Timmy fought to survive in the womb. Yet, in what the doctor called the biggest miracle he had ever witnessed, we both survived. Our baby boy was malnourished, though, so we asked our family and friends to pray that he would grow big and strong. God answered their prayers—and mine. That big and strong miracle baby was sitting beside me.

Timmy had clued Robin in that she should ask about the necklace I was wearing—one I rarely take off, because it's so meaningful to me. When Timmy got his first real job playing quarterback for the Denver Broncos, it was the first time he received a real paycheck, and it enabled him to buy generous Christmas gifts for everyone in the family. His special gift for me? A beautiful, sparkling diamond key necklace. On national television, my son sweetly shared that I was the "key" to his success. It wasn't because I taught him how to throw a football, but he believed my words, actions, and prayers over the years had an impact, helping to shape him into the man he'd become. I'm so thankful for the privilege of influencing my children!

Through these flashbacks and more, with my children and grandchildren standing in the background, I saw the big picture of influence unveiled before my eyes. Over time, through challenges and setbacks, stretches of monotony and anonymity, we each have the opportunity to positively influence others. Even when we don't realize it.

But my hope is that you will, indeed, realize it. That you will comprehend your God-given opportunities for influence—the ripple effects of how you live your life—and be inspired to influence on purpose.

RIPPLE EFFECTS

Seven pairs of eyes strained with anticipation to see what awaited us at the end of the long private road. It was 1992, and in an implausible "God story," our family had just acquired a home and acreage at a government auction a few days earlier. Even before we unpacked our boxes, our three little boys impatiently begged to explore our property.

It took me a while to understand my male counterparts, especially since our first two children are more like me—females. But by this point in my life, after years of living with a husband and three boys, I wasn't surprised when my little guys' first priority while exploring our new domain was to pick up rocks and throw them. Thankfully, on this occasion, their target was our lake and not each other. (My husband, Bob, refers to the small body of water adjacent to our woods as a pond, but *lake* sounds much classier to me.) Observing the boys' delight at the resulting ripples as they threw one rock after another into the lake, I took advantage of a perfect teachable moment. It's a mom thing!

Long before I discovered numerous inspiring quotes about "ripple effects," I used simple terminology to teach this truth to three impressionable little boys. While I don't recall all the details of the conversation, it probably went something like this: "Just think, if ripples spread out across our lake when you throw your rocks into the water, how do the words you say and the things you do affect the people around you? And then, how do those people affect the people around them?" As the boys continued to toss whatever they could find into the water, we talked about simple examples they could understand. "If you say something unkind to your brother, he will feel bad and might be unkind too. The unkindness spreads. We want to spread good things that honor God rather than bad things that don't." I knew the boys would be tossing things in the lake for years to come, and I hoped the "ripples" lesson would come to mind every time they did.

Years later, I had the opportunity to explain ripple effects to one of our grandsons. Just as his uncles did at his age, he instinctively threw whatever he could find into our pond, causing the fish to duck. "Just as ripples spread out when you throw a rock into our pond, the things you say and do affect the people around you," I told him. My young grandson looked up at me with his big blue eyes, armed with rocks in his bulging pockets. Even if he didn't have a clue about reverberating ripples, his mother would later teach him about the consequences of his words and actions. It's a mom thing!

When our three boys were older, two in college and one in high school, I wrote each of them a letter about the ripple effects of influence. (Although my daughters were already married when I composed the letter to their brothers, and they never felt compelled to throw rocks in the lake, there were many other opportunities while they were growing up to illustrate the ripple effects of how they live their lives.) The original letter is on some prehistoric hard drive buried under outdated paraphernalia in our storage room, and the boys' copies were most likely tossed along with college textbooks they were unable to resell. But even if they no longer have my exact words, I trust they remember our lifelong focus on positive influence reiterated through stories, verses, and visuals during their years in our charge.

In my lost letter to my sons, I illustrated ripple effects with the life of Daniel. One observation that struck me while studying this Old Testament prophet is that positive influence is not about living to please those around us. I have the tendency to be a people pleaser, and my heart ached to think that my people-pleasing ripples might negatively impact my boys. Thus, the goal of my letter was to encourage my sons to be God pleasers. To stand for what is right, even if they stand alone.

As kids, all my children loved the story of Daniel's courage when he was unfairly banished to the lions' den. Like Daniel, every one of us needs courage to face the temptation to compromise and conform to a world that rejects God. Although Daniel lived in a godless culture, he impacted nations, kings, wise men, and his friends by living a life that pleased the Lord. His ripples of influence expanded incrementally, leading to an impact he never could have predicted—one that extends to my family and yours almost three thousand years later.

Our life choices are like rocks tossed into a pond, producing ripple effects that inspire those in our spheres and beyond to think and act differently.

When we reflect God's character through the gifts and opportunities He gives us, we are like rocks tossed into a pond, producing ripple effects that inspire those in our spheres and beyond to think and act differently. My prayer for you is the same as my prayer for myself and the people I love—that we would aspire to this God-sized goal of far-reaching influence.

Those who are wise will shine as bright as the sky, and those who lead many to righteousness will shine like the stars forever.

DANIEL 12:3, NLT

I alone cannot change the world, but I can cast a stone
across the waters to create many ripples.

MOTHER TERESA

CREATED FOR INFLUENCE

Who has the power to impact a decision, inspire a positive action, prompt a helpful change, turn a life (or many) around for the better, and leave an eternal imprint? You do!

You do not have to be famous, rich, or successful. You don't need an impressive degree or lots of followers on social media. A specific age, nationality, or personality is not a requirement, and you're not limited by your job, location, or marital status. You, my friend, have the power to positively influence others.

"How can I ever influence anyone for good?" a young woman called out to me as I was leaving a speaking event.

At that moment, nothing was more important than responding to her question. "Influence" was not my topic that day, but I believe so strongly in a woman's need to make a difference in the lives of others that I intentionally weave it into my messages and conversations. Why is bringing up our potential for influence a priority? Because even the mention of how influence is both our privilege and our purpose seems to stir up a longing that already exists within the heart of every woman.

I was the first person this young woman told about her story, and I listened attentively. She had suffered from a heart-wrenching experience and continued to struggle so much that she wondered how God could use her. We talked and prayed and hugged, and then I encouraged her, saying, "God will use your story to powerfully tell His story." I quickly introduced my new friend to a woman I knew would care for her and stay connected. As I left, I glanced back to see the two women hugging, and I felt free to go. Later that night when

I returned to my hotel, tears formed even before I could slide my key card into the door. I wept out of gratitude for God's love and purpose for the precious girl I had just met—and for His love and purpose for you and me. Like this woman, we all need to know that we are part of a bigger plan. There is more to life than the daily routine; we are created to have an impact that echoes into eternity. God gives us the privilege to positively impact the lives in our spheres of influence and to motivate others to do the same.

You may be like the woman in my brief encounter who doubted her ability for positive influence. Maybe someone who should have encouraged you labeled you "good for nothing," and you've believed their "destined for failure" prediction. You might suffer from a poor self-image, crushing past experiences, or a barricade of overwhelming challenges—maybe some of your own making and others imposed on you through no action of your own. I understand, and I've been there too. I only had a moment of influence with the woman in this story, but for the first time, she understood her potential as I shared, "God uses flawed people like us to impact other flawed people." She got it! All I did was briefly share a biblical idea. Influence is not original with me. It is a contemporary word that expresses a timeless truth.

We are created to have an impact that echoes into eternity.

Our influence is not about whether we are adequate. It's about allowing God to use us and our experiences to leave an eternal imprint on the people we encounter in our lives.

GIRLFRIENDS

"You are just like us!" the spokesperson for the cute group of ladies commented. "We expected you to act like you are on another plane, but we think you are real and down-to-earth and could be our girl-friend. Can we take pictures with you?" It was nearly 11 p.m. when

Julie and her friends approached me. I was tired and hungry. I had arrived at the event before six for a "meet and greet," and I didn't speak until nine. I never eat before I speak; salad would surely stick in my teeth. It seemed as if I had been standing and talking for hours, but their comments perked me up. *They see that I'm just like them? Wow! Thank You, Lord*, I silently prayed.

Julie's reaction is always my goal, but at the huge event in New York City, this Southern girl felt a little out of place. As we talked and took pictures, I forgot all about my growling stomach. I was so encouraged by the response from this group of energetic, talkative young women.

I hope that like Julie and her friends, you think of me as a girlfriend, someone you can identify with. Someone just like you. We may be in different seasons and circumstances, but we are alike in that, in the midst of the challenges of life, we need purpose. A purpose that drives us. I cannot imagine any greater purpose than to have a positive impact on the people in our spheres of influence.

I believe that within the heart of every woman is the desire to be influential. My prayer is that you will be inspired as we uncover and explore the miraculous motivating power of influence women can have on this generation and the next, no matter where we are planted in life. Whether submerged in the trenches of endless diaper changes, climbing up the corporate ladder in stilettos, or serving the "least of these" here or abroad, we can engage our God-given opportunities for positive influence. And I believe that we women have the unparalleled opportunity to influence this generation and those to come.

We all need to know that our lives count. For more than just showing up at work, checking off items on a to-do list, or passing a class. For more than taking a dream vacation, achieving a "steps" goal, or crossing off items on our bucket lists. There is more to life, much more.

In the following chapters, I share stories from my own life as well as from many friends who are living with influence. All of these would have had different outcomes if God had not been involved. He uses ordinary women like you and me to star in extraordinary God stories—real-life narratives of purpose and influence. Although we're all imperfect and inconsistent, we can still be influential because of God's grace. We echo what Jesus said: "Apart from Him, I can do nothing" (see John 15:5). And apart from Him, you would not want to be my girlfriend.

FOUNDATIONS FOR INFLUENCE

For many years, I have had the privilege of encouraging women to use the incredible influence God has given us to eternally impact our world. My goal has been to explain what I believe are the key foundations that equip us for a life of influence and to clarify each point with Scripture, personal stories, and life application.

When I first began to develop my message on influence, I wrestled with constructing an outline. I agonized over the main points, scribbling my thoughts and crumpling pieces of paper as I worked. I love order, but I desired more than just witty organization. Every component needed to line up biblically. To make sense to women in all seasons of life. To fit in an easy-to-remember, take-home outline. To communicate the essentials of influence, not just in words but also in reality. To point women to the God who created us to be influential. In time, six major points on influence evolved: Master, Manual, Prayer, Mindset, Mission, and Passion. If we can do nothing without the Lord, then the key to having positive godly influence is to know Him and be connected to Him. All six of these points reveal how to increase our influence by drawing closer to God and allowing Him to change us and use us to impact those we come in contact with. We'll look at each of the six in more detail in the chapters to come.

In my quest for a short phrase to clarify the significance of influence, I repeated the first letters of each of my points over and over: *MMP, MMP.* In an unexpected burst of inspiration, I came up with a catchphrase based on this simple acronym that to me defines positive influence: *miraculous motivating power.* By God's grace, our positive influence has the potential to motivate others to do the right thing, make good choices, and—most important—seek Him. Whether or not we see results from our efforts, the Lord gives us the privilege to be part of the life-impacting process, which really is miraculous motivating power.

Ready or not, I began to speak on influence. As humbling as critiques can be, I welcomed constructive feedback, because from day one, it was essential to constantly improve my message—and it still is. In order for my life and my influence to change for the better, I must be a lifelong learner.

Years ago, a local television reporter, armed with a camera and microphone, cornered me as I walked into the Jacksonville convention center. He noted that I was the speaker for the main event later that day, but he questioned why I arrived hours early to attend other sessions. Then, without seeking permission for an interview, he positioned the microphone next to my lips and asked why I would bother to hear other speakers. My response to random questions is not normally quick or impressive. In this instance, however, my daughter Christy had called minutes before I entered the building and shared a quote from her favorite grad school professor, Dr. Howard Hendricks. I echoed his words as I replied, "I want to continually learn, so that I can be a fresh, flowing stream rather than a stagnant pool." A few friends who happened to tune in to the news that night commented on my "eloquent" remarks. I readily shared the humorous backstory with them as well as with the group I spoke to later that day. It made for a great introduction and a good laugh.

Although I am not as articulate as Dr. Hendricks, I agree with his premise. In my own words, continual learning really is a goal for my message and my life. You are smart women, so you get my point: I have only learned a fraction of what there is to know about our potential for life-impacting influence, but I'm grateful for the privilege to share what I have learned thus far with you!

Thank you for investing your time to read this book. My sincere prayer is that God will encourage you as only He can do, and that He will use you to impact countless lives for eternity with your miraculous motivating power of influence.

May He grant you according to your heart's desire, and
fulfill all your purpose.
PSALM 20:4, NKJV

Chapter 1

FINDING OUR PURPOSE

You may think that only a high-profile person can be influential, but as John Maxwell wrote, "If your life in any way connects with other people, you are an influencer."[1] And influence spreads. Whether it's your children, your husband, coworkers, or people you interact with at the grocery store, gym, school, church, office, or PTA, you have the potential to inspire those around you in a positive, life-giving, and God-glorifying way. Why? Because people are always watching us.

My youngest son discovered this truth when he was in high school. One afternoon, I picked him up after football practice, and on the way home we stopped at a nearby store. Timmy walked beside me as I pushed the red shopping cart up and down bright aisles. My eyes bounced from the grocery list to the white labels on the edges of the shelves, looking for evidence of a sale.

With a strong desire to be the best possible athlete, Timmy has always been nutrition conscious. And, like his mother, he has always been frugal. As we strolled down the cereal aisle, my focus still attuned to markdowns and clearance items, I noticed my son grab something from a shelf. With a sheepish look on his face, he tossed a brown box with three colorful elves on it into the cart. It happened to be selling at a super-low price.

When we rounded the corner, a father and his son passed by. The boy, a kindergartener at the school near where Timmy played football, recognized my son. He stopped and stared for a minute, his eyes bulging out of his head like a cartoon character's. I didn't know it at the time, but the boy snuck a peek at our shopping cart before he took off with his dad toward the other end of the aisle.

The very next day, this little boy stood up in front of his kindergarten class during show-and-tell. Holding up a box of Cocoa Krispies, he said, "*This* is the cereal Tim Tebow eats for breakfast!"

Well, it didn't take long for my phone to start blowing up with texts and calls from annoyed parents thanking me—sarcastically, of course—for influencing their kids to demand Cocoa Krispies for breakfast. In typical mom fashion, I used the Cocoa Krispies experience to teach Timmy about his potential for influence. I reminded him of the picture that hung in the bedroom he shared with his brother. A young boy in an oversize football jersey holds a football under his arm as he watches a group of high school–age boys studying the Bible under a nearby tree. The picture, printed by the Fellowship of Christian Athletes, is entitled "Influence."

Timmy and I both enjoy poetry, so I was thrilled to find the perfect poem to accompany the picture, and I placed them together in a frame. This visual duo has traveled with him to every dorm room and city where he has played ball.

There are little eyes upon you,
And they're watching night and day;
There are little ears that quickly

Take in every word you say;
There are little hands all eager
To do anything you do;
And a little boy who's dreaming
Of the day he'll be like you.

You're the little fellow's idol;
You're the wisest of the wise;
In his little mind about you
No suspicions ever rise;
He believes in you devoutly,
Holds that all you say and do,
He will say and do in your way
When he's grown up just like you. . . .

There's a wide-eyed little fellow
Who believes you're always right,
And his ears are always open
And he watches day and night;
You are setting an example
Every day in all you do,
For the little boy who's waiting
To grow up to be like you.

EDGAR GUEST, "HIS EXAMPLE"

This memorable poem served to remind Timmy that he is accountable to positively influence those little boys, and others, whose eyes are on him. Even at his young age, he understood that having influence also meant he had a purpose more life-impacting than winning football games. Whether we are fifteen or eighty, eyes are also on us. Our children watch and mimic us. Our neighbors, coworkers, church members, classmates, friends, relatives, and more observe us. What will they see? Because people are watching us, we must be intentional about the way we live if our purpose is positive influence.

INFLUENCE ON PURPOSE

When we know in our minds and believe in our hearts that God created us for a significant purpose, we are inspired to live differently. We need a purpose bigger than ourselves, one that gives meaning to the mundane tasks of life. A purpose so big that it is worth all the effort required to love and train one or many kids, work on our marriages, get to know neighbors, give our best to the job, prioritize our education, invest in grandchildren, serve at church, or volunteer time and give generously to worthwhile causes.

Because people are watching us, we must be intentional about the way we live.

An important purpose changes everything! It not only motivates us but also has the potential to make an eternal difference in the lives of the people we connect with.

I was in the midst of writing about this subject when I met friends for breakfast before I flew home from a speaking event in Oklahoma. Months earlier, I had spoken at the kickoff for a new pregnancy center in that city. Although this couple had been unable to attend the fund-raiser, I'd told them all about the center director. Her strong courage and faith reminded me of my husband's, but she lacked experience. The young woman and her ministry remained on my mind and on my prayer list long after the kickoff event was over.

My friends had experience working with nonprofits. The husband had run hospitals for years and had served on the boards of pregnancy centers, while his beautiful wife was gifted with creative and practical skills and had a genuine love for others. They also had some time on their hands as they tried to adapt to their new life as retirees. I knew they could be a wonderful resource, so I tried to connect them with the young director. When my first attempt failed, I debated whether to try again. But I sensed God was involved, so I made another effort. A special relationship resulted, and I received multiple texts of gratitude from everyone involved. The director had the passion and determination required for her job, but she needed my friends' wisdom and experience on her board. And the relationship wasn't one-sided; the retired couple also had a very real need that was fulfilled by their union.

As we enjoyed breakfast that morning, several months after I helped them connect, my friends shared details of their involvement with the pregnancy center. Then, as the waitress cleared the table, the husband paused, looked directly at me, and sincerely thanked me for giving them what they had lacked in their current situation: "God-ordained purpose."

My friends dropped me off at the airport to fly home, and I went straight to the restroom to check my mascara. As I pondered yet another God story, I couldn't stop the tears. For my friends, having a significant purpose gave their lives new meaning, erasing the ho-hum, let's-just-get-through-the-day attitude they'd been fighting since they'd moved. Retirement means that paychecks quit coming, but none of us really plan to retire from having purpose in our lives. Intentional purpose charged my friends' batteries and brought them joy. A few weeks later, I received the Christmas letter they sent to their friends and family. I smiled as I read the middle paragraph: "My friend Pam Tebow spoke at the opening banquet for the new pregnancy center. Long story very short, we were asked to be on their board. Way too much to tell, just know we're so excited to be part of what God is doing in these lives."

God gives us abilities for a purpose, and He weaves our abilities with His purpose into opportunities for meaningful influence. In other words, miraculous motivating power! God is the author of incredible stories. He wrote this one for my friends, and we can trust Him to write stories of purpose and influence for us, too.

In our Sunday newspaper, I was surprised to find an article reprinted from the *Chicago Tribune* on the importance of purpose: "A job's meaningfulness—a sense that the work has a broader *purpose*—is consistently and overwhelmingly ranked by employees as one of the most important factors driving job satisfaction. It's the linchpin of qualities that make for a valuable employee: motivation, job performance and a desire to show up and stay."[2]

The same article cites a study published in 2012 in the *Journal of Career Assessment*. According to research, the primary reason people skip work is not because they intend to quit or aren't satisfied with the job. It's because they find the work meaningless.[3]

Purpose makes a difference not just in a job but in all of life's activities. It prevents us from slowing down, giving up, or opting out, even when we face daunting challenges. Purpose rearranges our goals, mindsets, countenances, to-do lists, speech, and more. When we truly understand the power of our influence, like my son Timmy did when he was in high school, we understand that our purpose is to impact the lives of the people who are watching us. A significant purpose energizes us. It transforms our work ethic, inspires creativity, and wakes us up with more to look forward to than a cup of coffee. Like my retired friends, we are motivated to love, serve, give, pray, and keep on keeping on until our heads touch the pillow, encouraged to do it all over again tomorrow. How we live our lives matters—especially if we recognize our God-given purpose to use the influence He gives us!

DISCOVERING OUR PURPOSE

Do you have purpose? Have you identified people around you who might benefit from your influence? For some of you, your purpose and your audience are obvious. A baby is crying in the next room.

Your students await tomorrow's lecture. You serve preemies and their anxious parents as a pediatric nurse in the NICU. You care for an elderly parent who often forgets your name. I have close friends in each of these situations, and their purpose is apparent to them and to those they influence.

Or you may be overwhelmed with too many tasks and people you're responsible for, making it hard to hone in on one area of purpose. You are nodding your head in agreement if you are a working mom, one who returned to school, one who homeschools her kids, or any woman who wears more than one hat. I have been there and done that, and you may be there now! In a later chapter, I share how I survived that challenging season, one that stretched my faith and prepared me for greater influence.

For others, your season of life has changed. Your kids grew up. You retired from your job. You are no longer married. Health issues limit your activity. You may wonder who you can influence in these new circumstances. My friends in these situations are seeking new purposes or revised versions of their former ones.

Or you may be like my mom. She didn't think she had purpose. For most of her life, she believed the lie that she wasn't capable of influence, because the influential people in her life enslaved her with doubts about her self-worth. Even when she began to attend church and Bible study later in life, her fears and doubts quickly stamped out any sparks of truth and purpose—until she turned seventy.

To celebrate my mother's seventieth birthday, my two daughters and I planned a special luncheon at the charming women's club where she was an active member. We sent out hand-engraved invitations, purchased decorations and ingredients for our lunch menu, and traveled several hours to her home. Our plan was to arrive early to prepare lunch, decorate, and tend to all the other details, but the Lord had a bigger plan.

While I was busy with food prep in my mom's kitchen, I could hear my daughters talking to their grandmother about her involvement in various organizations. Mom lamented because, although she was busy, there seemed to be no point to all of her activities. She wondered if her life mattered. I listened and prayed as the girls encouraged her with ways she might make an impact on the groups she belonged to. One daughter suggested inserting a section for prayer requests in the club newsletter, since Mom was in charge of the club's member relations. And because she enjoyed sending cards to her grandchildren for every occasion, my other daughter suggested she send cards with handwritten notes to the club members who had birthdays, were sick, or had lost loved ones. And she could even add applicable Bible verses. Mom perked up!

Within a few months, both ideas resulted in significant influence. The prayer list became a staple in the newsletter, and club members were enlisted to pray. Then women began to share answers to their prayers, which inspired more women to ask for prayer. In an obvious God story, Mom's sophisticated, secular club eventually set aside a specific time each month for women to share how their prayers were answered. And the many cards Mom wrote to encourage members paved the way for meaningful conversations. Some of the ladies even joined Mom's Bible study. A few years later, my mother, who was once shy about discussing faith matters, began to leave little gospel tracts in the places she frequented. Members of another club she belonged to voted for her to be their chaplain, and she often discussed with me the devotions she was working on for her meetings. Mom's joy and fulfillment were evident during our regular phone calls, as she updated me on what she called her "ministry." It really was influential!

Purpose changed my mother. Our infinite, creative God wove together her opportunities, her personality, her gifting, and her season in life into a tailor-made way for her to significantly influence others. She had purpose, which eventually enabled her to believe that her life counted. Mom proved that it's never too late to discover our purpose, and she always insisted she found hers that day as we prepared for her seventieth birthday party.

While we were cleaning up after that party, she shared through her happy tears that it was the first birthday party she ever had. I did not, however, want it to be her last. We celebrated Mom's eightieth birthday with another party. My daughters couldn't make the trip because by then they were busy with families of their own. What a special occasion it was, though, with many sweet ladies attending the birthday luncheon. This time, a restaurant did all the work, while each of Mom's friends shared what my mother meant to her. I thought my heart would burst as I listened to stories of her influence on each of their lives. In my mom's words, her influence began when she turned seventy. In my words, it continued long after she went to heaven at eighty-six.

Mary's Influence on Purpose

I refer to Mary as my "alterations lady," but she is so much more. Mary is seventy-six, and she has loved and cared for the babies in our church nursery for more than forty years. Parents are able to enjoy the worship service because their little ones are safe in Mary's tender care. She understands that her service is influential, even though she doesn't receive a salary and churchgoers without babies probably don't know her name. A paycheck and accolades do not motivate Mary. Her purpose does.

Mary also does alterations, as you probably guessed from her nickname. Her dear husband of fifty years passed away about six years ago. She could retire and take it easy, but Mary continues to work. Why? Because her other driving purpose is to love on all the people God sends to her with their alterations. Over the years, Mary has led more people than she can count to a relationship with Christ. For those who visit the sewing room in her garage, Mary is often the only person in their lives who will listen, care about a health issue or a family problem, inquire about their relationship with the Lord, or offer advice when needed. She keeps her Bible near her sewing machine so she is ready for the people God brings her way. She is always busy. There is a bench outside her sewing room where customers wait their turn, and it is worth the wait.

Mary prays for the Lord to keep her mind sharp so she can continue to alter clothes—not for the income, but for her ministry. She is driven by her purpose to love lonely, hurting people. Mary's purpose has yielded positive influence for more than half a century! I'm glad when I have a dress that requires altering, because it means that I can listen to some of Mary's stories. My husband, who, like Mary, is passionate about the gospel, thinks she is one of the coolest people he knows. Even he does not mind waiting for an alteration or two.

Cristin's Influence on Purpose

Cristin is decades younger than Mary, but her purpose drives her, too. Cristin served as my hostess when I spoke at a women's conference, and I was immediately drawn to her joy. From her positive outlook and sweet spirit, one would assume all was right in her world. Years before, however, she suffered the consequences of an abusive homelife as a child and again as a young wife and mother. Instead of throwing a pity party when she became a single mom, Cristin turned her focus away from her challenges with a purpose to serve and encourage other struggling single moms with theirs. In her words, "God would give me a purpose through all the pain and abuse I had lived through." She started a support group and created a website for the single moms in her community. And Cristin organized and raised funds to treat every interested single mom in her area to a free event she calls Dare to Dream, a Saturday of fun, food, speakers, lovely gifts, and activities for children of every age. Cristin is a woman of purpose and influence who shares, "I want to use every last bit of my story for His glory!"

Every woman needs purpose. We have the privilege and responsibility to use our God-given gifts and opportunities to influence this generation and those to come. A purpose this big changes us from the inside out. The result: We will overflow with purpose, joy, and gratitude, because our mighty God uses our influence to impact people—for all eternity!

We have the privilege and responsibility to use our God-given gifts and opportunities to influence this generation and those to come.

BIG PURPOSE, BIG IMPACT

The streaks of orange and blue lit up the harbor in the early morning light. From the hotel balcony, I watched the sunrise on Plymouth Harbor, trying to imagine how the Pilgrims felt when their ship neared this historic coast in 1620. The voyage from England had been incredibly long and difficult, yet they anchored offshore. Why would 102 men, women, and children, who had lived in the hold of the ship for months, not use what energy they could muster to make landing the priority? My husband, the history buff, explained that the *Mayflower* anchored offshore while its passengers debated the rules their settlement would follow. The sea-weary Pilgrims spent one more week aboard ship while they wrote the Mayflower Compact, their guidelines for living in the New World. The enormity of their future influence was considered before a single Pilgrim's foot stepped onto Plymouth Rock.

These courageous men and women made a covenant "in the presence of God and one of another" to join together "for [their] better ordering and preservation." Looking ahead to life beyond their ship, they determined to write, enact, and obey whatever laws were needed for "the general good of the colony." The group's stated purpose in settling this land was "For the glory of God, and advancement of the Christian faith."[4]

To say that the Pilgrims were influential is an understatement. Many historians believe that the Mayflower Compact influenced the Declaration of Independence and the US Constitution. The Pilgrims' purpose to honor God in both their public and their private lives had a long-range influence on future generations of Americans.

What a lesson about influence for us! My husband and I did not come from Christian homes, and neither did most of our close friends. We weren't privy to any secrets for a successful family, so we asked questions. Observed people we admired. Read recommended books. We did not have a "Tebow Compact" or anything close, but we thought a lot about the importance of our future influence. Even though we were not nearly as mature or forward-thinking as we thought we were, God gave us the grace to realize that generations would be impacted by our present choices.

Years later, when Bob and I were speaking together in Boston, we chose to take an extra day to see nearby Plymouth, nearly four hundred years after the Pilgrims anchored in the harbor. During our brief visit, we explored the small historic community, hoping to find evidence of their spiritual influence. Not one of the promotional brochures in the small visitor center made any reference to God. The lovely old church founded by the Pilgrims was now a museum. Our hotel, one block away from where the Pilgrims landed, was the first hotel I ever stayed in that didn't have a Bible in the bedside drawer.

Even if modern historians attempt to negate the long-range spiritual impact the Pilgrims had on America, their courageous determination to influence on purpose still lives on in our laws, our churches, and our lives. The Pilgrims took their influence seriously, and because of that they set the tone for the rest of our American history. The Pilgrims set sail to further the "advancement of the Christian faith" in a new home. Like the Pilgrims, we can purpose to influence future generations by the intentional way we live now.

How does such a lofty goal become reality? Perhaps we start by thinking through what we believe. Are we willing to lay aside lesser goals in order to advance the glory of God? Should we think through our own versions of a Mayflower Compact? What would that look like? It could be active involvement in a local church. Reading the Bible as a family. Setting aside funds for local and foreign missions. Praying for our officials. Establishing family traditions to build strong bonds and keep members connected during the challenges of life. Serving people in our communities. Promoting character in our homes, schools, and workplaces. We may not spend a week in the hold of a ship or the basements of our homes to formulate a plan of action, but our personal and corporate accountability is worth contemplating.

This true story of the courageous Pilgrims should inspire us to take our potential for influence seriously. To pass on to our children values, beliefs, standards, morals, and ethics we hope they will pass on to theirs. One of my favorite Scripture prayers is Deuteronomy 30:6: "The LORD your God will circumcise your heart and the heart of your descendants, to love the LORD your God with all your heart and with all your soul, so that you may live." After my history lesson on the Pilgrims, I'm more determined than ever to pray that our family's influence will be long-range, impacting generations to come.

In 2020, the *Mayflower II*, a restored replica of the Pilgrims' ship, will sail into Plymouth Harbor. A $7.5-million makeover has been in the works, preparing the ship for festivities marking the four hundredth anniversary of the Pilgrim landing. There will be media attention and fans awaiting the ship's anticipated arrival. I hope there will also be mention of the Pilgrims' determination to influence their new world on purpose.

MASTER

What is the first step we take
to touch a life in our sphere
to initiate a ripple of positive influence
to impact our world for the better?

We need to meet our Master.

The first *M* in the miraculous motivating power of influence is *Master*. When I attempted to have influence apart from Him, I exalted self by trying to impress others. But when I began to grow in my relationship with my Master, for the first time, I experienced positive influence. And I never want to get over the joy that God can use me—and He can use you—for His purposes. We are transformed when we know the Lord and learn to trust Him. When people in our spheres witness the difference Christ makes in our lives, they are intrigued to learn more, and we have life-impacting influence.

Although we are tempted to search for other masters, God is the only One who is worthy ("I, even I, am the LORD, and there is no savior besides Me" [Isaiah 43:11]). He has the perfect Master plan, to give us "a future and a hope" (Jeremiah 29:11). Our choice to give Him the rightful place as Master is daily, even moment by moment. We face an ongoing battle for the right to rule our lives, but we will miss out on opportunities, blessings, and positive influence when we run our own lives or choose any other master but the Lord.

God's love drew me to Him initially and continually draws me. He knows everything about me—and you—and yet He loves us anyway. He loves us so much that He sacrificed His own Son, so that we could enjoy a personal relationship with Him and have real life now and for eternity. What love! The greatest influence we will ever have is to tell others about our wonderful Master and His unconditional love. God's love will have ripple effects for all eternity.

> On His robe and on His thigh He has
> a name written, "KING OF KINGS,
> AND LORD OF LORDS."
> REVELATION 19:16

Chapter 2

A MASTER PLAN

Recently I discovered a box of old papers—really old, yellowed, crinkled ones. Memories from my childhood. A poem I wrote about my dog. A birthday card from my mother. A postcard from a family vacation. Instead of excitement over my discovery, I felt disappointment that the tangible tokens and faint memories of my early years were void of spiritual significance. I couldn't find even one reference to God, a Bible story, church, or faith.

No such memories existed, because there was virtually no spiritual influence on my young life. At least none that I can remember. That changed one Sunday in the spring when I was twelve. My dad was playing golf as he always did on Sunday. My mom slept in. I woke up my eight-year-old sister, and we walked to church.

MY STORY BEGINS

For years I tried to jog my memory to figure out how I even knew about this church. Then, in what seemed like an old movie playing in my mind, I remembered my cousins getting dressed up for Easter. The two girls were four or five years older than me, and I idolized them for their fashion flair and cool talk. Their family was visiting us in Charleston, where we lived for two years. My parents impressed our relatives with an Easter egg hunt and a home-cooked meal, with church sandwiched in between.

That's how I knew the church was close, maybe only a mile away. My sister and I probably held hands as we walked to church that day. Life was different then, and it was safe for two kids to venture out alone on a main street. I can't recall the surroundings. But as if it were yesterday, I remember hearing for the first time in my life that God loved me. The preacher that Sunday morning explained the gospel clearly enough that a twelve-year-old girl could understand it. I'm so grateful the message of salvation is simple: God loves us so much that He sent His only Son, Jesus, to be born in a manger. To live as a man. To die a horrible death on the cross, even though He never sinned and didn't deserve to die. He did it for us, to pay for our sins and the sins of the whole world. He loves us that much! Three days later, He rose from the grave. He lives in heaven, where we will go when we die if we have a relationship with Him.

When the preacher spoke about sins, I knew that I was a sinner, in need of a Savior. I felt as if he were talking to me. When he said that all anyone had to do to enter into a personal relationship with Jesus was believe, I did believe—with the faith of a child. I was a child. Everyone who made the decision to trust Christ that day was invited to come up to the front of the church. I still marvel that I walked up all by myself. I didn't know one person in the church except my sister. I told whoever counseled me that I had just prayed that prayer along with the preacher. At home, I often said a singsong blessing before meals, but this prayer was different. I knew I was speaking to God.

Friendly people shook my hand and greeted me. Then my sister and I walked home.

I looked the same. I sounded the same. I even acted the same. But I would never be the same again. I had met my Master.

Well-meaning people from the church visited our home and gave me a Bible, but my parents were offended because they didn't know anything about my decision. They never let me return to that church, and life seemed to go on the same as before.

At the time, I didn't realize the impact of my decision; yet my eternity was settled forever in heaven. The Holy Spirit lived inside me. I wouldn't understand His presence until much later, but the fact that He took up residence in my life impacted me more than I will ever know in this life. My parents rarely discussed or warned me of the many pitfalls of youth, yet somehow I couldn't bring myself to do the crazy teenage things I observed others doing. Of course I was tempted. I made mistakes. I told lies. I had a sin nature. But the Spirit of God was real, even though I didn't comprehend His influence. He protected me. I had a conscience, and I grasped right and wrong.

I choke up every time I recall my story. There are no odds to explain it. All I knew was that God loved me enough to send His Son, Jesus, to die for me, but that was enough. I did nothing to deserve His love. It is unconditional. Nothing compares to that love. Nothing.

THE NEXT STEP

When I entered the University of Florida at age seventeen, I had met my Master, but I sure didn't comprehend much about my relationship with Him. Even then, however, I had a desire to be influential.

As a vain, self-centered coed, my idea of influence was to obtain an impressive résumé, which I systematically set out to acquire. My life was all about me, but somehow I knew it was meant to be more about God. How did that work? I had no clue!

One morning in the fall of my sophomore year, my roommate came home from her early class with a copy of the school newspaper. "You might want to take a look at this," she said as she flung the *Alligator* on my bed. When I caught a glimpse of the front page, I was struck by how superficial the girl in the photo seemed. That girl was me, posing for one of my campus activities.

I was searching for influence and significance through all my busyness, and I'd found it—in a way. But what I was really demonstrating was that the way to get ahead in life, at least in college life, was to exalt self. Campus involvement is commendable, but my motives were mostly selfish. My worth was centered on who I could impress and what I could achieve in my sphere of influence. I felt so confused and empty, and I reasoned that my many activities would fill the void. But instead, I questioned my purpose and my relationship with a God I barely knew. This sort of influence was obviously not fulfilling.

I found a poem that accurately described my life at the time:

I lived for myself,
I thought for myself.
For myself,
And no one beside.
Just as if Jesus never lived,
As if He had never died.

Upset, I skipped class that day. I didn't want to be either the girl in the poem or the one on the front page of the paper. Even though prayer was not a concept I fully understood, I was desperate enough to try praying. I really wanted to change, but I knew from previous failed efforts that I couldn't change myself. So I sank to my knees on the floor of my little room in the sorority house and cried out to God for help.

He heard me. God always hears us. Before I even stood up, there was a knock on my door. I opened it to find a sorority sister and her friend, who were inviting girls to a Bible study on campus. I motioned for them to come in. We talked, and I cried. They seemed to care. I knew God was involved; He had heard my cry for help and answered so quickly. *God must really love me*, I reasoned. I circled the day on the calendar, because I knew I would never be the same. I never was.

MY FIRST GLIMPSE OF INFLUENCE

The next week, I attended the Bible study the two girls invited me to. I learned a little bit, and then I returned the following week to learn more. I couldn't keep the amazing new truths to myself. Every week from then on, I taught the little bit I had just learned to a few of the girls who lived in my sorority house. And after a while, the most amazing thing transpired: We all began to grow in our relationships with the Lord and each other. For the very first time in my life, I felt as if I had purpose and significance. Why? I had positive influence! My life counted. Every other endeavor paled in comparison to investing in the lives of those girls. To write that it was worth the time and effort is an understatement. It was the most fulfilling opportunity of my young life!

After I asked Jesus to be my Savior at age twelve, nothing on the outside seemed to change. But this time was different. It took a while, but even people I didn't know well began to comment on the difference in me. There was a lot that needed to be changed. There still is. I'm so grateful that God is in the life-changing business!

That year, my friends and I grew in our faith, our understanding of the Bible, and our prayer lives. The few of us who gathered every week began to pray for the new girls who would join us the next year. One of those girls whom we didn't know yet but we prayed would join us, is now my dearest friend! I can still picture Nancy sitting on the edge of my bed crying—I can't remember why. I asked her if she was sure she had a relationship with Jesus. She wasn't. I had never led anyone to Christ, and I didn't want to mess it up. This was too important. I had a copy of *Four Spiritual Laws* from Campus Crusade (now Cru), and Nancy and I read it together page by page. When we got to the end, I asked her if she would like to pray to ask Jesus to be her Savior. She did, and we read the prayer together. She met her Master that day. She will never be the same either.

Influence does not end with the person whose life we have the privilege to impact. God takes our small offerings and multiplies them. I only knew a verse or two in my Bible, but I learned some truths and taught them to the girls who lived around me. The next year, some of the girls I taught started groups of their own. They wanted in on influence. (Some refer to this kind of influence as *discipleship*.)

God takes our small offerings and multiplies them.

Many years later, the girls in those Bible studies met for a reunion. I was the old lady in the group, but what a happy old lady! In fact, *happy* doesn't adequately describe my overflowing heart. I had the privilege of meeting many of the girls who were influenced by the Bible studies after I graduated. One woman, Donna, has since become a good friend. We met for the first time at that reunion, and I found out that she was influenced by a girl who was influenced by a girl who was influenced by a girl in our original little group. Ripple effects! Several times during the weekend I had trouble composing myself. I was so overcome and thankful that God allowed me, in a small way, to be involved in His big plan for these women.

THE CIRCLE OF INFLUENCE

As a freshman, my husband, Bob, and two of his friends started a chapter of Campus Crusade for Christ on our campus. In order to train students who came to Christ, Bob and his friends taught a Bible study—the same Bible study the two girls invited me to attend after I prayed for help. The Bible study where I learned truths about my Master—truths that I excitedly shared with the girls who lived in my sorority house and that changed our lives forever. God writes the best stories!

But our love story had a strange beginning. One day my freshman year, I was on my way to class when I heard someone call out to me from inside a rather large refrigerator box. I later learned that the crazy guy in the box was Bob, and the crazy guy leading him around by a rope was his friend Joe. They were advertising for a Christian speaker who was coming to campus. Although they were cute, my first impression was that they were religious fanatics. I was right!

Bob and I recently attended a fiftieth reunion celebrating what God did through the years in the lives of countless college students and even professors who came to know their Master through the group Bob helped to start. Two years after the first meeting, I became involved. Years later, our children were also impacted. Our son Peter was a student leader and then stayed at UF another two years after graduation to serve on Cru staff. Only God could orchestrate such an incredible story, and He gets all the glory. He alone knows the names of those who have been influenced and will never be the same, including my husband's, mine, and those we had the privilege to impact as the circle widened.

A couple of years ago, I was invited to speak at an event Cru was sponsoring for University of Florida sorority women. What an incredible opportunity for influence in the same place I experienced my first influence! I was beyond excited. My close friends were praying, and my sweet college friend Susan would be there to support me. The message was rolling around in my head. During my hour-and-a-half drive to the college, I prayed and went over and over each point. I arrived early and parked down the street from the Women's Club. I watched a young man put up a sign, while his buddies rushed in and out with trays of food.

But there seemed to be something missing from my message: a way to connect. I had so much in common with these girls. I had gone to UF. I was in a sorority there too, and so was my daughter Katie. Two of my sons graduated from UF. One had significant influence as a student leader and regular speaker for Cru, while the other had great influence as he lived out his faith through four seasons of football. Of course, the name recognition is the reason I was asked to be the speaker. But that wasn't enough; I needed to find a deeper connection with these young women.

Lord, I cried out silently, *I am so inadequate. With all my heart, I believe You orchestrated this privilege for me to influence these precious girls. During this season, they are making decisions that will impact the rest of their lives. I know You will come through. You have to. There is a battle raging for their souls. I really, really care. I care more than I thought possible. I don't know them, but I was just like them many years ago. Flood my heart with love for them. Actually, You already have, but please show me how to connect to their hearts.*

My heart was beating rapidly with anticipation as I entered the club. Would the girls even show up? The event was optional. They were busy preparing for sorority rush, and this was their only night off. But the free food in a lovely setting might draw them.

It was time. The doors opened, and most of the girls came in groups. I watched them, praying, waiting for the earthly connection that could impact their eternity. And then I knew. It wasn't lightning, but it was just as sudden and straight from the Lord. (We are never left on our own when our goal for influence lines up with God's.)

Nearly every girl who walked in had a backpack. What a simple visual that illustrated a profound truth. That was my connection!

I began with a couple of funny stories, although I am not naturally funny. I had the girls' attention because I had walked in their shoes. We were decades apart in age, but I could still relate. I shared my story of coming to the end of myself at the beginning of my sophomore year, when all the activities and accolades did not satisfy. Of crying out to God from my little room in the sorority house. Of God responding to my prayer. Of the beginning of influence, my life counting for the first time. Of sharing what I learned with my sorority sisters.

Then I used the illustration God showed me: Most of their backpacks were heavy, just like the burdens they carried and that I once had carried. Their burdens varied, but each one had them: poor decisions, broken relationships, lies, abortions, selfishness, pride, disappointments. No one is exempt.

"But," I encouraged them, "there is a solution. At your age, I learned that I could lay my heavy burdens down at the foot of the cross. Don't listen to the voice of the enemy who whispers in your ear, 'You have blown it this time. That sin is the one God does not forgive. There is no hope for you. The hole you dug for yourself is too deep.' All lies!

"Jesus came to earth to die for each one of those sins. He never sinned, so He could die for the sins of the whole world. For every one of us at the same time. For every single sin: past, present, and future. He willingly was beaten and nailed to a cross. He gave up His life because He loves us. 'While we were yet sinners, Christ died for us' (Romans 5:8). I keep a huge rusty nail in my makeup drawer to remind me of a love that defies reason. It is for freedom that Christ came to set us free. First John 1:9 tells us, 'If we confess our sins, He is faithful and just to forgive us our sins and to cleanse us from all unrighteousness'" (NKJV).

I paused for a moment, looking around at the young women in the audience. I knew that on many college campuses, unplanned pregnancies and abortions are common and had possibly impacted some of these girls. "You know that I stand for pro-life," I continued. "I did a Super Bowl pro-life commercial with Timmy. But please, don't think that abortion is the unforgivable sin. No sin is unforgivable, except rejecting God's offer of salvation. Don't let what happened in the past prevent you from having a great impact in the future. God can use your story to powerfully tell His story."

As I looked around the room, I saw tears in most of their eyes. I knew there were tears in mine. I had the privilege of a lifetime: to encourage the girls to lay their backpacks—their burdens—at the foot of the cross. I led them in a simple prayer of salvation.

Our son-in-law Joey Allen has written and illustrated a children's comic book tract with a beautiful prayer. I encouraged the girls to use their own words or Joey's simple ones:

Dear Jesus,
I know I am a sinner.
I can't save myself.
I believe You died on the cross to pay for my sins.
I believe You rose from the dead.
Now I put my trust in You, and only You.
Thank You for forgiving my sins,
For being with me,
And for giving me a home in Heaven.
Amen.[1]

I concluded with this encouragement: "If you just prayed that prayer for the first time, you are now a child of God. He will never leave you or forsake you. When you die, He will take you to heaven, where you will live with Him for all eternity. I am so thankful to have you as a sister in Christ!"

I reminded them to take some tracts to share with their friends. Our family loves giving them away. I watched girls stick some in their backpacks—the wonderful visual I have used many times since that night.

I stayed as long as the girls did, listening to their stories. I hugged girls and cried with some of them. I thanked the organizers for all their efforts. And then the tears fell like an open faucet when I got to the car. My heart was so full of gratitude to the Lord: for drawing me close when I was a student, for revealing the parable of the backpack, for the girls who loved Jesus and brought their friends to hear about His love, and for the precious girls who laid their backpacks at Jesus' feet that night and met Him as their Savior. They will never be the same, and neither will I. Nothing compares to being a very small piece of the very big puzzle God designed to influence lives for eternity.

Our Master could work in the lives of others without any assistance from us, so it is humbling to comprehend that He invites us to partner with Him. We have the God-given privilege of incredible influence that impacts lives for eternity! I never want to get over the miraculous motivating power of influence.

Your story will be different from mine; you may have different gifts or areas of influence. But every woman's story can be better than a Disney or Hallmark movie when we allow the Lord to be our Master director. Our stories can have dramatic plot twists when we turn them over to the God who has the best plans for us—"plans for welfare and not for calamity to give [us] a future and a hope" (Jeremiah 29:11). With God as our Master, there will still be challenges, adversity, and setbacks because

Every woman's story can be better than a Disney or Hallmark movie when we allow the Lord to be our Master director.

we have an enemy, one who wants "to steal and kill and destroy" (John 10:10). The devil hates our potential for spiritual influence. But when we know our Master, He blesses us with hope, purpose, and a happy ending (see chapter 13).

Don't settle for an ordinary life. Choose to live your life influencing people in your sphere on purpose.

A DAY WORTH CELEBRATING!

Today is a special day. A significant birthday—one worth celebrating. My child is thirty. There won't be a cake with thirty candles or well-wishes from friends. In fact, I may be the only one who remembers. Thirty years ago today, my precious six-year-old little boy ran to find me because he was ready to ask Jesus to be his Savior. He knew for certain he was a sinner, especially on that day when he had clearly demonstrated his self-will over and over.

I grabbed a Good News Glove, just like the one I'd used with his older sister. The gospel is simple. He already understood it. But now he was as desperate as a rowdy, towheaded little boy could be. He sat on my lap as we went through the gospel, and without hesitation, he prayed to ask Jesus to be his Savior. We both had tears in our eyes. Then he jumped up, happy, secure, and ready to run off to his next adventure. When Bob came home later that day, our family celebrated our son Robby's decision. And as a family, we celebrated it every year.

I chose to make each child's spiritual birthday a big deal. It is! There were meaningful gifts, favorite foods, and a time to reflect back on the details of when each child came to Christ. Our children were all young when they made their decisions, so it was up to me not only to remember the details but to enable my children to remember the most vital decision they will ever make in life. Later, when the enemy whispers in their ears that they don't really have a personal relationship with Jesus, they can combat his lies. A spiritual birthday celebrated every year recalls the details, etching a significant decision with a permanent marker in the mind of each child. Life-impacting influence!

These days, I may be the only one who acknowledges my children's spiritual birthdays. But one of my greatest joys is that my children now celebrate the spiritual birthdays of their own children. When my precious granddaughter Claire is asked about her birthday, she enthusiastically responds that she was born on June 19, and her spiritual birthday is April 1, April Fools' Day! Claire's family recently moved and joined a local church. At the end of an April service, the pastor invited anyone who had a birthday to come up to the front. Without hesitation, Claire, eleven, immediately hurried up to the front of the church. Her spiritual birthday is as real to her as her physical one, and that day she influenced the crowd as she sweetly shared about her spiritual birthday. The day a person meets his or her Master is a day worth celebrating!

Have you met your Master? I hope you know how much He loves you and all He has done for you through Jesus. If you have trusted Him for salvation, know that nothing can take away your relationship with Him. You are His child, safe in His arms. And every day you and I can learn more about what it means to allow Him to be in charge of our lives, directing us to a beautiful purpose.

Chapter 3

FIRST THINGS FIRST

Although it was more than thirty years ago, I vividly remember the day I sat on the edge of my bed in tears. I had envisioned handling life like Superwoman, with unlimited energy and capability. "What's the matter with me?" I sobbed.

I tried to pull myself together with logic: I was blessed to know the Lord and have a husband, a home, and three adorable kids. Adorable, yes, but . . . my curly-headed first-grade daughter, Christy, had blue eyes, dimples, and a superstrong will. Her cute four-year-old little sister, Katie, had big brown eyes, lopsided pigtails, and a mischievous streak. And my chunky, towheaded one-year-old son, Robby, had begun walking at nine months to everywhere he shouldn't go, touching everything he shouldn't touch. These three, however, were not the main cause for my loosened grasp on my Superwoman cape. Neither was my "out of the box" husband, Bob. Or the Bible study I taught. Or the sweet little girl I watched every day to help her newly divorced mom.

MY BATTERY NEEDS CHARGING

Only a week had passed since I'd spoken to a large group of women about "Priorities." Recently I discovered my faded notes from that event, typed on the electric typewriter I was proud to receive for high school graduation. Evidently I encouraged those women to formulate a plan: get organized, set goals, aim high, use time wisely, and find balance. I added subtleties like "If you just stick to your plan, work harder, get up earlier or stay up later, and do everything you are supposed to do in the way you are supposed to do it—then you will be successful!"

I even referenced Superwoman, who had become a cultural icon. There's a tendency for women to play her role in an earnest attempt to prove their efficiency, their skill, and their ability to multitask, to meticulously make a plan and stick to it without any room for margin, and to do it all with great hair and wearing designer shoes.

I apologize to any of you mature readers who attended that event. I've since learned that real life offers plenty of opportunities to remind us that no matter how sparkly our capes or how strong our capabilities, certain days, or even seasons, will leave us overwhelmed and drowning in responsibilities, without energy to spare. I don't know about your cape, but mine is a little tattered and snug, I have my share of bad hair days, and most of my shoes are so "last year."

When I spoke at that event, I falsely assumed that all we needed to be real-life superwomen was a good plan, the energy to carry it out, and a little help from the Lord. But our fictional heroine is no match for the incredible demands on our lives that can't be solved by sheer determination and a cute cape. Husbands, children, jobs, homes, bills, and more require time and energy. And we often run out of both! Even when we take vitamins, eat reasonably healthy, and make an appearance at the gym. Even when our alarms wake us up before the sun. Even when our friends on social media are impressed by our juggling abilities. In order to keep going, our internal batteries need to be charged, just like our cell phones, computers, and iPads.

As my real-life challenges increased, I didn't need just a "little help" from the Lord; I needed His continuous involvement—and a new plan. Without realizing it, I'd slowly bought into a version of "God helps those who help themselves," which is *not* found in any Bible on my shelf. Although I still desired to influence women as I had in college a decade earlier, there was an obvious difference. In college, I was a new believer and keenly aware of my limited knowledge and abilities. A few years later, pride crept in and I thought I had it together. My focus became organization: a planner, goals, an extensive to-do list. All of the above are helpful, and I still use some of those tools. But they're not enough. As I sat on the bed that day, humbled and discouraged, I faced the reality that all my efforts didn't eliminate the strain and stress I was feeling. I had influenced those women negatively by suggesting they just needed to work harder and more efficiently. My plan wasn't working!

Are you discouraged by your inability to do life the way you planned? What are you putting your hope in? What's becoming your master? Organization may not be your thing, but are you mastered by your intelligence? What about artistic or musical talent? Does your social status or appearance take center stage? Are you focused on your athletic ability or leadership skills? All of these are assets, blessings from the Lord. But no plan, ability, or person is worthy to replace God in His rightful position as Master.

No plan, ability, or person is worthy to replace God in His rightful position as Master.

While watching a cartoon with my grandchild, I was introduced to the goofy little yellow characters known as Minions, made famous in the *Despicable Me* animated movies. Minions always want to serve someone, and for some reason known only to the film creators, they always choose the most despicable master possible. I admit to being out of the Minions loop. But Minions aren't the only ones who choose unworthy masters. Those of us who choose to be our own masters aren't very far behind—or ahead.

COME TO ME

Even though the challenges I face in later life are, in reality, heavier than my earlier ones, my burdens seemed much weightier during the season of my Superwoman complex. I would have insisted that God was my Master, but I was convinced that everything depended on me.

Then in 1981, suddenly my life was turned upside down when Bob came up with the idea to teach our kids at home. *Homeschool* was not yet coined as a word. No one was discussing it on the talk shows because no one was doing it—at least no one we had ever heard about. Bob gave me a pass that first year, because Christy was enrolled in a fine Christian kindergarten, and I gave birth to our third child on her second day of school. We talked about starting the next year. To be perfectly honest, I thought that if I submitted to my husband, God would surely change his mind. But I started homeschooling my kids in 1982 and didn't retire from my teaching career for twenty-five years.

Our extended family was opposed to Bob's radical idea, our neighbors didn't understand our choice, and though our friends were gracious, they most likely were a little concerned. The discouraging prediction we heard over and over was "If you homeschool, your kids will never play sports or go to college." But I wanted my kids to go to college and have the option to play sports. I didn't want to be the odd woman out.

We kept the kids inside and the drapes drawn, so as not to attract attention. Reports circulated about parents who were arrested for homeschooling. No educational publisher would sell us curriculum because the legality of homeschool was questionable, so salespeople hung up on me. Most members of the church Bob served probably thought we were weird, and I couldn't blame them. Bob doesn't worry about what people think. His focus is usually on pleasing God. Well, I want to please Him too, but it would sure be easier with a few more people on my team.

And then I discovered these verses: "Come to Me, all you who labor and are heavy laden, and I will give you rest. Take My yoke upon you and learn from Me, for I am gentle and lowly in heart, and you will find rest for your souls. For My yoke is easy and My burden is light" (Matthew 11:28-30, NKJV). I knew this passage was in the Bible, but I didn't own it until my goal to crush life as the proverbial Superwoman fell apart and my energy was depleted. And I became desperate, which is usually my catalyst for spiritual growth. I was desperate enough to come to God, and the first burden I gave Him was homeschooling. I included my heartfelt prayer that if it was God's plan for my kids to play sports and go to college, then He would work it out as only He can do. That burden was just too heavy to carry myself!

Carrying my burdens was like carrying an extra-large bag of dog food—all the way home from the store. I was weary and needed rest. Not just physical rest, although sleep is essential, but rest for my soul. I can't explain "rest for my soul," but I know when I have it: peace, calm, hope, relief, assurance, recharged batteries, a load lifted, being able to breathe.

How about you? Is your burden weighing you down? Is it more than you can handle alone? Are the voices of despair and exhaustion overpowering the voices of hope and peace? Do you have high expectations you can't meet—while friends or family members pile on even more expectations of their own? You're trying, but it doesn't seem to be enough. You feel like giving up! That was me before I came to Him.

I'm beyond grateful that I accepted my Master's invitation to come. I came as I was, flawed and needy, with burdens galore. I came weary and discouraged, with expectations I couldn't meet, self-made laws I couldn't follow, and people I couldn't please. I soon realized that I didn't come to a place, a religion, or a set of rules. I came to a Person. A Person who loved me enough to suffer on my behalf. One who was willing to help carry my burdens and share the load. I didn't need to know all the details; I just accepted His offer. I pictured Jesus motioning to me with His arms open wide, inviting people like me and you, who are weary from carrying the heavy burdens of life, to come to Him. So I came to Him then, and I keep coming. I'll continue coming to Him until I meet Him face-to-face one day. And on that day, I will finally leave all my burdens behind.

As the verses describe, I yoked myself to the Lord, my Master. What does a yoke even mean? I had no idea at first. When we moved to the Philippines some years later, Bob showed me a real yoke. The native oxen-like animals, called carabao, are hitched to one another in order to carry a load or plow the rice paddies. One is the leader, carrying the brunt of the load, and the other walks alongside, carrying a lighter load. The double yoke links the two animals together. A spiritual yoke is like that: We still carry our burdens— burdens that keep us aware of our needs—but the heaviest part of the load does not rest on us. Thank goodness! The Lord is the lead burden bearer, and we follow with our smaller loads.

My oldest son, Robby, provided a great illustration of "yoking together" when he came home one weekend from college. (Yes, my children went to college after all!) His older sisters were married, and his younger brothers were on a mission trip with Bob. That left only me to help Robby move a large hand-me-down couch he was taking back to school in his truck. There was no way I could lift it, but my innovative son placed the couch on an old rug. Robby acted as the burden bearer, pulling one end of the couch, while I guided the other end as it easily slid on the rug. Actually, I just held on to the couch while Robby pulled. But Robby counted on me to do my small share. That's the way it is when we yoke ourselves to our Master. We don't bring much to our joint effort, but the Lord invites us to do our part.

When our granddaughter Claire was nearly three, she provided another illustration of working with the Lord to carry our burdens. Claire was determined to carry a bag of groceries up a long series of steps. The task was daunting, so she begged her grandpa for help. Bob scooped her up in his arms, and while she carried her load, he carried her. How like God to do the same for us when we come to Him with our challenging loads.

The overwhelming responsibility I felt for my children's education caused me to come to my Master regularly and yoke up with Him. And I learned from Him. (We'll talk more about learning from Him in the Manual chapters.) I came to my Master and gave Him one burden after the other, and I've been giving Him burdens ever since.

The Lord knows the end from the beginning. He knew that homeschool was the best for me and for our family; He knew I would need to begin homeschooling before He called us to the mission field a few years later. Although I didn't have homeschooling mastered by then, at least I had a head start before I encountered even greater challenges in the Philippines. He knew we would encourage other missionaries that homeschooling provided the option to keep their children with them, rather than send them off to boarding school. The Lord also knew long before I did that I had two dyslexic kids. Homeschooling enabled me to protect their tender hearts from disapproval and come to Him for wisdom. Timmy would later write about dyslexia in his books to encourage other kids with similar challenges. (More on that in chapter 10, "Love like Our Master.") God knew my dear friend Brenda would almost single-handedly get a miracle bill passed in Florida that would allow our homeschooled boys to play sports, two in a private school and one in public school. He put it on my heart to start support groups for homeschoolers in the Philippines and then when we returned to Jacksonville—back when support was needed because homeschooling was still so uncommon. He wrote incredible God stories by providing college scholarships for each of my kids.

The Lord knew all of the above. I didn't know anything except my need to be yoked to Him. I just carried the smaller burden of preparing the kids, while God had the large burden of orchestrating their future. I'm so thankful we yoked together to impact the lives in my charge.

Please know that homeschool is not the flag I fly. It was God's plan for us, but He has a one-of-a-kind plan for every person and every family, which is why we need to come to Him and seek His plan—a Master plan to give us "a future and a hope." And although "Master" is the focus of these chapters, our relationship with Him is woven into every topic of every chapter. After all, toward the end of the book of Revelation, our Master says of Himself, "I am the Alpha and the Omega, the first and the last, the beginning and the end" (22:13). There is no place, no area of our lives, where His love and power do not extend.

WHY "MASTER"?

Up to this point, this chapter has been about my relationship with my Master, but I believe that everyone has a master. Think about this: Who do you submit to? Who do you answer to? Who is your highest authority? Who do you feel a sense of accountability to?

Years ago, I chose the term "Master" to describe what the Lord is to me. But why "Master" when I could choose a more familiar designation? I am blessed (or sometimes stressed) to have a live-in Bible scholar. Bob is armed with several degrees, was awarded both a "Reverend" and a "Doctor" designation, knows the original languages the Bible was written in, and won't let me get away with wimpy theology. He encouraged me that my choice of "Master" to describe my relationship with the Lord is not just a forced *M* word for my outline. This might be more information than you want, but *Vine's Expository Dictionary* translates the same Greek word *kurios* as both "Master" and "Lord."[1] The disciples frequently called Jesus "Master" (see Luke 8:24, among others), and Jesus even used the word to describe Himself (see John 15:15). "Master" is also used to refer to God the Father, such as in Jeremiah 3:14. And it really does work well in my outline!

But why is God worthy of being the Master I submit to and trust for my life? My answer that "He just is" or "the Bible tells me so" is not enough for my husband. So as I made tiny scratches on the surface of studying the word "Master," I was encouraged by the wealth of verses backing my allegiance. Here's my "CliffsNotes" version: God has a rightful position as Master and Lord because of the following four *C*s and much, much more.

Creator: He is the Creator God (see Genesis 1:1; John 1:3; Colossians 1:16).

Character: His character is perfect (see Deuteronomy 32:4; 2 Corinthians 5:21; Hebrews 7:26)

Cross: His perfect love sent His only Son, Jesus, to the cross to pay for my sins (see John 3:16; Romans 5:8; 1 Corinthians 15:3; 1 Peter 3:18).

Coronation: He is King of kings and Lord of lords (see Revelation 19:11-16).

Referring to God as our Master is not original with me, of course. My husband was privileged to attend the funeral of Truett Cathy, founder of Chick-fil-A. Every attendee was handed a card stressing the importance of a master. It read, "Truett Cathy believed that a life well-lived is predicated by selecting the right Master. Truett chose Jesus Christ as his personal Lord and Savior and dedicated his life to serving Him."

The concept of God as Master shows up in the Old Testament, too. After the Israelites arrived in the Promised Land, Joshua instructed them to choose who their master would be. Would they serve the pagan gods of the people around them, or would they serve and follow the Lord? He declared, "As for me and my house, we will serve the LORD" (Joshua 24:15). While many people align with the ancient leader Joshua and Mr. Cathy, most of us choose to run our own lives and be our own masters. Bosses, parents, husbands, teachers, government authorities, and more may all compete for master status, but usually self wins.

The prophet Elijah dealt with the same choice we often face. He saw the people of Israel wavering between worshiping the Lord and worshiping the pagan god of the Canaanites, and he asked them pointedly, "How long will you hesitate between two opinions? If the LORD is God, follow Him; but if Baal, follow him" (1 Kings 18:21). The Israelites couldn't make up their minds which master to follow. We may have the same problem. Following Baal may not be tempting for most of us, but we don't always understand that we have a choice of masters. The frustrations that result from being our own bosses often drive us to relinquish the controls of our lives to the Lord. But we quickly discover that our choice is not "one and done." It's a choice we make daily, or actually moment by moment.

Even the apostle Paul, who had a dramatic conversion and wrote many of our New Testament books, admitted that the Christian life is a battle with our human nature. The very thing he wanted to do, he didn't do (see Romans 7:15-20). I can identify. I want God to be my Master, but when I'm stressed or discouraged, or when hormones are raging, I often revert to my default of "me" and take the controls back. I mimic one of our grandchildren, who claimed, "Me can do it myself." I may use better grammar, but I'm just like that toddler when I attempt to do life myself. Over time, though, we can refocus, shift our dependence from ourselves to the Lord, and develop consistent habits with our Master.

FIRST THINGS FIRST

It's not enough to believe that God has the right to be our Master. We have a free will, and God won't force us to turn over the control of our lives to Him. We must allow the God who created us and has a wonderful plan for us to be the Master of our lives. And if God is going to be the Master of our lives, then He must be the Master of each day.

How does that work? We need to take time each day to acknowledge the Lord and His role as the boss of our lives. To renew our decision to give Him control. It's different for everyone, and mine is not a one-size-fits-all solution. Come up with your own Master plan that works for you, but consider these verses:

> "Seek first His kingdom and His righteousness, and all these things will be added to you" (Matthew 6:33).
> "In the morning, O Lord, You will hear my voice; in the morning I will order my prayer to You and eagerly watch" (Psalm 5:3).
> "Choose for yourselves today whom you will serve" (Joshua 24:15).

During a recent hotel stay, I was intrigued by a small sign next to the coffeepot in my room: "We believe in a great breakfast, but first things first." I admit to preparing my coffee at night so it's ready to consume first thing in the morning. But even before my coffee, I attempt to focus on what should be my first thing.

I need to seek my Master first and foremost, and that means in the morning. I am such a morning person, but most of my family members balk at my a.m. enthusiasm. Many of you are reacting the same way. Waking up with my mind racing doesn't mean I am super-spiritual. In fact, morning people are often tempted to use their energy to scribble to-do lists or race to a job, exercise routine, or car pool.

For me, the ideal day begins when in my first conscious thoughts after I wake up, I pray Romans 12:1-2 to the Lord, picturing myself giving my day and my life to Him. It usually goes something like this: "Good morning, Lord! I give myself to You as a living sacrifice, holy and acceptable to You, which is my reasonable service of worship. I don't want to be conformed to the world but, instead, to be transformed by the renewing of my mind, so I can prove what Your good and acceptable and perfect will is for me this day."

It's natural to be conformed—assimilated into the world, "squeezed into its mold," trying to be just like everybody else. In middle school I tried so hard to dress, act, and talk like all the other girls. But conformity is not as cute on an adult. Without even realizing it, we are indoctrinated by our culture, and it can be hard to tell the difference between a woman who knows her Master and one who doesn't. When we begin each day by consciously giving our lives to the Lord, He reminds us throughout the day when we start to look like the world. He's in the business of transforming us.

Another favorite passage that reminds me to connect with my Master first thing is Jeremiah 29:11-14: "'I know the plans that I have for you,' declares the LORD, 'plans for welfare and not for calamity to give you a future and a hope. Then you will call upon Me and come and pray to Me, and I will listen to you. You will seek Me and find Me when you search for Me with all your heart. I will be found by you.'" Realizing that the Lord has good plans for us helps us remember that He is a good Master, One who wants to be found when we seek Him. I was excited to find another verse from Jeremiah that complements the one above. I altered it slightly to relate to women: "I know, O LORD, that a woman's way is not in herself, nor is it in a woman who walks to direct her steps" (see Jeremiah 10:23). The Lord directs our steps! Why would we stumble through the day like tourists without maps, when God has the best plans for us?

You may come up with different verses that remind you of God's role as your Master; cry out to the Lord in any way that works for you. My goal is to encourage you to come up with a plan to give the Lord preeminence in your life—beginning with each day—and for your plan to eventually become a habit.

I came up with mine out of desperation, my usual catalyst for change. One day when my kids were small and I was recovering from trying to be Superwoman, a friend referenced a bestseller by Stephen Covey entitled *The 7 Habits of Highly Effective People*. In that season, I was always so tired from a packed day that I rarely woke up during the night, unless a child was crying. But that night, I woke up long before the sun was up, grabbed a piece of paper, and wrote the title for my next talk: "The Seven Habits of the Highly Effective Woman." I regularly changed habits two through seven, but habit number one was consistently "Who's the Boss?" (At the time, there was a popular television show with that title, which proves I'm not too clever.) But to me, "Boss" and "Master" are identical twins; "Master" is just more spiritual sounding. The point is obvious, though: We need to make a daily habit of seeking the Lord first to remind ourselves that He is our Master.

I like to define *habit* as something that is repeated so often that it becomes almost automatic. And according to our copy of *Encyclopaedia Britannica* (purchased years before Google replaced encyclopedias), "the behaviour becomes more automatic with each repetition."[2] Supposedly we must repeat an act for four weeks before it becomes a habit. That's twenty-eight days, or one month. It's not easy to develop a new habit, and when we attempt to establish a new spiritual habit, as opposed to a practical one like making the bed or brushing our teeth, we can expect opposition. But the results are worth the effort. After a few outings, I retired the message on seven habits, but years of choosing to make seeking my Master my first habit have influenced me more than almost anything else in my life.

While I know and believe the principle of "first things first," my inherent tendency to be my own boss ensures that I'm not always faithful to apply it. Life is beyond busy, and some mornings pass without me even glancing up. And even when I do begin my day by giving it to the Lord as a living sacrifice, I can easily slide off that altar and grab the controls of my life. It happens regularly. But as soon as I realize I'm trying to be the boss, I try to copy our cute little grandchild whose response to being caught in the act is "I'm wong; peaze forgive me." I then return the authority of my life back to my rightful Master.

Relinquishing the controls of our lives allows our Master His rightful place as Boss. If He's not in charge, we won't have the kind of influence He intended for us. Too much is at stake for us to run our own lives. A few days ago, I lamented to my husband that I missed an important text because I failed to charge my phone. Bob reminded me that the Lord never goes off-line. What a relief, because I make a mess of life when I do it on my own! We need to be plugged in to the ultimate power source from the moment we wake up until we rest our heads on our pillows again at night.

If our Master is not in charge, we won't have the kind of influence He intended for us.

I was once asked in a Q and A, "If you could change anything in your life, what would it be?"

I immediately replied that I wouldn't attempt to be a wife, a mother, or anything else apart from the power of God. I said that I regret the many days I lived in my own strength, and I know that people close to me will attest to the difference when I am living with God as my Master. I then quoted a verse I was trying to apply at the time and still am: "I am the vine, you are the branches; he who abides in Me and I in him, he bears much fruit, for apart from Me you can do nothing" (John 15:5). "Nothing" means *nothing*!

I long for my life to bear fruit and have ripples of influence. I bet you do too. Pursuing God as our Master is the greatest habit in all of life because it is a dynamic relationship that changes our focus, rearranges our priorities, and transforms our characters. When we allow the Lord to be in charge, He provides opportunities for influence. Then the overflow of our lives will impact the people in our spheres with fruit that remains.

And sometimes pursuing God as our Master means we will go places we never thought we'd go . . .

Chapter 4

WHEN WE BELIEVE

It took me a while to get our three youngest children to bed that memorable February evening. I was on my own because Bob and Christy had left earlier in the day for a speaking event in a neighboring state. Eight-year-old Christy was so excited about her daddy-daughter time. I knew they would be driving late into the night; in fact, Christy was probably already asleep in the car.

Not long after I got the other three kids down, I headed to bed. After praying for the ones traveling and the ones sleeping, I closed my eyes and tried to rest. But something happened that does not normally happen to me. In fact, I don't remember anything like it ever happening before. I had what I can only describe as a very real prompting from God. There was no audible voice, just a sudden clear realization that God wanted Bob and me to go to the Philippines as missionaries.

A DIVINE STING OPERATION

You need a little background here to understand that this idea did not just come out of the blue. Bob had gone to the Philippines on a short-term mission trip a month earlier. We were both convinced that God had orchestrated the circumstances surrounding that experience. To this day, Bob laughingly refers to it as a "divine sting operation" because of all the details that had to fall perfectly in place for the trip to happen. The previous year, he'd attended a meeting where he learned about a mission trip to the Philippines for pastors. His first thought was that he would love to go, but the timing didn't seem right. Pastoring the growing congregation he'd founded three years earlier was more than a full-time job. There were too many responsibilities and not enough resources, so he dismissed the idea and promptly forgot all about the trip.

Months passed. Then, after a chance encounter with someone who was going on the mission trip, Bob learned the group still had spots open. He wondered if God wanted him to go, but he didn't see how he could since the deadline for airline reservations was fast approaching, and we didn't have money for the tickets—or the trip expenses. He told the Lord he was willing to go, and a local businessman came to mind. Bob decided not to call him, and prayed, *God, You have to do this.* Two days later, the man called—the first time he'd ever called Bob. The two men chatted awhile, and the businessman asked Bob what was going on in his life and ministry. When Bob shared about the mission trip opportunity, the man inquired about the cost. He not only thought Bob should go but also offered to personally pay half of the amount and then promised that his company would match the other half. He said he had money to give away, and the Lord had put Bob on his heart. It was obvious to Bob and me that the trip was God's plan.

That belief was confirmed when Bob returned home from the life-changing trip, which energized his passion for the gospel. His enthusiasm for the Filipinos' responsiveness to his preaching was surpassed only by his excitement at the births of our four kids. In two weeks of ministry, five churches were planted with the 230 people he led to Christ. I knew Bob would love to go on another mission trip if he ever had the opportunity, but once he came home, he quickly turned his focus back to our church, never mentioning the possibility of returning to the Philippines.

NEVER-ENDING QUESTIONS

As I tried to sleep that night, I had an unexpected awareness that God was speaking to me in an inaudible voice in my head. I know it sounds crazy. It was not the result of anything Bob had said or I had ever thought, but it wasn't exactly out of context either. As I pondered how God had worked out the details for Bob's trip and how excited he was about the response to the gospel, I had no doubt that it was God prompting me with the realization that His plan was for us to become missionaries to the Philippines.

How would you process an outrageous and unexpected prompting from the Lord? I wrestled with God for a good part of the night. I had a lot of questions. *How can we do this when we have four little kids? How could we possibly think about moving to the other side of the world? Where would we live?* The slides (I realize that dates us!) Bob had brought back from his trip, showing grass-covered bamboo huts with dirt floors, were flashing like strobe lights in my mind. *What will our families think? Where will the financial support come from? What will we do with our home in Florida?*

To me, these questions seemed perfectly logical, reasonable, and practical. I was a logical, reasonable, and practical person, and if it was God's plan for us to go to the Philippines, I needed answers to a few basic questions. Eventually the answers came—just not in the way I expected.

No sooner had I presented all my questions to God than a familiar Bible verse became fixed in the forefront of my mind. The words of the prophet Jeremiah not only addressed my questions but gave me much-needed courage for that moment and for months to come: "Ah Lord God! Behold, You have made the heavens and the earth by Your great power and by Your outstretched arm! Nothing is too difficult for You" (Jeremiah 32:17). Later, I connected it to another verse from the same chapter: "Behold, I am the Lord, the God of all flesh; is anything too difficult for Me?" (Jeremiah 32:27).

I felt as if I were in a tug-of-war with God that night, asking questions but receiving no answers. I went back and forth between my questions and what the verses said about God—the God who made the heavens and the earth. I had seen Him act on my behalf time and time again, and my faith had grown. Bob had taught our family that faith is like a muscle. The more you exercise it, the bigger it becomes. By this point, I often exercised my faith muscles for finances, homeschooling, parenting four kids, and Bible studies I taught, but this was something new.

Faith is like a muscle. The more you exercise it, the bigger it becomes.

I had developed a deeper relationship with my Master, and I usually granted Him permission to run my life, but did that include going to the mission field? Could I trust Him with the unknown? *That's what faith is*, I reminded myself. Put simply, faith is trusting God, even when we don't have a clue how His plan will unfold. And a trust relationship grows only one way: by making the choice to trust. Could I make that choice? Could I believe what I could not see? Could I trust that God would meet the needs of my family if He sent us to the Philippines?

I knew God was bigger than my questions. God stories flooded my mind as I remembered how He had always been faithful in the past. "Okay, Lord," I whispered, "I can't imagine how You will make this work, but I trust You." Then I gave up the fight and slept the rest of the night.

GOD'S GOT THIS

When Bob returned from his short trip with Christy, he could hardly wait to tell me the news that God had called us to go to the Philippines. I wish we'd had cell phones in those days so I could have snapped a picture of the look on his face when I smiled and told him, "I know; He called me, too!" When we compared stories, we realized we'd sensed God's call at about the same time the night before. But instead of questioning the call as I did, my husband, true to his bold, courageous nature, immediately responded. "I'll go, I'll go!" How gracious of God to call us simultaneously. That clear call would serve to encourage us during countless challenges in the years to come.

It also helped to counter the reactions of our families, who were not exactly enthusiastic. I understood. They were worried about our safety, and with good reason. The president of the Philippines, Ferdinand Marcos, was beginning to see his authoritarian regime threatened, and political chaos resulted. The nightly news from the Philippines caused legitimate concerns from our family and friends who cared about us.

During the next few months, Bob set up the board for the Bob Tebow Evangelistic Association and transitioned our church for his departure. From the moment God called us to the Philippines, we decided that we would trust Him to provide every resource we would need. Rather than ask for support, our plan has always been to work hard and share what God is doing in the ministry with those who are interested. Bob then returned to the Philippines to set up our ministry, with a God-sized goal of spreading the gospel throughout the nation's 7,100 islands. He also planned to secure a home for us.

His one promise to me was a flushing toilet, and I counted on him to keep his promise. Just as I counted on the two verses describing God's great power and outstretched arm.

During our time of preparation, leaving, and traveling, I clung to those verses in Jeremiah the way we firmly held on to the hands of our four young children as we maneuvered through crowded airports en route to the Philippines. We moved with a baby in arms, an overstuffed diaper bag, two suitcases each, and thirteen carry-ons (true story) hanging off Bob's two arms. I kept reminding myself that since our God made the heavens and the earth, moving a family of six halfway around the world would not prove too difficult for Him.

GROWING FAITH MUSCLES

I share this story to encourage you that the faith I needed as a young mother to journey with my family to an unfamiliar land is not that much different from the faith God's journey for you might require. He may ask you to follow Him by faith to an unfamiliar place of illness, job transfer, empty nest, financial crisis, or loss of a loved one. Can we trust God to be our Master in the unfamiliar, the difficult, the painful? Can we follow Him when our cheering section is non-existent? When our choice is not popular but we know it is right?

Faith in a good God who knows the future and what is best for us gives us courage to confront these challenges. This faith is not any different from the faith we had in the airplane that flew our family across the Pacific Ocean to the Philippines. Even though our engineer son Peter once created a prizewinning science project on the laws of aerodynamics, this concept still eludes me; yet I never doubted that the plane transporting our family would successfully arrive at our destination. I had faith in the airplane. And even if I had doubted its ability, the plane was still able to do what was promised when we bought our tickets. In the same way, God is trustworthy—able to do what He has promised—whether or not we believe Him. If we choose to believe, we will learn firsthand how truly trustworthy He is. If we don't make the choice to believe, we will never know God in the way He wants to make Himself known to us. And we may never have the courage that trusting God in tough times requires.

Our little bit of faith in a great big God enables us to trust Him. And when we do, our faith muscles grow. One of my role models of faith is Sarah, who, as we read in the first book of the Bible, certainly had to exercise her faith muscles when God called her husband to leave their home and everything they knew. She followed Abraham, who followed God, who did not give either one of them a clue where He was leading them. (See Genesis 12:1-9 for the beginning of their story.) At least I knew I was going to the Philippines, and I would have a house with a flushing toilet—or so I thought!

GOD IS BIGGER THAN OUR CHALLENGES (AND CRAWLY THINGS)

Our family of six arrived on the primitive island of Mindanao in the fall of 1985, in the middle of a turbulent political climate, shortly before the EDSA revolution. Soldiers carrying machine guns stood on every corner. I could handle soldiers better than I could handle the large assortment of crawly things in the tropics. I have often wished these creatures had not made it on the ark.

During this huge transition in our lives, I realized that my attitude would directly impact my children's attitudes, so I determined to exercise my faith muscles and be positive. My children copied me like little clones. If I believed that God would provide for us, they likely would believe it too. If I treated our change of continents as a great adventure, they would become young adventurers. If I resisted the overwhelming temptation to grumble (even about crawly things), then, hopefully, they would learn to refrain from complaining.

Mothers do not need to search for someone to influence. We have an audience who will mimic us, whether we want them to or not.

Looking back, I still marvel that I was able to trust my husband and the Lord, especially in view of the facts: The toilet in the house my husband found for us did not flush after all—because there was no running water. Our new city was only a degree or two north of the equator. Without air-conditioning, it was a major adjustment, even for a family from Florida. And let's not forget the crawly things.

I hadn't even adapted to the time change when my choice became clear: I could trust God even though at times it did not appear as if He were involved in our affairs, or I could give in to the temptation to do what came naturally—believe only what I could see around me. I was keenly aware that my crisis of faith would have long-range consequences not just for my impressionable young children but also for me personally. In the years preceding our present circumstances, I had learned both intellectually and experientially that God is a big God. In reality, He is "the same yesterday and today and forever" (Hebrews 13:8), so He does not actually become bigger. But my view of Him increases as I learn more about His character and choose to believe in His trustworthiness and sufficiency. I often refer to my "big God," because He continues to become bigger and bigger in my understanding as I trust Him more and more.

But was God big enough for the numerous challenges I was facing? I desperately needed to tap into the sufficiency of a big God for situations I could not have imagined when I was a fashion-conscious college student preparing for a career in public relations. Sweaty, exhausted, and overwhelmed, I prayed for strength, gritted my teeth, and chose to believe by faith that my Master was a big God. Ultimately, even more than providing my children with comfort and security, my goal was to demonstrate to them that we could trust God because He is trustworthy. It is one thing to quote Hebrews that faith is "the conviction of things not seen" (11:1) and what pleases

God (see 11:6), and it is another to live it out in front of my kids who are watching me. Over time, this faith, trust, confidence, and reliance in a very big God has become my personal objective for influencing my family—and others. You can trust a big God too, no matter what.

EYES ARE ALWAYS WATCHING

My faith muscles were a little flimsy when Bob left the kids and me with our Filipino friends while he traveled to Manila to renew our visas. We had only been given six-week visas when we arrived in the Philippines, but Bob had already had multiple opportunities to preach the gospel during those six weeks.

The original plan while he traveled was for us to be in the home he had rented, the one without running water, but plans changed, as they often do. How do we react when this happens? I am a planner, so changing plans is not easy for me—especially when I can't even envision the new plan. My greatest need was to trust my Master, who is free to alter our circumstances, and to demonstrate to my children, who were one, four, seven, and nine, that He is trustworthy. My accountability to influence them prevented me from throwing a pity party, although the enemy knew my biggest obstacle to faith. I have a vivid memory of lying in bed next to a screenless window while a variety of crawly things paraded by. We hired our first house helper because she could catch mice with her bare hands (another true story). Although dealing with bugs and other crawly things was not a life-threatening situation, it was, for me, one that called for supernatural faith.

The enemy knows our weaknesses, fears, and doubts. He appeals to our desire to know how our story ends before we finish the first chapter. Should we put down the challenging book we are living out and try to write our own version? Maybe your story began well, but the plot thickened until it became a story you never signed up to write or live. Unfortunately, that theme is all too common. Women I love are hurting because of a cancer diagnosis, financial setback, or husband's deceit. Don't give the enemy access to your pen or computer to finish your story. Remember that even challenges can be moments of influence. People in your sphere are watching you. They need to see if you can trust your God when your world falls apart. Is a happy ending still possible? Is your God big enough?

Jeremiah 32:27 was still playing in my head, reminding me that nothing is too difficult for God, and that was my lifeline. The God who created the heavens and the earth was powerful enough to sustain me. So even as we all dealt with fevers and pus-filled sores on our pampered American bodies, an unfamiliar culture, cold bucket baths, hand-washing our laundry (even cloth diapers), and more, I chose to believe that God was in charge and I could trust that His plan for us was good. These circumstances may not come close to yours, but please make the choice to believe Him too.

Not only were my children watching me, but our Filipino hosts were observing us closely, not to critique us but to graciously attempt to meet our needs. Many of the Filipinos around us—especially the friends sharing their house with us—took note of our upbeat attitudes and valiant (if sometimes less-than-successful) attempts at adjusting. They secretly began searching for more appropriate housing. Meanwhile, Bob was in Manila, trying hard to return to us. He could not have known that flights are booked months ahead during the Christmas holidays. He was forced to take a very slow passenger boat to return to us on the island of Mindanao.

Nearly a month passed while we waited. The kids and I rode tricycles (carts pulled by three-wheeled bikes of sorts), shopped in the open market, attended church, befriended the neighbors, and made up lots of Scripture songs (I'll talk about this later in the chapters on the Manual). And while we were waiting on God, He was acting on our behalf. "For from days of old they have not heard or perceived by ear, nor has the eye seen a God besides You, who acts in behalf of the one who waits for Him" (Isaiah 64:4).

A businessman in the church we attended knew someone with two homes, and he tried to talk his friend into renting one to us. The homeowner, who owned a fleet of fishing boats, had moved his family to another island but kept his home in our city. But he refused to rent his home. In an unbelievable God story, the man's wife had a vivid dream where God told her that they must rent to the American missionaries. She cautioned her husband not to disobey God, and he gave in. (We did not actually hear this part of the story until years later. The owner eventually became a good friend and shared this amazing God story.)

The kids and I were hopeful as we entered the gate in the wall surrounding the home, typical of nicer homes in the Philippines. As we toured, I had to hold little hands attached to little people ready to run and explore. I breathed a "Thank you" for the furniture I observed, since we hadn't brought any with us to the Philippines. It didn't fit in our twelve suitcases! The home was so much nicer than I had prayed for. We went through the kitchen, several bedrooms the kids could use, and a roomy master bedroom. Then I saw it.

We'd been taking cold bucket baths in a makeshift shower, really a piece of concrete with a drain and a faucet. Pouring cold water on my little eighteen-month-old son was not much fun—for me or for him. So imagine the look on my face when I walked into a bathroom that looked just like any American bathroom that I used to take for granted. Not only did it have running water and a flushing toilet, but it had a bathtub, which I later learned was the only bathtub in the city. I could hardly compose myself. We certainly could have endured the challenge of cold bucket baths, but God graciously gave us more than we needed or expected to show that He cared. My faith muscles grew that day.

STORIES BEHIND THE SCENES

The backstory to our housing crisis is a God story too. Our landlord had become a Christian years before when he read a Gideon Bible in a hotel, and his whole family eventually came to Christ. When he and his wife attended a Gideon convention in America, he decided he liked the American bathroom and eventually added one to his house. He even added hot water to that one room in the home, which to this new missionary made it a mansion. While we were singing our verses about waiting on God, He was, indeed, acting on our behalf.

Our Filipino friends helped us move in. A nearby pineapple plantation delivered a Christmas tree as a gift. We added a few handmade ornaments, and I went to a local store and bought some toys that broke in less time than it took to wrap them.

The day before Christmas, Bob returned from Manila, weary from his long boat ride but so thankful to be with his family in the home God provided. *Grateful* does not begin to describe our sense of awe and wonder at our God, who faithfully provided for our missionary family far from home on Christmas. We have been blessed with many amazing Christmases together, but our first Christmas in the Philippines serves as a monument to what the season is about—the love of God!

My older children remember the hardships of our transition to a new country, culture, home, and friends, but the permanent impression on their minds is that we trusted God, and He came through. Trusting God by faith is not easy, but it is worth it! The accountability to influence my children with my feeble efforts would lead to one of my favorite examples of influence. Our oldest daughter, Christy, now serves with her husband and two children on a difficult mission field. When they announced their decision twelve years ago, Christy exclaimed, "Mom, Joey and I can't wait to trust God for our missionary adventures, just like you and Daddy did." Wow! The same God I struggled to trust is the One who gave me the grace to cling to Him, resulting in ripple effects I will never know until heaven.

What are you trusting God for? No matter what it is, big or small, believe that He cares about you and your situation.

When we remember that God is our Master, we can trust Him to guide our every step. And when we do, our children and others who watch us will be encouraged to trust Him too. What are you trusting God for? No matter what it is, big or small, believe that He cares about you and your situation. And ask for grace to have faith in Him. The most effective way to influence people in our spheres to trust God is for them to watch us trust Him.

AN UNWELCOME HOSPITAL VISIT . . .
AND A GOD STILL AT WORK

After our first difficult year in the Philippines, I could not have imagined that the following year would hold even greater challenges. It started when we ate out for the only time while we lived in Mindanao. It was a cheap meal with a costly outcome. While Bob was away preaching, I was at home with the kids and developed a serious case of amoebic dysentery, which resulted in severe dehydration, the leading cause of death in the Philippines. I refused an IV, just as I had refused stitches for Robby on an earlier trip to the local hospital. Four-year-old Robby had climbed up on the kitchen counter and fallen off, resulting in a gash. When I witnessed nurses reusing a needle, I decided that a butterfly Band-Aid would be sufficient for his cut. I also assumed I could fight amoebic dysentery on my own rather than risk infection from an IV.

Robby's head healed quickly, but my situation declined rapidly. In those days, I could not reach Bob by phone or by any other means.

I lapsed into a coma. I will never know how the dear Filipino lady, the matriarch of the home we had lived in for a month when we first arrived, found out about my condition. She laid her tiny body partially on mine, and I still remember waking up from the coma to her singing and crying out to God to wake me up. I am sure He sent her.

Bob returned home later that day, and Christy quickly packed a bag for me. Bob picked me up in his arms, and we flew to Manila, where I spent eleven days in the hospital. If I had not been half-conscious, I would have resisted leaving my children at home with only a house helper, a woman who spoke poor English and had never been in charge of our children. The anguish I felt traveling so far away from my kids without any way to reach them could have consumed me, but I kept clinging to my faithful God. I prayed He would be strong on behalf of my precious kids. I knew Christy would try hard to mother them, but she had just turned ten. If only there were some way to communicate.

The next day, Bob finally left my side in the Manila hospital to get something to eat. In a God story that I rarely share because I can't get through it without crying, I learned that the Lord answered my heartfelt prayer for my kids' welfare while we were apart. Although we had no working telephones, God had a better form of communication for a praying mom. While Bob was walking back to the hospital, he "happened" to run into a Filipino man he recognized. The man told Bob that he had just seen our kids at the home of some missionary friends, who lived an hour or so away from us on Mindanao. The odds of connecting with this man in Metro Manila, a city of millions, were astronomical! Bob was overjoyed and rushed back to the hospital to tell me the news.

I can't adequately describe my reaction. I was filled to the brim with gratitude! I later learned that our friends had been on their way home from a meeting and felt prompted to stop by our house. They arrived shortly after we had left for the airport. When our children told them where we were, our friends did not hesitate to take our four kids home with them. But I would have spent eleven days concerned about their welfare if God had not orchestrated the "by chance" meeting. My faith muscles grew much bigger that day.

Some months later, I had a relapse but did not think it necessary to go all the way back to Manila. Bob and I saw a doctor on the closer island of Cebu, and I was prescribed some strong medicine. After taking only one dose, I read about the side effects, which included placenta previa and birth defects. I threw the medicine away—just in case . . .

Chapter 5

SPECIAL "GOD STORIES"

In the fall of 1986, Bob traveled to a remote village in the Philippines to preach the gospel, which was his ministry priority. He arrived with his translator, a large homemade screen, a projector, and the *JESUS* film in the dialect of the villagers. In those days, when Bob showed up unannounced, most of the villagers would come to the "only show in town," as he describes it. Between the first and second reels of the movie, he preached to the crowd, inviting those in attendance to ask Jesus to be their Savior. On this occasion, with the second reel playing in the background, he says he "became very aware of all the abortions taking place in America." He dropped to his knees and wept for those babies. It was in this context that he prayed, "Lord, if you give us a son, we will raise him to be a preacher. And we will name him Timothy"—which means "honoring God."

Bob always returned from his adventures to energetic kids who were ready to hug, wrestle, play, and climb all over Dad. They would eventually settle down (to some extent) and listen as he told them stories about his trip. This time, Bob seemed more eager than usual to convey the details. As he recounted his prayer for Timmy, my mind instantly switched gears to the prescription I'd tossed after taking the first pill. While our four kids were clapping in excitement about the prospect of a little brother named Timmy, I hurried to find the outdated *Physician's Desk Reference* a doctor friend insisted we take with us to the mission field. As I quickly shuffled pages in the fat book, I found the medication. My eyes locked onto the warning next to it, which confirmed what I'd read earlier: "Can cause birth defects." My reaction time was faster than usual, and I promptly prayed that those four words in tiny print wouldn't have a giant-sized impact!

At first, I was not nearly as excited as the kids about another little Tebow. I was older, already had four kids, had recently recovered from amoebic dysentery, and had firsthand experience with the less-than-desirable medical facilities. Yet it wasn't long before I was caught up in the anticipation of another child and prayed along with my family. And God answered our prayers quickly.

From the onset, the pregnancy was difficult. I had profuse bleeding and cramping, and we kept thinking we had lost the baby we prayed for. As we were dealing with my challenging pregnancy, a mission team came through our town. With no acceptable restaurant anywhere in the area, we invited the large group to lunch. I don't remember many of the details, but last year when I spoke at an event in California, I met a man who was in that group. He remembered how frail I was as I attempted to serve everyone the meal. He also recalled that his team laid hands on me and prayed for me and the child in my womb. He teased that he often takes credit for the Heisman Trophy winner. God weaves together the most interesting stories!

On the recommendation of another missionary family in the area, Bob and I made an appointment with the "best" doctor in our town.

She successfully delivered our friends' baby, but the baby also contracted amoebic dysentery while in her care. The doctor did some tests on me and, in a matter-of-fact manner, informed us that Timmy was "a mass of fetal tissue—a tumor." She felt I was in significant danger and insisted that I needed to abort immediately in order to save my life! Bob and I were both speechless. We left her office and never returned.

There was no "plan B" doctor, no alternative. I couldn't travel to better medical facilities in Manila because even slight movements caused my bleeding to increase. I did receive an encouraging letter from my doctor in Florida, who delivered our middle three children. Of course, his letter came slowly by sea, as did most mail to our area. In our current culture of constant connection, it's almost impossible to identify with our situation—a close-to-zero ability to communicate with anyone, except in person. Our phone rarely worked, and cell phones and personal computers were not yet available. But the positive aspects offset the negative: no rolling eyes, negative comments, unsolicited advice, or stories of others in similar (or not) circumstances. We tried not to dwell on the "what-ifs."

Despite the doctor's diagnosis, my husband and four kids remained optimistic, eagerly anticipating Timmy's arrival. I was a little more realistic. As much as possible, I tried to work through the possibility that I might not survive. If, I reasoned, God's plan for me was to give up my life in childbirth, then I somehow believed God would still be God. My faith rested in the reality of an unseen sovereign God, not in an emotion or a determination that I could dredge up, like hoisting a sunken ship from the bottom of the ocean. Both the process of lifting a heavy object and believing a trustworthy God require effort, but trusting God's effort over mine wins out every time!

Bob and I were convinced that our only choice was to leave my life and the life of our child in God's hands, so I made the conscious choice to trust God. Each time I chose to believe Him for a hard thing, the next time seemed easier. I wasn't ready to compete in the Olympics, but my growing faith muscles were noticeable. The Lord wrapped us tightly in a cocoon of trust and hope. We had committed our little boy in the womb to our Master, whose plan we trusted.

I made the conscious choice to trust God. Each time I chose to believe Him for a hard thing, the next time seemed easier.

While the months passed, I kept busy homeschooling the kids, reading them books, singing along with kids' tapes or to Christy's piano accompaniment, and playing games with the family—all from my bed. After the kids went to sleep, I often spent time in the Psalms, my go-to for encouragement. I remember making up many tunes to various verses that I clung to. Recently, one of our children asked me to count the verses from Psalms I put to tunes. I was shocked to record nearly fifty, many from those challenging months. One of the verses I sang was Psalm 9:10: "And those who know Your name will put their trust in You, for You, O Lord, have not forsaken those who seek You." Another was Psalm 55:22: "Cast your burden upon the Lord and He will sustain you; He will never allow the righteous to be shaken." And one of my favorites was Psalm 31:14-15: "But as for me, I trust in You, O Lord, I say, 'You are my God.' My times are in Your hand." Across the Psalms, I wrote, "God is good, but life is hard."

Toward the end of my pregnancy, the bleeding stopped unexpectedly. Bob flew us all to Manila, where I met with a highly recommended American-trained doctor. Bob, taking no chances, quizzed him about just how many babies he had delivered. The doctor responded that he stopped counting at twenty-five thousand. That was good enough for Bob, especially since we had no time to explore other options. The Lord graciously allowed us to set down our suitcases in a rented home (more on that God story in another chapter) just in time for me to give birth. My cousin Lawana flew to Manila to take care of the kids, who adored her. God seemed to orchestrate every detail—except the traffic as we drove to the hospital. But He even parted the cars in one of the busiest intersections in Metro Manila. As Bob flagged down the policeman, I cried out in pain, which helped our cause. The sympathetic policeman ensured that every car in every direction came to a sudden stop. And unknown missionaries were treated like royalty, at least on that day!

"He's a miracle baby!" the relieved doctor exclaimed. Bob stood next to him when Timmy entered the world. I'll spare you some details, but Bob will never get over his amazement at the tiny piece of placenta that had been Timmy's lifeline and his shock at the huge ball of blood that followed. There aren't words to describe how I felt when I heard the sweet sound of my baby's cry. "Thank You, Lord," I whispered then and countless times since.

It wasn't easy for a doctor who had delivered so many babies to explain how Timmy survived. This was the biggest miracle he'd ever been part of. After Timmy's traumatic months in the womb and challenging delivery, it wasn't surprising that our little boy was malnourished. But there were working telephones in the capital city, which enabled us to call family and close friends with the happy news of Timmy's birth and the urgent request to pray that he would grow big and strong. People sure took us up on praying, because if you have seen him lately, you know the Lord answered their prayers and ours.

After Timmy's safe arrival, our doctor informed us that he had been monitoring a huge cyst he'd discovered during my first exam. Knowing I was more concerned about our baby than myself, he neglected to mention it but administered strong antibiotics to prevent further infection. After mom and baby were out of danger, our knowledgeable doctor stunned us with his certainty that if I had remained on Mindanao, Timmy would have had zero chance of survival, and uterine shock from the untreated cyst would have taken my life as well. But he was determined neither death would occur on his watch. A few days later, I had surgery to remove the dangerous and intensely painful cyst. The details are better left untold, but from my perspective, it seemed like my baby weighed much less than the cyst. I was so thankful to recover from both.

RIPPLE EFFECTS

Endless stories circulate on the Internet concerning Timmy's birth story, with varying degrees of accuracy, but they have one common thread: He truly was a miracle baby. At the time, however, only family and close friends were aware of the details of Timmy's birth. When he was nominated for the Heisman Trophy in 2007, an ESPN reporter videotaped a two-hour interview with Bob and me to gain footage for the upcoming telecast. Three days later, as we sat in the audience at the Heisman Trophy celebration, in what is now the PlayStation Theater in New York City, we were shocked to watch a video clip of my testimony of trusting the Lord and refusing to abort my son. It aired live on national television immediately preceding the announcement that Timmy was the first sophomore ever to win the Heisman Trophy. A story that I had only shared in small groups was shouted from ESPN, resulting in an instant national platform for a pro-life message. Only God could have orchestrated such an unexpected sequence of events that resulted in an incredible ripple effect. I arrived home from our weekend in New York to phone messages inviting me to speak at pro-life events.

A decade after Timmy won the Heisman, I had the great privilege to share our story in Washington, DC, at the annual March for Life in front of four hundred thousand people, with thousands more tuning in to the live broadcast—including one woman who especially needed to hear it. A few weeks ago, that woman contacted two of my favorite influencers, Jeannie and Mary, the incredible organizers of the March for Life, and shared her experience. At the very moment a doctor pressured her to surgically remove her baby, saying there was no hope for life, my story flashed in her mind, and the similarities in our circumstances gave her the courage to refuse the procedure. A friend recommended another doctor, who heard a heartbeat and continues to treat her and the baby growing in her womb. This sweet mother-to-be reached out to thank me for my influence.

Only God writes stories like this! I could not have envisioned that our experience would be told in New York and Washington, and that I would have the privilege of sharing it personally in all but four states in America. I even had the joy of telling our story to a wonderful group in Anchorage, Alaska. God uses the most unlikely people for influence—in my case, an anonymous missionary, home-school mom. There are no odds to explain it. God alone is the author of our God stories!

I wouldn't have chosen to literally broadcast my crisis of faith in a public arena. But a worldwide audience of people cries out for solutions to the challenges in life, for a plan or a person to turn to in the midst of adversity. When the lab test is positive. When the divorce is final. When exhaustion is the norm. When the funds are insufficient. When the rejection e-mail is in the in-box. When giving up seems like the only option. People need the hope that can only come from our big God, and life-impacting influence takes place when we share our hope with those who are desperate to know its source.

FAITH MUSCLES

Most of the stories I share in this book have happy endings. But my life is just like yours, full of trauma and trials, offering plenty of opportunities to build faith muscles. So how do we cope with "stuff" we don't sign up for? How do we handle it when we're faced with severed relationships, tarnished reputations, and financial setbacks? When people we count on disappoint us and our dreams never materialize? When we endure broken bones, broken promises, and broken hearts? Much like a recent thunderstorm in our area that destroyed a transformer, the storms of life leave us in the dark, tempted to give up. We're like kites in the wind, blown in unexpected directions.

The way we respond to tough circumstances reveals what we believe about God. It's human nature to question and doubt Him. We wonder, *Is my faith big enough to handle the hard things? Is my God trustworthy?*

The Lord uses hard things to bring us to a point of need and dependence. As He meets our needs, we learn to trust Him. And our best reference book for faith is the one written by Jesus, "the author and perfecter of faith" (Hebrews 12:2). Knowing we needed assistance from that book to grow faith muscles for our new life on the mission field, Bob and I and our older children memorized the first chapter of 1 Peter. We learned a key point about faith: In the same way our physical muscles are tested by weights, our faith muscles are tested by trials (see 1 Peter 1:6-8). James echoed this truth and emphasized that we should "consider it all joy . . . when [we] encounter various trials, knowing that the testing of [our] faith produces endurance. And let endurance have its perfect result, so that [we] may be perfect and complete, lacking in nothing" (James 1:2-4). Sounds like our rocky road to "perfect and complete" may require a vigorous workout schedule, updated athletic gear, and closed-toe shoes, but we'll be glad we made the journey.

As we've seen with our three sons, working out builds big biceps. And trusting God through trials builds a strong faith. People I meet often joke about the contrast between my size and the size of my boys. My physical muscles may not be noteworthy, but I strive for big faith muscles! At this point in my life, I stake my faith in a very big, faithful God. And through time and experience, He has proven Himself trustworthy.

But how can our faith be steady when circumstances are up

and down, like the waves pounding on our Florida beaches? Do we trust our own wisdom and efforts or trust an all-powerful God? My reference book has the answer: Our faith doesn't rest on the wisdom of men but on the power of God (see 1 Corinthians 2:5). Since I'm directionally challenged, a favorite verse is "Trust in the LORD with all your heart and do not lean on your own under-standing. In all your ways acknowledge Him, and He will make your paths straight" (Proverbs 3:5-6). I would choose straight paths over crooked ones any day! And since I'm regularly confusing my right and left (honest), I'd rather have an all-knowing God as my GPS instead of Siri. Isaiah 30:21 says, "Your ears will hear a word behind you, 'This is the way, walk in it,' whenever you turn to the right or to the left." Long before Siri, I often prayed for help when I lost my way, both physically and spiritually.

What you believe about God determines how you react to the twists and turns in a busy life.

What you believe about God determines how you react to the twists and turns in a busy life. Walking by faith involves sloshing through muddy messes, hiking up towering mountains, and trudging through the grind of daily challenges. But we don't walk alone, nor will we lose our way. (Whew!) As a woman walks by faith, I picture the Father pointing her out to His Son, say-ing, "She believed Me today." And the Son responds, "And I was with her every step of the way." The life of faith is a result of exercising our faith muscles day after day, year after year, until we arrive home.

A sweet friend presented me with a tiny mustard seed in a small glass bottle. In his Gospel account, Luke compared small faith with a mustard seed. The tiny seed with a humble beginning grows into a large flowering tree where birds can rest. In the same way, our little bit of faith in a big God has the potential for great influence. People in our spheres search for evidence of the validity of our faith in God. When they see that our faith is solid and real, they will begin to consider that God might really be who He says He is. That we can trust our Master with a Master plan that is beyond our scope of imagination.

Faith was often my topic when I first began to speak at women's events. I concluded those events with the following:

> Here is the test for the reality of your faith—on whom does your life depend? If your life can be explained logically, in temporal terms, then you need to exercise those faith muscles. If, on the other hand, your life can only be explained supernaturally, then the world will sit up and take notice of a life that reveals your faith in your faithful God. We will never regret trusting God with our lives! An ordinary woman is made extraordinary by her faith.

My longtime friend Gennene displays extraordinary faith. Cancer hasn't robbed her of her faith or her joy. When we talk or text, she's ready with praise for her God. Blessed with a beautiful voice, Gennene responds to her trials with praise songs for anyone who'll listen. She even texts me the words to the hymns she sings and the verses she quotes, like Romans 11:36: "From Him and through Him and to Him are all things. To Him be the glory forever." She encourages others in her situation by making cards for patients in the chemo lab and doctor's office. Whether her cancer returns or goes into remission, she knows for certain that she can trust her Master, and He will never leave her alone. I attempt to encourage her, but her sweet faith also encourages me. And when we get together, we're instructed by our Manual to encourage one another, "each of us by the other's faith, both [hers] and mine" (Romans 1:12).

THE BLUE DRESS

I could not have envisioned that trusting God for the life of my son would one day result in the ripple effects of extraordinary influence. But it made trusting Him for the less important aspects of life much easier—like a special dress.

I once heard a speaker comment that we shouldn't bother God with the small details in life. I disagree. How often do you whisper a prayer for help when you misplace your car keys or forget a password? I commented to a friend recently that the Lord is constantly rescuing me when I forget, misplace, and overlook necessities like car keys, a cell phone, and reading glasses. I really believe God cares about even the tiniest details. Even a not-so-minor detail like the perfect dress for a daughter's wedding.

I needed a great dress at a reasonable price, and it was just two weeks before Christy's wedding. Before you gasp, there are some facts you need to know. This was 2003, before online shopping, and I was in the midst of the busiest season in my life. We were planning two weddings—one for our firstborn and a second for her sister eight months later. Our youngest son had just begun spring football at a school across town. His brother Peter was on the track team at another school and was about to graduate from high school. My husband and I divided and conquered. He took Timmy to spring ball and attended as many of Peter's track meets as he could, and I attended all of them. I was also planning graduation for all the seniors in our homeschool group, which by this time had become sizable. The graduates had voted to have me as the speaker, even though I graciously attempted to decline. Then, although Peter didn't actually attend the school where he was running track, we were asked to host the track team party at our home—in addition to the graduation party and Peter's birthday party. I remember composing the wedding guest list in between track events. When I had a rare free moment, I shopped for a dress in our local stores, without success. And there was no optional time to travel in search of a dress. But I reasoned that if God beautifully dresses every lily in the field, He could certainly dress me.

Right after her engagement, Christy and I decided that her wedding would be "by faith," because we wanted God to do more than we could plan. We even wrote the words "A Wedding by Faith" on the cover of Christy's wedding notebook. Our goal was to pray through every detail, and our main request was for her wedding to have an impact on everyone who attended. We wanted God to get the glory for bringing two people together who had both committed their future spouses to Him at an early age, and we hoped to influence the younger attendees that they could trust the Lord for their love lives. And we had to do it all on a limited budget.

Two weeks before the wedding, I still hadn't found a dress. Out of obligation, my bride-to-be daughter and I represented our family at a wedding near the beach, an hour from our home. We heard about a small, exclusive dress shop located in the same area, so before we headed home, Christy begged me to check out the store.

The clients in the upscale shop looked as if they could afford pricey designer dresses. The saleslady rushed to assist me. "I need a dress for my daughter's wedding," I told her.

"When is the wedding?" she asked me.

"Two weeks from today," I responded.

She couldn't hide her obvious disdain. "What kind of mother are you?" she questioned.

I bit my tongue, but what I wanted to say was "The kind who is doing the best she can! I plan ahead, love to organize, and usually have my act together." *But not this time*, I admitted to myself.

In an attempt to hide from the saleslady's disapproving glare, I began to sort through a rack of lovely dresses. Then I saw it! My eyes locked on the dress of my dreams. I knew it immediately. It was the exact color I wanted—the color I hadn't shared with anyone but the Lord. It was the perfect style, the perfect size, the perfect everything—except the perfect price. After I peeked at the price tag, I was reluctant to try the dress on, but my daughter insisted.

"Mom!" Christy exclaimed as I stepped out of the dressing room. "It's the most beautiful dress I've ever seen. I know God intended this dress for you!"

Everyone in the store looked too—the customers, the saleslady, even the well-dressed lady who appeared to be the manager. "You have to buy it!" my daughter insisted. It seemed as if every woman in the small shop nodded in agreement.

"Honey," I explained to Christy as I placed the dress on the padded hanger, "this dress does not fit our budget."

"But Mom," Christy responded, "just ask them to hold it."

I knew I couldn't justify the expense. We were already over our wedding budget, and her sister's wedding would follow soon. But I hated to disappoint Christy. So I thanked everyone, left my number with the manager, and then quickly exited the shop.

Lord, I prayed throughout the course of a busy weekend, *I believe You care about my dress for the wedding. I trust that if the beautiful blue dress is not the one, then You'll enable me to find another one. You have to accomplish this for me, because I can't do it on my own.* Then I moved on to the tyranny of the urgent—as if needing a dress in two weeks is not urgent! Okay, it was urgent, but not life-and-death urgent.

How often are you so wrapped up with the needs of those in your charge that your dreams seem secondary? You want to scream, "But what about me?" You don't, though, since you doubt that anyone would listen. But Someone does. Early in the wedding planning, I found a verse in Psalms that became mine: "I will cry to God Most High, to God who accomplishes all things for me" (Psalm 57:2). Could I still trust the Lord when my plans unraveled? When everyone around me was focused on his or her own plans? *This wedding,* I reminded myself, *is a wedding by faith. Do I trust God or not?*

I reasoned that if I couldn't afford the blue dress, I still had a week and a half to find something else. Maybe I could borrow one. *It's just a dress,* I told myself. And then I sensed God's supernatural peace—a peace I can't explain in words. I would be okay with or without the dress. Although it was my dream dress, I couldn't let that focus consume me. I still had a myriad of other details to tend to.

My phone rang early Monday morning, and I recognized the voice of the kind lady I'd assumed was the manager of the dress shop. "Mrs. Tebow," she began, "I'm filling in for my friend, the store owner, who is on vacation. While you were shopping on Saturday, I watched closely how you treated your daughter, the other shoppers, and especially the rude saleslady. I was touched by your spirit, even when I perceived you couldn't afford the dress you loved.

"I'm a Christian too," she continued, "and all weekend, I sensed the Lord impressing on me very clearly that He intends for you to have that dress. Could you tell me the figure you have budgeted for the dress?"

Fighting back the tears, I caught my breath and told the gracious woman what I could afford.

"It's yours for that amount," she said, "and I'll also include any necessary alterations. The owner gave me authority to make decisions like this one, and I am delighted to do so for you."

I thanked her, and the tears flowed even before I hung up the phone. I couldn't wait to tell Christy and my friends who had been praying for me. I'm aware, of course, that this was just a dress, not a cure for cancer or an end to war. But God answered the prayers of a woman trying to trust Him with all her heart for the desire of her heart.

Our wedding by faith was all we prayed it would be and much more. A few months into the planning, I'd put a Scripture praise to a tune, sensing that my own words wouldn't be adequate to express my gratitude for all God would do as we trusted Him. As Bob and I walked hand in hand from the lovely reception to our car, I sang my praises over and over in my heart: "I will praise You forever, because You have done it; and in the presence of Your saints I will wait on Your name, for it is good" (Psalm 52:9, NJKV).

When we experience firsthand the love and faithfulness of God, we can trust Him with the big and small details of our lives. Then, with real conviction, we can influence those around us to trust Him too. Faith in a big God—our Master—is miraculous motivating power and the cornerstone of an influential life.

MANUAL

When God becomes our Master, we've taken the most critical step toward positive influence. But how do we grow in our relationship with Him, establish priorities for our lives, and develop godly character, wisdom, mindsets, and more?

The Word of God draws us to the person of God. Everything we need to know about life and godliness can be found on the pages of the Manual, the second *M* in the miraculous motivating power of influence. Nothing has influenced me more than reading, studying, engrafting, and applying verses of Scripture to circumstances in my life. In the Bible I've discovered hope for despair, courage for fear, gratitude for bitterness, freedom for bondage, and a peace that passes all understanding for anxiety. I've learned how to combat doubt, insecurity, and discouragement, and I've found purpose and direction for areas in my life like marriage, parenting, work, and ministry.

Thankfully, we don't need to be scholars to derive benefits from the Bible. We can begin with one verse, as I did. When we know first-hand the life-changing impact of a verse or a passage, we can show people in our spheres that the Bible is a book worth reading and inspire them to open the Manual and experience its influence for themselves.

Reading, memorizing, and meditating on Scripture has had an unmistakable impact on me, and it has served as one of my greatest opportunities to influence others—with ripple effects on my family, my friends, and the people I meet along the way.

> All Scripture is inspired by God and profitable for teaching, for reproof, for correction, for training in righteousness; so that the man [or the woman] of God may be adequate, equipped for every good work.
>
> 2 TIMOTHY 3:16-17

Chapter 6

WHEN ALL ELSE FAILS
(READ THE DIRECTIONS)

After a lifetime of driving a variety of used cars, I bought my first new one. It's pretty high-tech. I, however, am not. In the glove compartment sits a manual that contains all the information I need to operate my car. But instead of taking it out and reading it, I punch buttons, I turn dials, I tap screens. And I usually waste a lot of time and get frustrated in the process, because I still can't figure out what's what.

My resistance to reading manuals is not a new problem, as the next story illustrates:

"Wow, Mom, you bought a new toaster oven. It looks fancy. How do I toast a bagel?" one of the boys asked while he was home on a college break.

"We haven't figured out how to use it yet, but I think the lower button toasts," I responded.

"How long have you had it?" my son asked.

"Oh, about eight months, but we haven't read the manual yet!" I replied.

A few days later, a friend came to lunch and asked to use the toaster oven to heat up her sandwich. "We have an oven just like this one," she informed me.

Hopeful, I said, "Oh, good! You can teach me how to use it."

In a matter-of-fact manner, my young friend explained, "Well, we have had it for a while, but nobody wants to read the manual, so we are still using the old one."

These true stories can be filed with the one about my inability to change the clock in my old car. I didn't want to read the manual, so every time we sprang forward, my solution was to wait six months until the time was correct again.

If I really felt guilty about my recurrent failure to read manuals, I wouldn't share the sordid details. Truth is: I hate reading directions! And devoting the required time, in the midst of a busy life, to reading a comprehensive book providing detailed operating instructions goes against my human nature. But then, there's not much at stake with a toaster oven or clock radio. There *is* a lot at stake for a wife, mother, student, friend, employee, or neighbor—in short, for all of us. We need the directions to life! Is there a manual for that?

A few years ago, I read an article about a man who did an experiment for a year. Every morning, he opened a fortune cookie and tried to live by the directions he received in his fortune. Among other things, he took a forty-eight-hour vow of silence, got a tattoo, and played the lottery with his so-called lucky numbers (with disappointing results).[1] He wrote a blog about his experiences, which generated a lot of attention and became popular for others in search of directions for life. For believers, a fortune cookie is definitely not our go-to for directions, but if we're honest, we often look for guidance from friends, the Internet, television, magazines, books, or even ourselves. But there's a better place to find the real directions. When I first attended that college Bible study years ago, I learned the answer to my question: There is a Manual for our lives, and God wrote it!

You may be like I was. I only knew a verse or two when I went to my first Bible study. I couldn't locate the lesser-known books like Amos or Philemon or even the more familiar ones that everyone else seemed to know. I started slow. But I started. That was decades ago, and I continue to learn—and learn. Bob often reminds me that the definition of *disciple* is "learner." The Bible has since become the Manual for my life. And my goal is to study the directions, in order to learn and to have eternal influence on the people in my sphere. One of the first passages I learned speaks to that desire: "All Scripture is inspired by God and profitable for teaching, for reproof, for correction, for training in righteousness; so that [we] may be adequate, equipped for every good work" (2 Timothy 3:16-17). Influencing others is a good work. We'll be made adequate and equipped to influence by our Manual, the Bible.

The Manual draws us to the Master. On the trustworthy, inspired pages of the Bible, He lifts a curtain to reveal Himself to us, explaining truth in words we can understand. He discloses His program and His plans, allowing our faith muscles to bulge as we see truth lived out. The Manual is where I learned the principles I taught my children and share with others. Where I discovered my purpose. And where we can find wisdom, hope, encouragement, peace, courage, strength, and—as the verses above promise—everything we need for good works. Reading the directions may not be critical for a toaster oven, but reading the directions in the Manual is destiny-changing!

The Manual draws us to the Master.

A TRUTH FILTER AND LIFE CHANGER

Our oldest daughter, Christy, was once asked following a speaking engagement, "What was the most important thing you learned growing up in your home?"

She responded that it was engrafting the Word of God, because it gave her a grid to filter everything through. She could filter in truth, like "'I know the plans that I have for you,' declares the LORD" (Jeremiah 29:11), and filter out error-filled thinking, such as "I can make my own plans and run my own life, and there won't be consequences."

Giving our family this kind of life-transforming grid may have been my greatest influence. The grid of God's Word creates ongoing ripples in the lives where it makes its home. My husband and I didn't grow up with the advantage of that grid, and maybe you didn't either. But anyone can pick up the Manual anytime and begin reading. Bob determined that long before our children could read the directions for themselves, we would read the directions to them. He took seriously the words in Deuteronomy 6:6-7, "These words, which I am commanding you today, shall be on your heart. You shall teach them diligently to your sons and shall talk of them when you sit in your house and when you walk by the way and when you lie down and when you rise up." Our goal as parents was to weave God's Word into the fabric of our children's lives through discussing it during the routine of ordinary days.

So years ago, when our kids were young and our lives were less complicated, our family began reading from Psalms and Proverbs almost every day. I went along with my husband's wishes, but I wondered if our children were too young to get much from it.

As it turns out, little minds take in more than we know. A favorite application example from Proverbs took place when we moved to Manila, where our rented home came equipped with a television. Thankfully, at that time, very few programs shown in the Philippines were in English, and the fact that those were broadcast from the United States—a twelve-hour time difference—narrowed the choice even more. I left the room while the kids were watching a "safe" program, only to return to our three-year-old son holding his chubby little hands over his eyes. That day we'd read, "The prudent sees the evil and hides himself" (Proverbs 22:3). Our little boy had no idea what *prudent* meant, but even at his young age, he knew "evil" when he saw it. He followed the directions: He hid his eyes from evil.

I'll never know the full impact of reading Psalms and Proverbs over the course of many years, but I believe it marked all of our lives for eternity. We learned about our Master's character, His faithfulness, true wisdom, and so much more from the Psalms and Proverbs.

A few years later, in an effort to motivate our kids to memorize those verses we'd been reading, we rewarded (or should I say, "bribed") them with "Daddy's Dollars." Our creative Christy designed and printed them on our first computer. The dollars could then be redeemed for computer time and a favorite television show, one that had no "evil." Our competitive daughter Katie always had the most dollars, and her brothers begged her to share.

I saved a few "dollars" in a box of memories, but they probably aren't worth much now. In reality, however, their value is priceless because they helped my children hide Scripture in their minds and hearts. God's Word residing in our hearts is better "than thousands of gold and silver pieces" (Psalm 119:72).

MAKING A JOYFUL NOISE

When our oldest child was seven and Bob was serving as a pastor, he gave the men in his Bible study an assignment: Put a Scripture verse to a tune for your family. Bob delegated this task to me. Later, we discovered that all the other guys involved in his Bible study had also delegated their assignments to their wives. I chose Luke 6:38, probably because my husband is a giver, while that's a weak area for me: "Give, and it will be given to you; good measure, pressed down, shaken together, running over, they will pour into your lap. For by your standard of measure it will be measured to you in return." My tune was simple, but the surprising result was that everyone in our family learned the verse quickly—and still remembers it today.

Years later, the ease with which we learned verses set to music was confirmed by a speaker's comment: "What is learned in song is remembered long." Just think of the commercial jingles you remember. Or a hit song from your past you're embarrassed to admit that you know word for word. Words put to a catchy tune spin around in our heads, facilitating memory and recall. Numerous examples dot the Scriptures. The psalmist wrote, "Your statutes are my songs" (Psalm 119:54). In Deuteronomy 32, we read that Moses composed a song incorporating more than forty verses, so the Israelites would set their hearts on those words and teach their children to observe them (see verses 44-46). I'm thankful my husband didn't give me that assignment, since I'm pretty certain my kids wouldn't have been enthusiastic about memorizing forty verses—especially from Deuteronomy.

The other wives from the Bible study were more musical than I was. One played the piano for our church. Another had a lovely alto voice. I don't have much musical ability or a great voice, but I've continued to put verses to tunes ever since. My original goal was for my family to remember Bible verses, but even though my kids are grown, I continue to make up Scripture songs just for me. My goal has enlarged to influence women—those I speak to at events or in private conversation—to engraft Scripture songs. That's why I sing my verses for others, even with a "not so great" voice. It helps to be older, because I don't take myself so seriously. And I know if I had a good voice, very few people could identify. One of my favorite comments was after an event, when a woman who had heard me speak and sing verses years before shared enthusiastically that she had been following my lead with her family ever since. I've been blessed to receive notes and hear many similar comments. Influencing people to engraft Scripture by whatever means works for them is one of my favorite types of influence!

The years of singing Scripture songs provide many special memories. A personal favorite took place the morning of an important day in the life of our son Robby. He walked into our kitchen singing, "For the LORD God is a sun and shield; the LORD gives grace and glory; no good thing does He withhold from those who walk uprightly. O LORD of hosts, how blessed is the man who trusts in You" (Psalm 84:11-12). Later that day Robby signed his letter of intent to play college football. He grew up on the mission field and was homeschooled, giving him limited opportunities to play organized sports. Because of state laws and his late start, the odds were not in his favor. But the Lord gave grace and glory, and our son will never get over it!

SONGS FOR HELP, HOPE, AND COURAGE
Help

"I need help!" I cried. "Who is there to help me?" I lived in a land so far from home. I had four little children who needed me. When Bob traveled to preach, he was often gone for long periods of time, without any means to connect with us. And communication with friends and family was so infrequent. I was overwhelmed with countless challenges. Where could I go for help?

Unlike in flat Florida, picturesque mountains dotted the landscape of our first home in the Philippines. One morning, when the neighboring roosters woke me up as usual, I opened my Bible and prayed, crying out for help, "Lord, open my eyes today to wonderful things in Your Word" (see Psalm 119:18).

My loving Father answered my prayer as I read Psalm 121:

I will lift up my eyes to the mountains;
From where shall my help come?
My help comes from the Lord,
Who made heaven and earth.
He will not allow your foot to slip;
He who keeps you will not slumber.
Behold, He who keeps Israel
Will neither slumber nor sleep.

The Lord is your keeper;
The Lord is your shade on your right hand.
The sun will not smite you by day,
Nor the moon by night.
The Lord will protect you from all evil;
He will keep your soul.
The Lord will guard your going out and your coming in
From this time forth and forever.

It always seemed to happen this way for me: In desperation, unable to handle things in my own strength, with my own wisdom, I cried out to the Lord. And when I opened my favorite book, I would find a specific phrase, sentence, or, in this case, whole chapter that encouraged me. "My help comes from the Lord, who made heaven and earth."

Last month, as I flew to Anchorage for a speaking event, I had a visible reminder of the truth God showed me from His Manual that morning many years ago. Grateful for my window seat, I was mesmerized by the majestic snowcapped mountains, a stunning visual of Psalm 121. The same God who formed the mountains is my help—a profound truth that gives me assurance and hope.

When my sweet granddaughter Claire was five, Christy called one day from the mission field where they served. (We're thankful that cell phones are now common even in that country.) Claire sang Psalm 121 to me—the same song I taught her mother years earlier. Claire calls it a "Grandma song." My daughter taught her daughter that our help is from the Lord, who made heaven and earth.

Scripture powerfully influences us with a reminder of who God is and what He has promised. When we read it, study it, and hide it in our hearts, it changes us and enables us to influence others. The Bible also provides us with help, hope, and courage in all kinds of situations.

Hope

We live in a world that's desperate for hope. You sense it as I do. Everywhere we look, people are stuck in hopeless situations. Television and the Internet are replete with world and local reports that make our hearts ache and our stomachs hurt. Hopelessness abounds—not only in far-off places but also in our neighborhoods, our offices, and even our own families.

Where do we turn when we are tempted to lose hope? Our resource is God's Word. "For whatever was written in earlier times was written for our instruction, so that through perseverance and the encouragement of the Scriptures we might have hope" (Romans 15:4). The Bible is jam-packed with specific, applicable verses that are more powerful than a two-edged sword. They can pierce our souls and enable us to keep on when our world crumbles around us.

Years ago, when we lived in the Philippines, our daughter Katie required surgery. Although the surgery was minor, it was major to this mom. I remember sitting in the hospital, without any family for support.

Lord, I prayed, *please show me some verses that will keep me from losing hope, no matter how the surgery goes.*

I opened my Bible and began to read the Psalms, where I often camp out. My prayer was answered as I read Psalm 62:5-8:

My soul, wait in silence for God only,
For my hope is from Him.
He only is my rock and my salvation,
My stronghold; I shall not be shaken.
On God my salvation and my glory rest;
The rock of my strength, my refuge is in God.
Trust in Him at all times, O people;
Pour out your heart before Him;
God is a refuge for us.

I read it again and again, allowing the powerful words of the psalmist to sink deep into my soul. *These verses are mine*, I thought to myself. As I waited for the doctor to speak with me, I began to hum and quote, weaving the words together with a simple tune. By the time the surgery was over, I knew that these verses would forever be my security verses.

Where do you find your security? Is it in a home, a husband, a job, a bank balance, or the number of followers you have on social media? Our children all had a security "something" they held on to when they were in a strange place or Mom turned out the light. One had a doll, another a blanket, and still another a small pillow. What is our source of security when the storms of life are approaching? Too much is at stake for us to fall apart. People are watching us—people we influence. Can we trust the God we read about and pray to? Security verses serve to remind us that our hope is secure in the Lord.

Our storms are not just full of wind, rain, and thunder, like the ones we encounter during Florida's hurricane season. Storms can also be physical, economic, spiritual, or emotional. We need to prepare for these devastating crises that take us by surprise and wreak havoc on our security.

I encourage you to find your own special security verses and make them yours. (Putting them to a tune isn't required.) There have been times in my life when all I could do was lay my head on my pillow and sing my verses to myself. But somehow that was enough.

One day I had lunch with a close friend whose world was crumbling. She shared that her husband of many years was having a midlife crisis, and he had left her and her three children. With tears in my eyes, I responded that I hadn't been in her situation, but I asked if I could share my favorite verses. I don't think I sang them, but I explained that I learned in a Bible study that the word *hope* means "a strong cord or attachment." "God will always hold on to you," I told her. "He will never let you go. You need to hold tightly to Him no matter what. He is your hope!"

Some months later, I received a card from my friend to thank me for sharing my "hope." She wrote, "Your visual that God wouldn't let go of me enabled me to make it through the divorce proceedings and everything else I had to go through. I hung on to God with all my might. And He never let go of me."

Please understand that I didn't do anything magical. I just shared applicable Scripture that I love, but it influenced her to place her hope in her heavenly Father. We offer a supernatural hope transfusion when we attach a truth about God to a circumstance in life. To quote my husband, "Hope is the battery in our lives that charges us with resolve and keeps us going."

The fruit of our influence often requires time to grow. Over time, I realized that people in our spheres catch our passion for His Manual from an overflow of our lives. I can talk about the Bible and quote a verse or two, but when my life is transformed by its power, I can't keep it to myself.

Years ago, I was preparing to teach on my favorite verses in Psalm 62 at a local women's gathering. As I hurriedly finished typing my notes in preparation, I tapped the wrong key and everything disappeared. I started to panic, but my daughter Christy said, "Mom, go get dressed and I'll print out your notes for you." Grateful for high-tech kids, I got ready, grabbed my notes from her, and ran out the door. As I stood up to speak, I opened my notes and noticed that the first point was slightly different than I remembered. The same thing was true of the next point, and the next. At first I was confused, but then I was overcome with emotion when I realized what had happened. I really had erased my notes! But I loved the passage so much that I'd taught it to my daughter, who then taught it to the Bible study she led when she was in college. Christy wasn't able to retrieve my notes, but her thoughts on the passage had been shaped by my influence and were pretty close to mine. The most effective way for us to influence others to love God's Word is for *us* to love it!

Courage

"I am so, so afraid I'll blow it! I have three kids. Please give me advice." The woman's voice was urgent as she grabbed my arm in a desperate attempt to prevent me from walking through the door into an event. I love to encourage women, but I was already late. I only had seconds.

"Fearful mothers have fearful children!" I warned her. "You need to cry out to the Lord for the courage you need. Read Psalm 56." And then I slipped through the door.

Fear about all sorts of things can paralyze us. Like this woman, you may fear "blowing it" with your kids. You may fear a suspicious lump, an uncertain economy, or news about unfriendly countries testing nuclear bombs. Women share with me their fears of remaining single or becoming single again after a divorce. Are you too fearful to sign up for a mission trip or attempt another challenge way outside your comfort zone? What about carrying a baby whom doctors say will have special needs? Some of the most courageous women I have ever met face this life-altering decision.

> *The most effective way for us to influence others to love God's Word is for us to love it!*

Bob and I wanted our children to be courageous, to stand alone. To try out for the part in the play or the position on the team. And later, to go after their dream jobs or run for political office. We prayed that they would have courage to handle the challenges of life.

I was forced to face my fears during our first week in the Philippines. Bob needed to leave for a week in order to secure a more permanent home for us on the southern island of Mindanao. He arranged for us to stay in a mission house in Manila run by a missionary from our home church. We both agreed that it was a safe place that would allow us to acclimate to our new country.

The morning he left, I prayed with the children, asking the Lord to work out every detail for our home and ministry. As I prayed, I sensed an urgency to move the cash we'd brought from America to help us purchase a car and set up our home and ministry. I immediately took the money from the army footlocker that had belonged to my father, which we'd brought on the plane (back when airlines had no weight limit for baggage), and I carefully hid it in my clothes in a dresser. Later that night, as my four children and I were sleeping in our one room, I was startled awake by a loud noise. Through the veil of darkness, I saw a man in black clothes rummaging through our drawers and suitcases. Paralyzed by fear, I remained frozen in bed as he moved quickly through the room. I opened my eyes just enough to watch him hover over each of my sleeping children. I held my breath when he opened the trunk and rummaged through our supplies, apparently not spotting anything worth taking. On his way out the door, he grabbed my purse. We found it later on the patio, minus a few pesos.

Although I was grateful the robber didn't harm us, fears began to surface as a result of the incident. Before I left America, I thought I had dealt with my fears. It was a struggle, but a few years earlier, I gave the Lord my concerns about homeschooling. When we left the security of a church ministry and formed our nonprofit, I trusted the Lord with our finances—or the lack of them. Even moving to the Philippines during a time of political upheaval did not sidetrack me. I managed to get all the way to Manila without exhibiting fear. But could I trust God with the lives of my precious children?

The made-up tune to Joshua 1:9 played in my mind: "Have I not commanded you? Be strong and courageous! Do not tremble or be dismayed, for the LORD your God is with you wherever you go." I love that verse! I put it to a tune for my little boys, as it seemed to be intended for wannabe soldiers.

The solution to my fear problem seemed to be more applicable Scripture! My go-to book of Psalms had more than enough verses to address fears. Tucked away in Psalm 56, I found more of *my* verses:

When I am afraid,
I will put my trust in You.
In God, whose word I praise,
In God I have put my trust;
I shall not be afraid.
What can mere man do to me?

VERSES 3-4

I made up a tune for the verses, so I could sing it to myself. I then sang it to my children every night for as long as they allowed me to tuck them into bed. I prayed that God's truth about fear would influence them. It did!

Some years ago, when our son Peter was in college, he spoke at a weekend conference for guys. "I sang a verse to them," he told me when he called to tell me how it went.

"You did what?" I replied. He couldn't see me, but I was grinning.

"I was trying to show them how important it is to memorize Scripture," he explained.

There was no need to ask Peter which verse he sang. Every time

I questioned one of the kids about his or her favorite verse, it was always from Psalm 56. Why? Because God used it to calm their fears when we had to evacuate our home in Manila during a coup, when tanks rumbled down our street and planes shot real bullets overhead. It calmed their fears when Mom had amoebic dysentery and was suddenly flown to a hospital hundreds of miles away, with no communication for eleven days. And it still calms their fears as they face the challenges of life as young adults. How can one passage have so much power? Because these are not just nice-sounding words. They are words from God, and He can use them to teach us the truth about Himself. The Bible is *the* book of influence—life-changing influence!

One of my fondest verse stories took place a couple of years ago. I joined my two daughters and their five children at Katie's house in Atlanta to celebrate two kids' birthdays. After a packed day of partying with children, games, cake, balloons, and presents, the girls assigned me the privilege of putting tired little kids to bed. I told them a story, and then they begged me to sing to them. A good voice doesn't matter to grandchildren. I sang a couple of songs, and then finished with my favorite: "When I am afraid, I will put my trust in You."

To my surprise and great joy, every one of my grandchildren sang along with me. They knew each word, because their mothers sang the verses to their children, just as I sang to them. Influence! My grandchildren dozed off to sleep, and I went to my room and cried happy tears. Lots of them!

Chapter 7

THE DOUBLE-EDGED SWORD

"Would you like to see my sword?" Bob asked young men who visited our home for any reason—just in case they had an interest in one of our two daughters. For years, an engraved, oversize sword, handmade in the Philippines, was strategically placed in a prominent spot in our kitchen, the most popular room in our home. Bob would often remove the cover, exposing the razor-sharp double edges, as a deterrent to any guy with thoughts he shouldn't be thinking. Our house was a revolving door for multiple gatherings, and over time, the word about Bob's sword got around, which was exactly his plan.

Bob also flashed the sword to illustrate the impact of the Bible on our lives. Hebrews 4:12 says, "The word of God is living and active and sharper than any two-edged sword, and piercing as far as the division of soul and spirit, of both joints and marrow, and able to judge the thoughts and intentions of the heart." We had a ready-made "show-and-tell" to demonstrate that a two-edged sword would cut deeper than the common metal sword with one sharp edge. Grateful for Bob's protective instincts and his desire for our family to be students of the Manual, I let him handle the sword and the application. When he teaches this truth, he often explains, "The God of heaven has life within Himself, and He is the One who gives life. This life comes to us directly through faith in Christ and is nurtured by the living Word of God. God has put His character into His words and statements."

Most of us are not theologians like my husband, but we don't have to be. Options to help us study the Bible abound with a variety of great printed Bible studies, online learning, neighborhood gatherings, classes at a church or Bible college, Bible apps, and more. I've done all of the above during different seasons. Experiment and discover what works for you.

The great thing about the Bible is that we can pick it up at any time and begin reading. Whether in the morning, in the evening, or in between, studying God's Manual is as essential to our spiritual lives as nutritious food is to our physical ones. I can go a little while without a balanced diet of time in the Scripture, but when too much time passes, I become spiritually malnourished, unable to feed the people in my life I'm responsible for influencing. The myriad of responsibilities and distractions tempts you and me to do everything else first. In a culture of endless voices, however, we must seek God's voice through His Word. I don't hear Him speak audibly but visually through the words on the pages of the Manual.

Studying God's Manual is as essential to our spiritual lives as nutritious food is to our physical ones.

But there have been seasons when I lived in the desert of distractions—empty and starving for wisdom, direction, purpose, hope, peace, strength, joy, and the encouragement to keep on keeping on. My solution sat on my nightstand, unopened.

My mother's Bible sat unopened for years. Later in life, she carried it to church but then came home and set it on the shelf. Mom was almost fifty when my dad died of a heart attack. After being with her for a month to provide emotional and physical support, I returned to my husband and job many miles away. But when I left, the compassionate women who brought Mom meals and loved on her also invited her to a Bible study. Eventually she went. What an influence those sweet women had on my mom as they shared their love for God's Word with her. In later life, her Bible study became a priority.

A Bible study was also important to our son Peter. One day when I visited him at college, he gave me a tour of the apartment he shared with several other guys. Knowing our male counterparts have a different perspective on decorating, I inquired about the four couches arranged in a square, with a fifth couch behind, almost in a second row. "Oh, just like the other couches, the extra one was discarded by a kid graduating," Peter explained. "He left it beside the road, where all the grads leave their stuff for someone who might need it. The 'new' couch is for the overflow crowd at my Bible study." Makes sense to me!

Years have passed since Peter graduated, but when we return to the campus for a football game or other event, Bob and I are often stopped by young men who want to tell their stories of how Peter impacted their lives when they were students. He exposed them to the powerful Word of God, leaving a lasting impact.

MEETING THE AUTHOR

If we aren't in the Manual, we won't know the Master! And knowing God is the greatest privilege in all of life. Years ago, I was stuck in traffic on one of the many bridges where I live. Since I was doing a Bible study in Isaiah at the time, I decided to use my time to memorize one of the passages I'd been reading: "'You are My witnesses,' declares the

Lord, 'and My servant whom I have chosen, so that you may know and believe Me and understand that I am He. Before Me there was no God formed, and there will be none after Me. I, even I, am the Lord, and there is no savior besides Me'" (Isaiah 43:10-11).

I love these verses, because as they penetrated my mind and then my heart, I began to comprehend the significance of really knowing my Master. And as the passage reminds me, when we get to know God, we can believe Him. And then we can influence others to know and believe Him too!

My grandson provided a sweet illustration of the impact of knowing the Author. When our missionary family—our oldest daughter, her husband, and their two children—is home on furlough, Bob and I look so forward to sitting with them in church. Joe usually snuggles up under his grandpa's arm, and sweet Claire sits by me. Joe, seven when this story took place, had lots of wiggles, which he kept under reasonable control in church. I remember my boys having the same issue. Joe half-wiggled through a couple of songs, but then as we transitioned to the next song, I witnessed an instant transformation. Joe stood straight up with perfect posture and sang as loud as he could, with a huge grin on his cute face. He obviously knew the song, because I could hear each word distinctly. Curious about his enthusiasm for this song compared to the others, I asked my daughter about the contrast.

Then I got it! It turned out that the composer of that song, a popular Christian artist, was a close friend of Joe's uncle Timmy. Joe and his family were staying in Timmy's home while they were in the United States on furlough, and the composer had also spent a few nights there that week to work on a joint ministry project. That morning in church, we sang the song the composer had sung the night before for a private audience of one: my grandson. Joe had a personal relationship with the one who wrote the music and the words of the song he was singing, and that visibly impacted him.

You get the analogy! Our personal relationship with the One who wrote the words in our Manual makes a world of difference. Passages in the Bible are no longer mere words on a page. They are words spoken to us by One we know and love. Shouldn't we be more enthusiastic? I know we've never met Nehemiah, Abraham, or Paul, but if we're believers, we've met Jesus. We know the Author, our Master.

The Author also knows you—and me. He knows our heartaches and challenges. Our shortcomings, strong wills, and strong suits. He knows when we're desperate to draw close. And as I've learned over the years, desperation is often the catalyst for growth. At first, I opened the Bible the way I take prescribed medication: I know it's beneficial for me, but I don't look forward to it. Eventually my inadequacies for handling the responsibilities of lives in my charge became like an arrow aimed toward the target of the Manual. Now I think of the Bible as good food, nutritious and nourishing, providing what I need for each day's challenges. Over time, the Lord has enabled me to see how life-giving His Word is.

MEDITATION IS NOT JUST FOR YOGA ENTHUSIASTS

Interest in meditation has increased in light of scientific research that supports claims of its health benefits. Articles circulate the Internet extolling the power of meditation to counteract the stress of multitasking and much more. My knowledge of meditation, I admit, is limited to meditating on the Manual. I'm not Webster, but I define meditation as thoughtful reflection on Scripture, appropriating its truths personally and applying them to life.

Job 22:22 encourages us to "establish His words" in our hearts. A worthwhile practice is to cement meaningful verses and passages in our minds as bricks are cemented together. Make them yours. Meditation is more than just memorization. Memorization means you know the verse well enough to recite it, while meditation goes a step further. It's thoughtfully reflecting on the verse and personally applying its truths to life. The goal is to weave God's Word into the fabric of our lives. The verses I include in the pages of this book have become mine over the course of time, as they have given me courage, strength, hope, direction, and more. They are in my head, and God brings them to mind when I need them. He's established truth from Scripture in my heart.

With many verses on meditation to choose from, I picked a few of my favorites:

- "O how I love Your law! It is my meditation all the day. Your commandments make me wiser than my enemies, for they are ever mine. I have more insight than all my teachers, for Your testimonies are my meditation. I understand more than the aged, because I have observed Your precepts" (Psalm 119:97-100).

  I take these verses literally and meditate on select passages of Scripture. Even though you and I might have degrees or high-level jobs, we still run short of wisdom, insight, and understanding. I ran short of wisdom when I began to have children, started to homeschool, moved to the mission field, and moved back again. I needed understanding and insight to deal with a variety of learning styles, personalities, and love languages. In the midst of all of the above, I began speaking to varied groups, which required insight to match my message with my audience. Meditation on God's Word can give us the wisdom we need to handle the challenges we face in life.

- "Finally, brethren, whatever is true, whatever is honorable, whatever is right, whatever is pure, whatever is lovely, whatever is of good repute, if there is any excellence and if anything worthy of praise, dwell on these things" (Philippians 4:8).

It's easy to focus on what's going wrong in our lives or the world, but the apostle Paul encouraged the Philippians to dwell on what is good. Because I don't want to become the "grumpy old lady," this is another passage I work on. Paying special attention to the goodness of God and remembering His specific blessings is an exercise I recommend.

- "This book of the law shall not depart from your mouth, but you shall meditate on it day and night, so that you may be careful to do according to all that is written in it; for then you will make your way prosperous, and then you will have success" (Joshua 1:8).

  This is my favorite. I was once asked to speak on raising successful children. When I looked up *success* in the Bible, the only reference I found was Joshua 1:8. The world may have a different measure, but I believed my children would meet God's standard of success if they engrafted His Word and applied it to their lives. The Scripture I taught to my children continues to influence them even now—long after they left our home. And it's an understatement of huge proportions to say that I have been impacted as well.

- "His delight is in the law of the Lord, and in His law he meditates day and night" (Psalm 1:2).

  I take this verse literally too. We can meditate on Scripture when we wake up, when we're waiting in line, when we're driving to work, anytime we find ourselves with a few free minutes, and my favorite—when I'm falling asleep.

- "As those who have been chosen of God, holy and beloved, put on a heart of compassion, kindness, humility, gentleness and patience; bearing with one another, and forgiving each other, whoever has a complaint against anyone; just as the Lord forgave you, so also should you. Beyond all these things put on love, which is the perfect bond of unity. Let the peace of Christ rule in your hearts, to which indeed you were called in one body; and be thankful. Let the word of Christ richly dwell within you, with all wisdom teaching and admonishing one another with psalms and hymns and spiritual songs, singing with thankfulness in your hearts to God. Whatever you do in word or deed, do all in the name of the Lord Jesus, giving thanks through Him to God the Father" (Colossians 3:12-17).

Each morning, just as I put on clothes for the day, I try to consciously "put on" (as the passage indicates) each of the qualities mentioned: compassion, kindness, humility, gentleness, patience, bearing the burdens of others, forgiving others just as God forgives me, and, above all, loving others. Letting God's peace rule me, and expressing gratitude. Letting God's Word live in me, using it to teach and encourage others. And whatever I say or do, doing it in the name of Jesus, thanking the Lord.

I'm well aware of my weaknesses. Aren't you? We try to fool others, but we don't usually fool ourselves. When my shortcomings have been exposed over the years, I've found verses to think about and meditate on. This passage covers a lot of battleground—minefields where my old and new natures battle each other, because not one of the qualities in this passage comes naturally for me. I can't will myself to demonstrate any of the above spiritual characteristics, but I believe that meditating on verses like these, over the course of time, results in gradual changes that are evidence of God's transforming power.

- "Wait for the LORD; be strong and let your heart take courage; yes, wait for the LORD" (Psalm 27:14).

• "I wait for the LORD, my soul does wait, and in His word do I hope" (Psalm 130:5).

Although I wrote about waiting for our first home in the Philippines in an earlier chapter, it also fits here as an illustration of applying the verses above. In a desperate attempt to patiently wait on the Lord, I found two related verses and meditated on them, combining them into a song. After I taught them to the kids, we sang them together in rounds throughout the days we waited on Bob to return to us and on God to provide our home. We waited with fevers and open sores that appeared on bodies ill-equipped for our new environment.

Meditating on verses, over the course of time, results in gradual changes that are evidence of God's transforming power.

As we meditated on truth by singing our verses, we were living examples of the unmistakable impact Scripture had on our minds. It was no longer a theological point I read about. The reality of the verses we focused on transformed my attitude about waiting; and as we sang those verses repeatedly, my children's spirits became patient too.

Besides verses like the ones above, I've learned the most about meditation from observing our cows. Although I'm joint owner with Bob of a bunch of cows that roam our property, I tell my family, "I don't do cows." I don't give them hay or chase a calf who escapes under the fence, but I do like to observe them chewing. One benefit I derive from the cows, besides grass-fed steak, is the obvious illustration of meditation. Cows have four stomachs and chew their cud. They eat grass, then spit it up and chew it again and again and again, absorbing every possible nutrient from the grass. I rarely see a cow who isn't chewing. I realize this visual is a little disgusting, but what a great example for us of meditating or "chewing" on specific verses—thinking about them, perhaps memorizing them, going over and over the meaning, and planning specific ways to apply them.

PASS ON YOUR VERSES

Share verses you love with your friends, coworkers, and family members. Your enthusiastic discovery of a new verse will inspire others to find a great verse too. Talk to kids naturally about your favorite Scriptures. It doesn't have to be in a formal setting, and you don't need to be an expert. I learned along with my kids. You don't need to have it together. Who does?

My mother, like most of us, had a tendency to be anxious. When she was in her seventies, my daughters encouraged their grandmother to find a verse to combat her nervousness. She found Isaiah 26:3, and it became hers: "The steadfast of mind You will keep in perfect peace, because [she] trusts in You." (She changed the *he* to *she*, which I'm sure didn't bother the Author.) She wrote her verse on a card and took it with her everywhere. When she shared her verse with someone, she would tell me, "I gave her *my* verse." It was so sweet! We need to carry "our" verses with us on cards or in our hearts, prepared to impact those we share them with, keeping in mind their potential to impact us.

BE THANKFUL FOR EVERYTHING?

Some of the verses that have been most influential for our family deal with attitudes like thanksgiving and humility. A reporter once asked our son Timmy how he dealt with losing a football game. Since guys don't often share many details, I was grateful to read his response in the newspaper: "When I was young," he answered, "my mom taught me a Bible verse about how to handle disappointments." I immediately knew which one he meant. As a young mom, I realized quickly that Scripture carries more weight than my words alone and has a longer impact, so when my children lost the game, didn't make all-stars, or had to watch some other kid get the position they wanted, we came back to 1 Thessalonians 5:18: "In everything give thanks; for this is God's will for you in Christ Jesus." (Of course there's also a tune for that.) When the boys were young, they would bow their little heads and pray, "Dear Jesus, thank You that we lost our game." They weren't happy about the loss, but there was instant relief when they gave their disappointments to the Lord.

I recommend teaching lessons like this at age five, six, or seven. Learning such countercultural concepts at nineteen or twenty is much harder when a loss in the SEC Championship means playing in a bowl game instead of the national championship.

Decades ago, I was early to pick up a child from a youth activity. I hate wasting time, so I checked out a nearby store. Not finding anything of interest, I walked out again. In a split second, an eight-foot piece of molding fell from above the doorframe onto my head. I still marvel that my first conscious thoughts were *"In everything give thanks . . ."* What an obvious God story!

I sustained serious injuries, and the aftermath of the incident is ongoing. Yet that verse—and the grace of the One who put it in our Bible and brought it to my mind—prevented me from potential bitterness. Insurance lawyers were brutal, evidence and witnesses disappeared, no million-dollar settlement was awarded, and no miraculous healing occurred. But in what I believe is a spiritual miracle, I have never had a moment of bitterness. The nerve damage in my face remains twenty-five years later as a reminder of the incredible power of the Word of God! I can't type these words without tears, because only God has the power to use a verse for a lifelong ministry in my heart to overcome my potential for bitterness.

Bitterness usually results in complaining, an unpleasant trait Bob vetoed for his family and his mission trips.

NO WHININ'

"No whinin'," Jackson babbled to his daddy, as he and our son Peter FaceTimed us. Jackson's parents were attempting to teach their little two-year-old not to complain. Our grandson is so adorable that "whinin'" seems acceptable. But complaining, grumbling, and whining are not as cute on our lips.

Since childhood, I have had an inner-ear vertigo issue, which makes me highly susceptible to motion sickness and can make traveling a challenge. Recently, in my middle seat on the long return flight from California, I worked on my to-do list. The women on each side of me seemed to be working on theirs too. As we approached Atlanta, the pilot warned of turbulence and made the familiar announcement "Return to your seats and buckle your seat belts." I was probably the only one on the plane who winced as we flew into the storm, preparing to land. I checked for the security of my prescription patch behind my ear. Apologizing to my seatmates for the unusual odor, I added an herbal oil concoction. I put on wristbands. I swallowed a pill for motion sickness. The plane continued to shake, and I realized the weather was too intense for my "bag of tricks." Bracing for the worst, I took the little white bag from the seat pocket. As the turbulence increased, I asked one of the ladies for her bag too.

Here we go, Lord, I prayed as the plane landed. *Please give me grace to make it to the restroom.* My prayer was answered. The ladies' room was directly across from my gate.

Normally I leave the large stall for those who need more space—unless I'm desperate. I was desperate. I needed room to lay my head on my carry-on bag in between "episodes." For the next four and a half hours, that oversize stall became my domain. The restroom attendant was aware of my presence, and she would periodically update me on my connecting flight, which was delayed because of the storm. *No whining*, I reminded myself. Because of my vertigo,

I have been there (or somewhere) and done that more times than I can count. But I refused to complain. Why? How?

Don't put me on any pedestal, especially if it spins around. I'm just as tempted to complain as any other woman. This true illustration is not included to provoke empathy. My seatmates, the flight attendants, and the airport employee were not the least bit sympathetic. I didn't expect them to be. But on that day, I knew for a fact that God loved me, and He had this! I also knew that I couldn't let a "woe is me" thought form in my already challenged brain.

All of us deal with real problems that can't be solved with fluids and a day or two of rest. Perhaps you have a child with special needs, pending surgery, a broken marriage, or bills you can't pay. Your teenager is rebellious. Your husband is too preoccupied to notice your needs. You're exhausted from caring for your elderly parent. Your home is too small, and your to-do list is too big. Working and going to school is just too much! For most of us, a legitimate grievance list is longer than this chapter. So why not complain, at least to ourselves? I grew up complaining with my lips and in my mind. Grumbling, complaining, or whining is an acceptable practice for women, especially when we get together. There may be a tinge of guilt, but pity parties assure us our girlfriends are in the same boat, with a cargo of complaints.

Long before our precious grandson was born, my husband uttered words similar to Jackson's: "No complaining!" He based that on Philippians 2:14-15: "Do all things without complaining and disputing, that you may become blameless and harmless, children of God without fault in the midst of a crooked and perverse generation, among whom you shine as lights in the world" (NKJV). Learning to live without complaining makes us stand out in our world, allowing us to "shine as lights" and highlight the grace of God in our lives. It changes our attitudes and enables us to be more content. It allows us to look beyond our temporary circumstances to what is eternal.

This "no complaining" rule came to be in 1994, when Bob took twenty young people on the first of many short-term mission trips. He noted that if one summer missionary complained, grumbling spread like lice and pink eye. (Since both of these unpleasantries were experienced during the early years of those trips, it's an appropriate comparison.) When they faced challenges like cold bucket baths, uncomfortable beds, and bumpy travel on unpaved roads, Bob reminded the group that nothing would happen to them that was worse than what Jesus suffered on the cross. What could anyone say in response to those words?

All of us have some legitimate complaints, and our compassionate God is aware of every difficult circumstance. Many verses in Scripture encourage us to come to Him with our complaints. When David fled from his persecutors, he prayed, "As for me, I shall call upon God, and the LORD will save me. Evening and morning and at noon, I will complain and murmur, and He will hear my voice" (Psalm 55:16-17). When my daughter Christy held training for abused, trafficked women in the country where she serves, she taught them how to cry out to God with their complaints. She shared verses like "I pour out my complaint before Him; I declare my trouble before Him" (Psalm 142:2) and "Pour out your heart like water before the presence of the Lord" (Lamentations 2:19). The women were so impacted by this revolutionary truth—that God loved them enough to draw them to Himself and hear their cries. Each woman was encouraged to write her own psalm of complaint to God. Christy wept as she shared with me about the transformation she observed in the women. For the first time, many believed that God really loved them and cared about their hardships.

You may not have faced the same circumstances, but all of us have scars, visible and invisible. We, like these precious women my daughter ministered to, can bring all of our complaints to the Lord, whose compassion never fails. I love the visual of pouring our hearts out like water before the Lord. Some of us are blessed with a close friend we can share heartaches with, but all of us can go straight to the throne of God with every complaint, and He alone can use our trials for our good and His glory.

There is, however, a big difference between complaining to the Lord and complaining to others. As I write, I can hear the raindrops on the window. It rained all day yesterday, and more rain is forecast for tomorrow. Proverbs 27:15 reminds us, "A constant dripping on a day of steady rain and a contentious woman are alike." There have been too many times when I've grumbled and my name could have been inserted in that illustration. Yours too? Please don't stop reading, because the Lord promises to help us. That's why I remain desperate for Him, even after years of learning and applying biblical truths. You and I will have our propensity for complaining until we go to heaven. And we just can't help but complain when we are in certain situations—or can we?

Some of you are probably too young to remember the popularity of conversion vans. To say we were thrilled when we bought a used conversion van is an understatement. A friend spotted it at a dealership—just in time, because our Suburban was near death. At first it was fantastic. The kids loved watching videos in their bucket seats, and our two youngest sons didn't even mind the long drives to Tennessee to watch their brother's college football games. But once on a family trip to the mountains for vacation, the van's transmission went out. Since Bob's "no complaining" rule had been in effect for so many years, we didn't grumble as we waited for hours in a small town while it was being fixed.

Time passed, and our youngest son, Timmy, was the last one I drove around in the van. That year we had fun together, and I learned a little about country music. In his bucket seat, he watched his favorite inspirational movies before high school football games. Then one day, the air-conditioning went out. Since it would have cost more than the vehicle was worth to fix it, we decided to keep driving the van as is until it died. Wishing for its early death didn't help. Since Timmy and I were the only two people who rode in the van, we made a pact, promising each other that we would roll down the windows and not complain. It was doable in the winter, but then spring came. Just so you get the picture, we live in Florida. It's hot! Summer arrived, and the van kept going. Then my window stuck closed and never did go down again. Despite it all, Timmy and I continued to remind each other of our agreement. The "no complaining" rule continually flashed in neon lights on the billboard of my mind—and his.

How do we influence others not to complain? We have to set the example. I certainly didn't volunteer to be the living illustration of someone with issues to complain about, but our children and others watch us closely. The ripple effects of complaining are obvious, as they can lead to widespread negativity. We must learn to halt the thought before it generates a bad attitude and then a word of complaint or "whinin'."

My friend Sue is not a complainer either. When I was stuck in the airport restroom that became my home away from home in the story I shared earlier, my husband was out of the country and I knew I couldn't drive home from the airport. I called Sue. When she answered, I could only whisper, "So sick in Atlanta." She didn't need to hear more. She assured me she would check flights and be there with her husband to pick me up. It was past midnight when I was wheeled to her car, carrying my little white bag with me.

Sue also understands the impact of combining "thankfulness for everything" with "no complaining." She actually wins the prize! Some years ago, she called to tell me that the MRI revealed breast cancer. Instead of saying, "Why me?" she said, "Why not me?" As she lost her hair and her strength, there was no complaining! How could she respond to such devastating news with a grateful spirit and a determination not to complain to others? Because Sue chose to trust God's Word rather than her circumstance. The ripple effects of that choice have impacted many lives, including mine. I'm so proud to call her my friend. I often share her life-impacting story. What influence!

THE MANUAL'S RIPPLE EFFECTS

When I spoke at a women's conference in the city where my daughter Katie lives, she brought all of her girlfriends. I sang a number of my Bible verse songs during the event, and afterward I asked her, "Honey, how many of those verses do you remember?"

She replied, "Mom, I remember all of them!" My mom tank was filled to overflowing! That's the point of working on verses day after day, year after year, and influencing those we love to take God's Word with them wherever they go in life.

I'm forever grateful for the many challenges in my life that drove me to God's Manual for answers. Nothing has impacted me more than the Word of God. We influence the people in our spheres to love God's Manual because we love it.

Don't try to influence in your own strength. Read, study, and prepare yourself for a life of influence with the life-transforming Manual God has given us. It really is miraculous motivating power!

PRAYER

Prayer, the third component of miraculous motivating power, is as necessary for our souls as breathing is for our bodies. Prayer is an essential tool of influence because it connects us to our Master, who has all power in heaven and on earth (see Matthew 28:18). When we talk to God in a simple conversation and listen as He speaks to us through His Word, the Manual, or in our inner person, our relationship with Him deepens. We can pray as King David did in a long psalm or like the apostle Peter when he was sinking in the water and cried simply, "Lord, save me."

Although the Bible doesn't distinguish types of prayer, for the sake of explanation, I divide prayer into three categories: prayer that influences us, others, and the situations we pray for. All three are important, and it's worth setting aside time to ask the Lord to work on behalf of the people and circumstances we bring to Him in prayer. What could be more influential?

As God answered my prayers through the years, my faith grew more than I once thought possible. And when I share the God stories that occurred in answer to my prayers, others are encouraged to talk to the Lord about their simple requests or deepest needs. The ripple effects of our prayers are impossible to comprehend with our finite minds. As we draw close to the Lord, our mighty, loving God can do more than we ask or think according to His miraculous motivating power (see Ephesians 3:20).

Let us draw near with confidence to the throne of grace, so that we may receive mercy and find grace to help in time of need.

HEBREWS 4:16

Chapter 8

A RUNNING CONVERSATION

"Prayer is just a running conversation with God," I heard my youngest son tell a group of young boys. "You can talk to Him when you throw the ball, when you are on the bench, when you are in the huddle." Talking to God all the time is what the apostle Paul meant when he encouraged us to "pray without ceasing" (1 Thessalonians 5:17). We tend to pray when our world detonates or we are at our wits' end. Yet the Bible instructs us to pray before we do anything at all.

I can't remember praying as a child except to repeat a singsong poem before meals. Prayer seemed to be just for preachers and super-spiritual adults. When I was twelve and walked to that little church with my sister, I prayed to invite Jesus to be my Savior. He answered that prayer, so I should have known I could talk to Him anytime about anything. But I didn't comprehend the power of prayer, and I missed years of connecting with my heavenly Father. My husband did too. We wanted to do things differently, so we began praying with our children as soon as they could say a few words. We hoped that talking to God would become as natural as hugs from Mom and as significant as a special date with Dad.

The responsibility of influencing our children to pray was a spotlight exposing the holes in my own prayer life. If prayer were not natural to me, how could it be natural for my children? Keenly aware that prayer was one of my weaknesses, I attended a prayer conference by a well-known pastor, who kept a detailed prayer journal and got up at 4:30 every morning to pray. I thought the solution was to copy him, but I failed miserably. I set my alarm, got up, and prayed. But I also was up in the middle of the night with a baby. (My sleep-deprived state occurred years before all the YouTube videos on how to get your baby to sleep through the night in a week.) Tired and discouraged, I gave up on the 4:30 idea, believing I would never grasp the reality of prayer.

You may be in a crazy busy season of life now, whether your baby sleeps through the night or your babies have already grown up. You might be spending late nights at the office, or writing term papers or a dissertation, unable to take on one more assignment. And you may do all of the above with a job, a husband, kids, and a to-do list so long that you can't imagine adding even one more responsibility. If prayer is on your list, it's positioned between "run to the grocery store" and "help with homework." Lots of us plan to make time for God, but the tyranny of the urgent shoves our prayer lives out of the way as one of my little boys shoved his brother when he thought I wasn't looking. My son got caught and put in time-out, while we get away with lives void of prayer. No one else knows if we pray or not. When I believed that taking time for prayer was just one more responsibility, it was shoved aside. But prayer became the domino that caused all the other dominoes to fall. Our enemy wins a great battle when we cease to pray.

Jim Cymbala wrote in his book *Fresh Wind, Fresh Fire*, "Prayer cannot truly be taught by principles and seminars and symposiums. It has to be born out of a whole environment of felt need. If I say, 'I *ought* to pray,' I will soon run out of motivation and quit; the flesh is too strong. I have to be *driven* to pray."[1]

Our enemy wins a great battle when we cease to pray.

Most women I know do not pray because they are supposed to. They pray because they have no other recourse. I remain in that category of women who are desperate for God's involvement. You probably are too. When our burdens are the heaviest, we are driven to pray. Years ago, I wrote in my journal (one of only a handful of entries that year), "Lord, at this season in life, I am driven to pray. Life's problems are so complex. I know for a fact now that there is no human who can meet my needs; yet so many humans depend on me."

I'm so thankful that in the midst of a busy life, God's grace drew me to Himself. I followed the example of the disciples, who begged Jesus to teach them how to pray, and I prayed to learn about prayer. I learned the most simply by praying. I learned not just intellectually but experientially that I could talk to God on the go. I can pray as I drive, do laundry, jog on a treadmill, lie in bed, sit at my desk, or watch a ball game. After all the years of trying to grow in the area of prayer so I could influence my children with its importance, I remember crying happy tears when I heard my son quote me: "Prayer is just a running conversation with God."

As I was in the process of reading over this manuscript for publication, I spoke at a "moms' encouragement" night. I shared the story of teaching Timmy that prayer is a conversation with God, one that takes place as we run, walk, dance, work, drive, or anything else. The next morning, I was preparing to speak again to the group when a lady in tears approached me: "I never knew I could talk to God all the time," she began. "I thought I had to kneel beside my bed in order for my prayers to be heard. I drove an hour and a half to hear you today, and I prayed all the way. I've never had such freedom!" When I shared that story with my family, they encouraged me to add it to this chapter—in case other women mistakenly believe we need to be in a prostrate position for our prayers to be heard. I'm as thankful as the sweet woman who approached me that we can, indeed, pray on the go, and God hears us.

A SPECIAL RELATIONSHIP

Writing on prayer is, for me, like trying to explain why the waves crash on the shores of our beautiful Florida beaches. My comprehension on the vast subject of prayer is limited. Yet the God who created the oceans, the tides, and the waves also opens His arms wide, inviting us to come to Him, talk to Him, spend time with Him. The Creator God desires a relationship with you and me through prayer.

And prayer really is a relationship. We value communication with the people we love. When Bob is on a mission field where communication is a challenge, I miss our interaction. When my missionary family is out of reach, I can't wait to talk to them. We've probably all experienced missing out on the latest with family and friends because we forgot to charge our cell phones. Talking with those we love keeps us connected, even when we aren't face-to-face. That's the way it is with prayer. We simply talk to God. I tell Him everything that is on my mind and heart. He already knows, but it's so freeing to tell Him.

In the next chapter I'll offer a framework for prayer that has been helpful to me, but my suggestions aren't rules to follow. There is no perfect strategy, set time, or course of action for prayer. We can join a prayer group, kneel by our beds, or pray on the go. Prayer is not about a set of rules or requirements; it is a relationship between two people who love each other. It's as natural as breathing and as fulfilling as connecting at the heart level with your best friend. Over time, when I began to comprehend that God loves me so much that He wants to spend time with me, my prayer life began to change.

If you are into college athletics, you know that the NCAA has strict recruiting rules. In the spring of our youngest son's junior year of high school, college football coaches were allowed one phone call to our home. I was often the one to take the call. The first coach phoned at 12:01 a.m., the exact day and minute coaches were allowed to call. Most of the coaches did their homework on our family and attempted to connect in some way, leading to conversations about homeschooling, missions, and multiple children. Even though I understood their motives in talking with me, I would hang up in awe that I had just chatted with a well-known coach.

Many coaches representing schools across the country called our home (when landlines were the norm). Their names were ones you would recognize—if you're a college football fan. After one of those calls, I was struck with this thought: *As impressive as college football coaches are, I have the incredible privilege of talking to the God who holds the whole world in His hand.* I remember wiping away tears at the realization that I can go straight to the throne of God anytime I choose. Hebrews 4:16 says, "Let us draw near with confidence to the throne of grace, so that we may receive mercy and find grace to help in time of need." Do you ever take for granted your privilege of connecting with the Lord through prayer? I sure do. Too many times!

I don't think I ever took for granted the sweet connection I had with my mom in her later years. I still remember the last time I drove to see her when she was still able to live alone. She lived about three hours away from us in Tampa, and finally I made it through traffic to her street. Usually I would pull into the driveway, knock on the door, and wait for her to unlock her three locks. But not this time! She knew I was coming, and she was waiting for me near the curb. When I spotted her, she had her arms wide open, ready to hug me.

That was a sweet reminder that our Savior has His arms open

wide, waiting for me (and you) to come to Him with every need, hope, concern, heartache, joy, and more. I didn't have to knock on Mom's door; she was waiting expectantly for me to arrive, excited to catch up on even the smallest details of my life. God is the same way. When I comprehended that He loves me and desires to be closely connected to me, I was no longer concerned about using spiritual-sounding words when I prayed. Instead, I talked to the Lord as I talked to my mom. And in the process, a relationship resulted, one I wouldn't trade for anything!

PRAYER'S VAST INFLUENCE

When I first began speaking to women on "Influence," I talked about three different components that prayer influences: us, the people we pray for, and the situations or circumstances we pray about. The Bible doesn't necessarily designate prayer categories, but a simple outline helps me to make sense of the big picture of prayer.

Prayer Influences Us

As pastor Ray Stedman wrote in *Talking with My Father*, "Prayer is not so much a channel by which we influence God as it is a channel through which God influences us!"[2] Prayer is not my strength, but over the years, prayer has changed me. Prayer connects me to my heavenly Father at every level—intellectually, emotionally, and physically.

Prayer was still new to me when Bob and I moved far from home, right after our wedding, to attend grad school. We had lots of wedding presents but not much money. We found an apartment and jobs. Most of our friends in grad school were poor like us, and we enjoyed cheap fun like potlucks coupled with playing board games. I think I was born frugal and made every effort to stretch what little we had. But one Saturday morning, the cupboard was bare and we had no money to buy food.

I had never experienced a lack of food or any other basic need. My parents took great care of me—until Bob and I were married and took off across the country. I didn't let them know we were struggling, because they would have preferred that Bob choose another vocation besides ministry. I didn't want to reflect negatively on our stated plan to trust God for our future, especially when we were just a few months into it, so we chose not to tell anyone but God about our needs. Of course, He already knew. Bob quoted Matthew 6:33: "Seek first His kingdom and His righteousness, and all these things will be added to you." A few verses earlier, Jesus instructs us not to worry about what we will eat or drink or wear, because God already knows that we need these things, and He will care for us.

This was a first for me; I had never prayed about such things before. But we were hungry, and we prayed humbly, asking God for food. We were standing in our tiny kitchen by the empty refrigerator, and Bob prayed, "Father, You said if we seek You and Your Kingdom first, then we would have everything we need. To the best of our ability, that's what we've been doing. As You know, we have no money, and we have no food. Would You please feed us? We're hungry. In Jesus' name, amen."

Gas was cheap in those days and we had a full tank, so we went for a ride in the scenic city we lived in. We prayed as we drove. God's peace invaded our minds and hearts, but our stomachs were still growling. Although this story took place decades ago, I will never forget arriving home and walking up the stairs to our little apartment. There, in front of the door, were two sacks of groceries! Not just someone's castoffs, but sacks full of meat, vegetables, fruit, snacks, cheese, and milk. We cried and thanked the Lord, and we never got over God's answer to our prayers.

We never lacked for food again. But if God could meet that basic need of food, couldn't He also meet our needs for grace, mercy, energy, wisdom, direction, hope, and so much more? We learned to pray specifically. We learned to trust God. God's amazing answer to our prayer showed me that God really cared about my needs. And for the first time, I knew beyond a shadow of a doubt that I would never have to handle life on my own.

One of the zillions of times I could not handle life on my own was in 2009. Our family sat in the stands at the University of Kentucky football stadium as our youngest son lay lifeless on the field. He had been hit in the front by the Kentucky defensive end, who knocked him backward. The back of his head hit the knee of his own offensive tackle. As we waited for what seemed like an eternity, the cameras found our family in the stands. I have often been asked what I was doing while I waited for Timmy to gain consciousness.

My family held hands and prayed. Then, as we stood silently, I sang Psalm 61:1-3 (another one of my Scripture songs) in my mind: "Hear my cry, O God; give heed to my prayer. From the end of the earth I call to You when my heart is faint; lead me to the rock that is higher than I. For You have been a refuge for me, a tower of strength against the enemy." God was the strength I needed when my heart was faint. As we prayed, the Lord gave us His supernatural peace, which allowed us to have a calming influence on the doctors, coaches, teammates, and fans as we counted on God to be our tower of strength.

Prayer Influences the People We Pray For

The story above also fits in this next category of prayer influencing others—those we pray for. I compiled a fat folder of letters and e-mails from people—everyone from kindergartners to grandmothers—who wrote to encourage us that they prayed as Timmy lay unconscious on the football field. The game was nationally televised, and later, as I traveled to various locations around the country for speaking engagements, many people shared that when they watched Timmy get hit, they immediately dropped to their knees and began to pray for him. People continued to pray as he healed. More than four million people indicated on Facebook that they were praying.

The neurosurgeon at the University of Kentucky medical school was watching the game. When he saw Timmy fall, he believed with certainty that our son had suffered a spinal cord injury. He immediately drove to the hospital, expecting to deal with a serious medical issue. Every other doctor we talked to later also believed that Timmy had injured his spinal cord, based on the way he fell. Only heaven knows how prayer influenced his situation, but he was able to walk out of the hospital and return to Florida with his team. Timmy played in the game two weeks later against LSU—and his team won!

Just as I stacked the letters and e-mails from those who prayed for my son, I picture myself stacking up prayers for the people I want to influence the most. We all have significant people in our lives: family, friends, and others God puts on our hearts. One of my favorite Scripture prayers for those special people is Colossians 1:9-12:

[I] have not ceased to pray for you and to ask that you may be filled with the knowledge of His will in all spiritual wisdom and understanding, so that you will walk in a manner worthy of the Lord, to please Him in all respects, bearing fruit in every good work and increasing in the knowledge of God; strengthened with all power, according to His glorious might, for the attaining of all steadfastness and patience; joyously giving thanks to the Father, who has qualified us to share in the inheritance of the saints in Light.

I choose different verses to pray for various people, but the passage above is my "go to." I love it because it reminds me to pray not just for circumstances but also for what is more important. We can pray that others would draw near to God, know Him better, be comforted by Him, glorify Him in both joy and struggles, and be made more like Christ each day. We are blessed with the freedom both to pray our own words and to use verses in the Bible that express the desires of our hearts.

On another occasion, I only whispered a quick prayer that was answered by our mighty God. Although it was years ago, I remember well the challenges of moving back to our home in Jacksonville from the Philippines. All of us were experiencing some culture shock. At first I resisted the move because I knew we were called to missions, and I was also aware that American life, by contrast to life in the Philippines, is hectic and fast-paced. But I submitted to Bob's board, who believed that we needed to recover from health issues and that Bob would be more effective traveling back and forth from America to the Philippines. As it turns out, the board was right: Our health improved and the ministry grew—and life was, indeed, crazy busy. My prayer list was long, but I recall my burden for our bubbly second daughter, Katie. It's not easy during the early teen years to join a group of kids who have known each other since kindergarten. Although Katie was outgoing, I sensed that she needed to feel special during this season. I prayed for the Lord to handle that in His way, and then I quickly moved on to my numerous responsibilities with four other children and fitting back into American life.

Katie asked if she could try out for a special part in the Christmas musical at the large church we belonged to. She hadn't prepared anything, but I let her go to the audition with friends of ours. By this time, I had forgotten about my specific prayer for Katie, but God hadn't. A few weeks later, she learned she'd been chosen for a starring role in the musical—quite an honor considering that hundreds of kids were involved. Katie wore a beautiful costume and sang a solo that showcased her sweet voice. Her role provided an instant opportunity to take part in something so significant and unforgettable. The girls she practiced with became her best friends.

I later learned that Nancy, the wonderful musical director, diligently prayed over all the casting decisions. She asked the Lord for wisdom to put the right person in each role—not just to make the musical a success but also to have life-impacting influence on each child chosen for a special part. Nancy had never met Katie before she tried out, but after much prayer, she knew that Katie was perfect for the part and the part was perfect for Katie. The Lord answered prayers in a way I could never have planned, and a sweet and sensitive homeschooled missionary kid was encouraged. Katie and dear Miss Nancy continue to enjoy the special relationship God brought about in answer to the prayers of all three of us! What a reminder that the Lord loves the people we pray for even more than we do, and He uses even our seemingly insignificant prayers for significant influence.

The Lord loves the people we pray for even more than we do, and He uses even our seemingly insignificant prayers for significant influence.

Kelly is a friend who is mighty in prayer. I call her a prayer warrior because she wages war against the enemy with her faithful prayers, and I'm so blessed that she prays for me. Kelly memorizes and meditates on verses the Lord leads her to, and she prays applicable verses for her family and others the Lord puts on her heart. Recently I spoke at a huge event. There were more influential men and women in one grand ballroom than I could count. In the midst of this situation that was certainly not in my comfort zone, I sensed an unmistakable peace that seemed to envelop me. Even though I had prepared and prepared, I didn't feel confident in my preparation or my abilities, but I had an over-powering sense that God would come through in a way only He could do. My overwhelming focus was to glorify Him. Kelly sent me a prayer text, and I read it again right before I spoke. Her words, which were actually God's words, had a supernatural impact. As extraordinary as it sounds, as I spoke that day, I sensed her prayers. This is the prayer text she sent:

> "You are worthy, O Lord our God, to receive glory and honor and praise." Rev. 4:11. "Come let us tell of the Lord's greatness, let us exalt His name forever . . ." Psalm 34:3. "I love you, Lord; you are my strength." Psalm 18:1. "You will keep in perfect peace all who trust in you, all whose thoughts are fixed on you! Lord, our heart's desire is to glorify your name." Is. 26:3, 8b. "Now all glory to God, who is able, through his mighty power at work in Pam, to accomplish infinitely more than we might ask or think as she speaks at this event and beyond." Eph. 3:20.

For decades, our family prayed for the salvation of my husband's mother. She was intelligent, well traveled, and active in the community, but she was not interested in spiritual things. Bob tried many times to talk to her about a relationship with Christ, but she wouldn't listen to him. In her late seventies, Mom suffered from ovarian cancer, and we hoped that she would finally be ready to talk about her faith. But when a good friend visited her in the hospital, she was thrown out for talking about spiritual issues. The only one Mom let discuss such things was our daughter Christy. Christy loved her grandmother and wept as she begged her to consider what Jesus did for her on the cross. During her visit, Bob sat outside the hospital room and prayed. He was amazed and hopeful, as he timed the visit and realized that his mother had let Christy stay for twenty-two minutes. But as Christy left the room in tears, his mom yelled to her son that she would not be another one of his evangelism statistics.

Knowing she was near death, we asked everyone we knew to pray for her salvation. Mom was moved to hospice, where family and friends frequently visited. When Bob and our son Peter arrived one day, they were surprised to find her alone. Bob didn't walk into her room with a plan, but he instinctively asked her if he could pray. Very few people turn down prayers on their behalf, especially when they are so near death. She said, "Yes," in a barely audible whisper. Bob held his mom's hand, and without realizing at first what he was saying, he began to pray the prayer that he always uses to lead people to Christ in the Philippines: "Dear Jesus, I know that I'm a sinner and need a Savior. Thank You for dying on the cross for me and rising again. I open the door of my heart and ask You to come in. Save me, Jesus. Thank You for saving me. Thank You for coming into my heart. Thank You that God is my Father and I am His child. Thank You that I have a home in heaven and I will come and live with You someday. In Jesus' name, amen."

His mother's countenance slowly transformed as he prayed. Bob was stunned. He questioned, "Mom, did you just pray that prayer with me?" In her faint whisper, she responded, "Yes." He asked, "Where is Jesus now?" She pointed her slim finger at her emaciated chest and said, "Heart." Bob then asked, "If you were to die today, where would you be?" She pointed up and mouthed the word "Heaven." That was the last word she ever spoke. We believe she is in heaven now, and we will rejoice with her there someday.

I share this story to encourage those of you who long to see people you love come to Christ. Never give up! Pray and pray, and enlist your praying friends to pray with you. A person's eternity is at stake! Until we take our last breath, it's not too late to meet our Savior and have the assurance that we will spend eternity with Him.

Prayer Influences the Situations We Pray For

You have heard the popular quote "Prayer changes things." It's true! Prayer can change our circumstances.

When we moved back to Florida from the Philippines, we didn't leave behind our ministry in the Asian country we love. Bob continued to travel back and forth, and in 1994, he began taking groups several times a year on mission trips. The summer trip is the largest, drawing youth, who are required to be at least fifteen years old. A few summers ago, I made plans to go, and Bob and I were surprised and overjoyed when our sons Timmy and Robby were able to arrange their crazy schedules to join us for the first week of our summer mission trip to the Philippines.

I knew that Timmy's burning desire was to preach in a prison while he was there. Bob tried to make that happen while we were on the island of Mindanao, but the local jail let all the prisoners out for the weekend. And although Timmy wanted to preach in the jail, an empty one was not exactly what he had in mind. Aware of Timmy's heart for prisoners, I prayed and prayed and prayed, crying out to the Lord to grant the desire of my son's heart. I kept praying, begging God as the widow begged the unrighteous judge in Luke 18.

When we returned to Manila, my husband tried all of his contacts in an attempt to make Timmy's desire a reality, but to no avail. Our longtime friend Mark has many friends in the Philippine government, but he came up short too. Mark sent one last text as I silently prayed, *Please, Lord, let this be the person who will open that door for Timmy to preach to prisoners.*

The Lord did use Mark's text to get results, but not in a way we could have ever anticipated. Mark accidentally sent his text to the wrong number, but as only God could arrange, it went to the right person—someone none of us knew, but who had the clout to open the prison doors. An influential senator texted back, "If you mean that it is Tim Tebow who is requesting to speak in a prison, then YES!"

The senator and his wife, also a senator, not only had the necessary authority to open the prison but were also committed Christians who welcomed Timmy. As they commented, "He was born in the

Philippines and loves our country and our people." So our son stood before six hundred prisoners and shared that God loved them and sent His Son, Jesus, to forgive their sins and give them eternal life. If there were any prisoners who did not accept God's free gift of salvation, they did not identify themselves. Every one indicated that they received Jesus as Savior.

Another incredible aspect to the story is that at least one hundred men were released from prison that day, but every man chose to remain long enough to hear what Timmy had to say. When those one hundred men exited the prison later that afternoon, they left with new hearts.

All I did was pray—and pray. But God did so much more! That's the way it is with prayer. Not all prayer stories are this dramatic, but often we do not have such stories because we do not pray. What situations in your life seem insurmountable? Never give up praying about them. Prayer can be your most significant act of influence. Trust God's love and concern for you as you pray "without ceasing."

Chapter 9

PRAYER PRIORITIES

Prayer is as necessary for our souls as breathing is for our bodies, but how do we actually pray? There are many different models for prayer, but there is one that has been especially influential in my life. I try to give credit where credit is due, but I have no idea who came up with the acronym ACTS as a method of prayer. Talk about ripple effects! These four letters, standing for *adoration, confession, thanksgiving,* and *supplication,* greatly impact my prayer life, which, as I illustrated in the last chapter, impacts me and all the people and situations I pray for.

Because prayer isn't my strong suit, I'm grateful for a simple tool to remind me of my prayer priorities. But ACTS is *not* a formula that has to be followed in exactly the same way each day! I tend to be a rule follower, but not in this case. I love the freedom and creativity we have in prayer, which I encourage you to take advantage of. Getting through all four segments of ACTS in one sitting is only doable on my dream day, one void of distractions, interruptions, and a myriad of obligations and responsibilities. My real day is beyond full, just like yours! So I often pray as I go, or have a "running conversation," as Timmy described prayer to the boys he spoke to.

While racing through life, women tend to establish priorities for our significant relationships. ACTS serves as a reminder to prioritize our incredible relationship with our mighty God!

A *IS FOR* ADORATION

Adoration means praising the Lord for who He is—holy, compassionate, mighty, just, merciful, and more. We honor Him when we worship Him. When I'm drawn to the Lord in worship, something takes place in my heart that I can't adequately describe. For a few moments, my "soul" focus is on my heavenly Father, not on my to-do list or current challenges. Even when I'm already on the go, the *A* in ACTS reminds me to pause long enough to tell the Lord how much I love Him—or, as the acronym suggests, "adore" Him. It's often a struggle to stop my mind from racing, but I find inner refreshment when I focus my attention on the person of God. I'm always glad I resisted the tyranny of the urgent, if only for a few minutes, to adore the God who created me, sacrificed His Son for me, and, to my amazement, desires to spend time with me.

I find inner refreshment when I focus my attention on the person of God.

We are free to express our love for the Lord in our own words, but I also borrow words from the psalmists. I search for appropriate verses to quote back to Him or put to tunes to sing to Him. A great voice or melodic tune isn't a requirement. God gave me my voice, so He is aware of my limited ability. And putting verses to tunes certainly isn't necessary; it's just my favorite means to remember meaningful passages. The Bible verses are easier for me to recall when they're attached to a simple tune. It helps to have the songs in my head, because I often praise Him while still in bed, while in the car, or anytime when only the Lord can hear me. Below are a few of my favorite "songs":

Your lovingkindness, O LORD, extends to the heavens, Your faithfulness reaches to the skies. Your righteousness is like the mountains of God; Your judgments are like a great deep. O LORD, You preserve man and beast. How precious is Your lovingkindness, O God! And the children of men take refuge in the shadow of Your wings.

PSALM 36:5-7

Praise the LORD, all nations; laud Him, all peoples! For His lovingkindness is great toward us, and the truth of the LORD is everlasting. Praise the LORD!

PSALM 117

O may Your glorious name be blessed and exalted above all blessing and praise! You alone are the LORD. You have made the heavens, the heaven of heavens with all their host, the earth and all that is on it, the seas and all that is in them. You give life to all of them and the heavenly host bows down before You.

NEHEMIAH 9:5-6

Praise the LORD! Praise, O servants of the LORD, praise the name of the LORD. Blessed be the name of the LORD from this time forth and forever. From the rising of the sun to its setting the name of the LORD is to be praised.

PSALM 113:1-3

It bears repeating that adoration is not a rule to follow or a measurement of spirituality; it's a brief moment in time when a woman basks in the love of her heavenly Father. Adoration draws us close to the Lord and aligns our minds and hearts with His priorities.

C IS FOR CONFESSION

Confessing our sins to God is an obvious and necessary part of prayer. While it's not my favorite, I'm grateful for the reminder to begin my day with a clean slate, by asking for and receiving forgiveness for words, attitudes, thoughts, and actions that don't honor the Lord. *Confess* means "to admit," and the *C* in ACTS provides built-in time to admit to the Lord what He already knows. Confession is for our benefit, since it encourages us to stop pretending that we're okay and remember that we can seek and find God's forgiveness. And forgiveness is amazing and freeing! It's a privilege only believers enjoy.

Following a recent event, a woman stopped me to say that she appreciated most of my message, but she rebuked me for confessing to the audience that I have a sin nature. I used myself as an example when I shared that as believers, our sin nature will war with our new nature in Christ until we go to heaven. I went on to express that when I spend a few minutes recalling the latest examples of my tendency to sin, I'm reminded why I need a Savior. I can't speak for the woman who stopped me in the hallway, but I can speak for myself: "All have sinned and fall short of the glory of God" (Romans 3:23). I'm one of the "all," and there's no doubt I'm a sinner with "stuff" to confess.

Two verses from Psalm 19 revealed an oversight in my prayer life: "Who can discern his errors? Acquit me of hidden faults. Also keep back Your servant from presumptuous sins; let them not rule over me; then I will be blameless, and I shall be acquitted of great transgression" (verses 12-13).

The first part of that passage reminds me that even though I'm not always aware of my errors or hidden faults, I'm still held accountable for them. Who should I ask about my hidden faults? You know the answer! I began to ask the Lord to reveal them but to do it gently and, if possible, not in front of a crowd. Shortly after I began praying about this, a friend mentioned a verse that impacted him, and the same verse instantly shed light on a sin of mine I hadn't been aware of. Our Master is gracious to answer prayer and to gently correct me when I'm teachable.

At a recent event, I used our family meal philosophy as an analogy for the benefit of dealing with faults early instead of late. In years past, after my gang sampled a new dish, we took a vote. Thumbs-up meant "Add it to the recipe collection," thumbs-down meant "Never again," and thumbs in the middle meant "So-so." Only the thumbs-up recipes made the cut. You get the point. I wanted immediate feedback. Twenty years from now, I really don't want to learn that I regularly served a recipe that was shoved around on plates and "saved" for later. And in the same way, years from now I don't want to discover that I've been regularly saying or doing something that hinders my relationship with God. But the stakes are higher if I repeatedly commit an offense for twenty years than if I serve oatmeal patties (thumbs-down by a six-to-one vote!).

By contrast, the second part of the Psalm 19 passage talks about presumptuous sins, and we're usually well aware of those. They're the ones we know we shouldn't commit but we go ahead with anyway. As the psalmist says, presumptuous sins rule us. They take control and run our lives. They're all we think about when we wake up or go to bed. Like an unwelcome guest, guilt over these sins invades our lives and refuses to leave. I want my Master to rule me, not my sin. He has the best plans for me, but His rightful place can be fraudulently assumed by unconfessed willful sin, a despicable master.

If you're like me, you confess the obvious. So this is the perfect spot to confess, at the insistence of our youngest son, that one Sunday Bob and I drove separate cars to church, and neither of us returned home with Timmy. In case you mistakenly elevated us to Hallmark family status, we really did leave him at church! A security guard called to inform us of our obvious neglect, which, apparently, we'll never live down.

Getting back to presumptuous sin, we fool ourselves when we justify our sinful response because others wrong us. I remember the season when bitterness and unforgiveness imprisoned me in a gloomy self-imposed cell. Our family was on a short furlough from the mission field, and I had five kids ranging from newborn to twelve. When the seven of us exited the plane in Florida, we plopped into a whirlwind life, so unlike the slower-paced one we'd left. Still recovering physically from the aftermath of giving birth to our miracle baby, I sat on an odd-shaped blue pillow, alerting observers to my issues. Coming from the tropics, we had no appropriate clothes for winter. I attempted to homeschool amidst the chaos, without much success. Overwhelmed, I had no interest in traveling. But we all packed into a van and traveled to visit supporters and speak at supporting churches.

In the middle of our trip, I had a birthday. Since it fell on the same day we were meeting old friends for dinner, it was logical to assume we would celebrate. I was wrong. My birthday isn't easy to overlook because it falls on or close to a major holiday. That year, it was forgotten. Completely! I'm not usually sentimental, and such things have never bothered me before or since, but it had been a challenging few months for me. I allowed Satan's whispers to render me useless, bitter, and unwilling to forgive and move on. Running through my mind was *Nobody really cares about me, even when I do so much for them.* I fell into the obvious trap of the enemy, and it took me a few weeks to find my way out. I should've known better. I've known women who were eaten up with bitterness. For a brief time, I was one of them.

I remember the day I gave up and forgave. I laid my wound at the foot of the cross—my hurt at others' thoughtlessness, as well as my own sinful response. Jesus already died for those sins and every other sin of mine—and yours. In Galatians, Paul wrote, "It was for freedom that Christ set us free; therefore keep standing firm and do not be subject again to a yoke of slavery" (5:1). Why do we choose slavery over freedom? Because we are hurt. Confused. Fooled. Proud. Angry. Jealous. Greedy. Tired. Weak. Sick. Scared. I'm not proud of my bitter response and my refusal to overlook a wrong, but I admit my sin in order to enable another woman to recognize hers.

I had to forgive something minor, but I'm very aware that many of you have endured major hurts. Today's women have more freedom to speak out against the perpetrators of serious offenses. Rape. Incest. Trafficking. Adultery. Abandonment. Abuse in all forms. How do you forgive such gigantic offenses? I haven't walked in your shoes, and I would never minimize your pain. I honestly wept through this section. I wept for those of you who have suffered unimaginably. For the devastating impact on your life. For the trauma of abuse in many forms. For the sleepless nights. I'm so very sorry! But I still believe the Bible. Those who abuse us win a double victory when past abuse leads to future enslavement to our abuser because we don't forgive. Forgiveness frees me—and you! It also stuns a culture where people are bent on protecting their rights and getting what they think they deserve. Our example of forgiveness can help others consider God's mercy. And we forgive big offenses the same way we forgive smaller ones.

For months, I've been memorizing and meditating on Colossians 3:12-17. I camped for a while on verse 13, because forgiveness doesn't come easily for me: ". . . forgiving each other, whoever has a complaint against anyone; just as the Lord forgave you, so also should you." This verse influenced me to forgive in the story below:

I won a victory today, but I wasn't awarded a trophy. No blue ribbon or championship ring. There was no applause. No one else knew, but I celebrated anyway. I had been wounded and became bitter and angry, the results of not forgiving. The enemy was up to his old tricks, but this time, I was onto him. Failure to forgive hurts me, not my offender! Jesus defeated Satan when He died on the cross and rose again. So in reality, a man from Galilee won the victory for me more than twenty centuries ago. He paid the penalty I deserved so I could have victory over my sin nature—my desire to be right, to have the last word, to come out on top. I can forgive even if my offender didn't ask for forgiveness. None of us can depend on feelings. What woman feels like forgiving? But I was exhausted from wrestling, and I chose to obey. In the same way God forgave me, I forgave someone. And I'm free! Forgiveness is a choice. Please choose forgiveness.

Forgiveness and confession are two sides of the same coin; we can't have one without the other. Everyone has stuff to confess. But it's much better to address sin at the time, anytime, all the time. We'll not be free of our tendency to sin until we go to heaven, but there's a great plan in place for us to deal with it until then.

T *IS FOR* THANKSGIVING

Adoration is thanking God for who He is, and thanksgiving is thanking Him for what He does. I desire to do both, and it helps to have a designated *T* time to express my gratitude to God for all He does on my behalf and for the people I care about.

Just as a passage from Psalm 19 influenced my understanding of confession, a Bible story in Luke 17 influenced my practice of thanksgiving. To summarize the passage, ten lepers approached Jesus. With loud voices, they begged Him to have mercy on them. All ten were healed, but only one returned to thank Jesus. "Now one of them, when he saw that he had been healed, turned back, glorifying God with a loud voice, and he fell on his face at His feet, giving thanks to Him" (verses 15-16). Jesus asked him, "But the nine— where are they?" (verse 17).

Although I'd heard this story many times, one day it mattered. I wondered if I were more like the grateful leper or the other nine. How many times has the Lord answered a prayer? Provided for my needs? Surprised me with an unexpected blessing? Did I thank Him, or was I like the nine lepers, ungrateful and entitled, simply going on my way? It's a valid question!

The same passage from Colossians 3 that reminds me to forgive also instructs me to be thankful: "Whatever you do in word or deed, do all in the name of the Lord Jesus, giving thanks through Him to God the Father" (Colossians 3:17). My favorite influential verse on thanksgiving, "In everything give thanks; for this is God's will for you in Christ Jesus" (1 Thessalonians 5:18), has a big write-up in the Manual chapters.

I'm grateful that my children are influencing their children to pray with thanksgiving. It helps to start young. My two oldest grand-children and I were enjoying lunch together a few years ago. Both girls wanted to ask the blessing. Claire, then three, opened her eyes and pointed as she prayed, "Dear Jesus, thank You for the carrots and the fruit and the lemonade, but I'm not sure about the sandwich." Abby, two at the time, prayed, "Dear God, thank You that me and Mommy had haircuts-es! Amen." What a great reminder to thank the Lord for His specific provisions.

Praying with thanksgiving enables us to focus on the good in our lives, reminds us of God's faithfulness, and changes our perspective from ungrateful to content.

S *IS FOR* SUPPLICATION

The previous chapter included some favorite examples of supplica-tion or, put simply, prayer requests. Do we always get what we ask the Lord for? Like any wise father, He knows when to say "yes" and when to say "no." My husband often rattles off "Bob" quotes that I scramble to write down. One recent quote explains why God's response to our prayer requests varies: "The difference in getting a 'no' answer and a 'yes' answer to our prayer request is the wisdom of God—not the love of God." I'm glad I found my pen in time!

I'm sure not an expert on prayer, but women seem to listen more intently when I describe prayer as "fighting for the people we love and long to influence." Nehemiah, who led the Israelites in rebuilding the wall around Jerusalem amid serious opposition, exhorted them, "Do not be afraid of them; remember the Lord who is great and awesome, and fight for your brothers, your sons, your daughters, your wives and your houses" (Nehemiah 4:14). That's good advice for us, too. The spiritual battle is raging, but I've witnessed many women fighting for their husbands, children, and friends through persistent prayer. Often we're asked to join them in the fight. What a privilege to cry out to our great God on behalf of a loved one longing for a husband, baby, home, or job. For those in bondage to drugs, depression, or pornography, or in need of forgiveness, hope, support, or a new start. For a loved one who threatens to leave our home and our God. At such times, we're in a tug-of-war. The enemy, who comes to "steal and kill and destroy" (John 10:10), is pulling loved ones in one direction, enticing them to follow bright lights and false promises, while we pull in the other direction with our powerful prayers to our mighty God.

I describe prayer as "fighting for the people we love and long to influence."

I believe women can be both tender and tough, especially when it comes to prayer. We can express our unconditional love but also our determination to fight and never give up. *Prayer warrior* is an accurate description, because we war against the forces of evil.

We serve a mighty God who is "able to do far more abundantly beyond all that we ask or think" (Ephesians 3:20). Please don't give up or give in when you are weary from fighting. Link arms with sisters in Christ to pray against the enemy of our souls. And even if we lose a battle, it doesn't mean we've lost the war. God has the final say!

Before the battle for our loved ones becomes intense, there are countless verses to pray on their behalf to equip them to stand strong in our challenging world. As I mentioned in an earlier chapter, Colossians 1:9-12 is a favorite. I have it in my head, so I can pray on the go. Paul prayed specifically for Christians in Colossae to

Be filled with the knowledge of God's will
Gain spiritual wisdom and understanding
Walk in a manner worthy of the Lord
Please God in all respects
Bear fruit in every good work
Increase in the knowledge of God
Be strengthened with all power to attain steadfastness
   and patience
Give thanks to the Father for their spiritual inheritance

In my file of "influence notes," there's a recent one from a friend who thanked me for influencing her to pray. Years ago, she invited me to speak on prayer to a group of young women gathered in her home. As I shared above, prayer is not my strength, but I passed along my special "prayer" verses like the ones above. My friend wrote, "[This] blessed me with godly instructions on prayer. What an important influence on my life!" Choose your own special verses to pray and then share them with those in your sphere. Heaven will reveal the ripple effects of your prayers.

The Piano Story

Praying for the people we love is ongoing. They're in our minds and hearts, and we whisper prayers for them as we travel through our days and our lives. Below is a prayer story about one of the special people in my life.

When our oldest daughter, Christy, was six, she begged to take piano lessons. At the time, we didn't have money for either a piano or lessons. I wanted to teach Christy even at a young age that she could talk to the Lord about the desires of her heart, so we prayed about it together. Christy continued to pray on her own. No lofty words, just a little girl talking to God. She believed He cared. He did.

Life was full during that first year of homeschool. I was so busy teaching Christy and caring for a four-year-old and a toddler that piano lessons were not my priority. Meanwhile, Christy shared her desire with her grandmother, who offered to let us borrow her piano. I took piano lessons as a child, so I attempted to teach Christy the basics. I lacked ability but tried to be the answer to her prayer. I'll never forget the day a woman called to inform us that she was being paid anonymously to come to our house every week to give Christy piano lessons. I hung up the phone in awe of God. He did care about Christy's prayer, and so did a generous friend.

Christy looked forward to her lesson each week. Piano seemed to come easily for her. But several years later, when God called us to the mission field, we returned the piano to my mother.

"What about piano lessons?" Christy asked. Next to my husband, she was the most excited about our missionary adventure, but she still hoped to continue piano lessons.

During the season of uprooting and leaving the known for the unknown, I wasn't sure how to handle the "piano subject." I stopped packing long enough to encourage Christy that it was God who planned our move to the Philippines, and she could trust Him with her concerns.

As a nine-year-old, Christy already had a big view of God, but it grew even bigger when she witnessed Him answer our earnest prayer for a home in a somewhat uncivilized area of the Philippines, as I talked about in an earlier chapter. And while I was busy adjusting to missionary life, Christy continued to pray for a piano. In an effort to encourage our daughter, Bob purchased a guitar for her. Christy was delighted when a Filipino man who worked for her dad gave her guitar lessons. With her piano background, she learned to play the guitar well enough to lead the music for the neighborhood outreach she urged me to start.

As a result of our ministry to the local children, Christy has a special memory of four little Filipino girls who became close friends. She prayed diligently for her friends to know Jesus, because she longed for them to be in heaven with her someday. We spent time together learning how to explain the simple gospel. Her love for the girls transcended the language barrier, and before our move to Manila two years later, God answered her prayers for her friends. Christy experienced the joy of leading all four friends to know Jesus.

Although Christy enjoyed playing the guitar, she continued to believe that God would provide a piano. I can't recall the exact timing, but some months after our move to Mindanao, we welcomed unexpected visitors. In the area where we lived, working telephones were rare, which meant communication usually occurred the old-fashioned way—face-to-face. Only one other American family lived in our area, so the kids and I were excited when a missionary family who lived a couple of hours away stopped by to catch up and ask a favor: "When we leave for our yearlong furlough, would you consider babysitting our piano? We want it to be in a protected place," my friend Connie explained.

I couldn't get the words out fast enough. "Of course," I responded.

I was stunned, but Christy wasn't, because she never doubted God would answer her prayer. We hired the church pianist at the Filipino church we attended to give Christy lessons. During that year, both Christy's faith in the Lord and her ability to play the piano increased.

"But what about a piano?" Christy exclaimed when my difficult pregnancy with her little brother necessitated an unexpected emergency move to Manila. I genuinely cared about my daughter's desire to play the piano, but at the time, there were much bigger issues. I had been sick for months, without medical care. We had an appointment with an American-trained doctor. As soon as I was able to fly, we left for Manila.

Our family temporarily resided in a mission house. Some missionaries were passing through on their way to other destinations, while other families, like ours, were looking for homes to rent in the area.

"There was too much furniture in that home," I overheard from a woman who had just checked out a home for rent.

"I thought so too," responded another missionary.

Our ears perked up when we heard about a home with furniture because we had very little furniture of our own. Since our house in Mindanao had been furnished, we hadn't purchased any. We needed a home immediately, but I was so weak from my challenging pregnancy and our move from Mindanao that I just couldn't house hunt and risk further complications. I begged the Lord for enough energy to check out *one* home.

Right away, we made an appointment to see the home with all the furniture. Our whole family stood at the gate while Bob rang the bell. I leaned on Bob for support and prayed silently, *Please, Lord, let this be the one.* We prayed together as a family, too. A servant opened the gate and guided us to the front door. As it swung open, the very first thing Christy and I spotted was a piano. It wasn't just any piano; it was a Yamaha baby grand. I couldn't speak. Tears filled my eyes.

Christy shouted, "Mom, there's a piano!" We didn't need to see any more. Of course this was the home for us! I was also excited, though, about the large room our boys would occupy, complete with bunk beds. There was also a room with a double bed for the girls. The landlords had left the country quickly for Canada in the midst of political chaos. That explained why they left furniture, an equipped kitchen, toys on the shelves—and a piano.

The homeowners, we learned, would only rent to American missionaries. We qualified and moved in later that day. The impact of trusting God for a piano and seeing Him provide not just one but three so far increased the size of Christy's God. "Jesus Christ is the same yesterday and today and forever" (Hebrews 13:8), but our view of Him changes as we walk by faith, trusting Him with the deepest desires of our hearts. God's provision of a piano influenced Christy, showing her that she could trust Him with even bigger concerns in the future.

The piano story continued. Some years later, when God prompted us to move back home to America to expand my husband's ministry, we bought our first piano with the money we made selling the stuff we couldn't transport. Christy continued to take piano lessons from our church pianist, an excellent mentor and piano teacher.

"My major in college will be music," Christy stated whenever her friends discussed their college plans. But as Christy approached her senior year in high school, we still hadn't met any homeschoolers who went to college. We informed our kids early on that not only would God have to open the door for their acceptance to college, a door that most people assumed would remain locked, He would also need to provide scholarships. Undeterred, Christy reasoned that if God could provide pianos in remote locations, then He could do anything! Her faith had grown to the point that she didn't doubt that if college were God's plan, He would make a way.

Long before homeschooling became more acceptable and states developed academic requirements, we attempted to cover the necessary subjects. I assumed Christy should take a foreign language, but teaching one was a roadblock for me. Although I had taken three years of French in high school, I had forgotten most of it. And at the same time, I was also responsible for four other needy students.

A language requirement was probably the last thing on my mind when I answered the phone one afternoon. A lady with a slight accent asked if I would be interested in her teaching my children Spanish. Speechless for a moment, I then asked how she knew to call me. She explained that she had mentioned to a friend that she would love to teach her native language but had no students. Her friend knew about our homeschooling family from a mutual friend. I'm not sure I ever understood the connections, but I know the ultimate Connector.

"Yes, that would be wonderful," I exclaimed, excited but apprehensive about the cost. "Oh, I don't want any payment," she explained. "I just have a desire to teach my native language to eager students. If you could bring your students to me, then that will be enough."

As much effort as I put in to prepare my children for life and college, it was the Lord who wove together their résumés in a way that only He could do. There was never a doubt in my children's minds that God did it! And their faith increased as they witnessed His unique plans for them unfold. All of our children have their individual God stories, but Christy's story seems the most dramatic, because she was the first homeschooler we knew to apply to college.

Armed with standardized test scores, a homemade transcript, two years of Spanish, and a memorized complex piano piece, Christy applied to the music departments of three local colleges. Going away to college didn't interest her because, as she explains it, she has ATMS disease—"afraid to miss something!" She didn't want to miss any of our family and ministry adventures.

At the first two auditions, Christy played her piece perfectly, and she was offered full scholarships to both schools. Her first choice, however, was an expensive private school with an excellent music department that had its choice of worthy students.

The day of her audition was also the day that another family story took place—the day we almost destroyed our property with a "controlled burn." (More on that adventure in another chapter.) Christy probably smelled like smoke when she arrived for her audition.

Christy knew her difficult piece, just as she knew the Lord would spare our property, even though she couldn't be there to help put out the fire. Although she'd played her selection perfectly at the first two schools, halfway through this performance, her mind went blank. She knew she'd blown it—her one chance to attend the school of her choice. The school with the best reputation, with recognized teachers, and where she felt the most comfortable.

"Pick up your music and continue," the judges encouraged her, so she continued to play where she'd left off. After she finished, Christy braced herself for rejection. The judges looked at each other, as if to agree on their decision, and then they offered her a scholarship to the school of music.

Christy waited until she got into the car to cry. In His unique way, the Lord confirmed, "I've got this! You thought the scholarship depended solely on you. But nothing can thwart My plan for you." Christy would never forget God's display of love and grace. His blessing didn't depend on her faith but on His faithfulness.

There were still challenges. The music department only gave half scholarships, and we couldn't afford even half tuition at the expensive private university. In another amazing sequence of events, the school also gave her an academic scholarship, which covered the other half.

One of our favorite stories occurred during Christy's junior year in college. The tuition was raised significantly, but her scholarships remained the same. Christy begged me to go with her to discuss finances with the dean of admissions. He was gracious and expressed his hope that Christy could remain at the university. He thumbed through various unclaimed scholarships and discussed a few possibilities. Then he looked up from his file and asked, "Where did you graduate in your class?"

"Well, I was the *only* one in my class," Christy responded, puzzled at his question.

"It looks like I found your scholarship," he said with a sly smile. "We are officially awarding you the valedictorian scholarship."

Christy's piano story is what I refer to as a God story, one that's impossible apart from the power of God. It's a heartwarming story about the prayers of a little girl who talked about the desires of her heart with the God she trusted. Her close relationship with a big, trustworthy God dramatically influenced her future in stories yet to be told.

How is the piano story a story about ripple effects? This God story influenced Christy, her siblings, her friends, and others we shared it with, showing them that God is trustworthy, so we can trust Him with everything—from the smallest to the most important issues in our lives. Christy's siblings were influenced to trust God to write His special stories for each of them, too. Her story influenced her friends, who wanted their own stories. It influenced all the children Christy taught piano to during her college and grad school years. It influenced scores of young women who attended her seminars entitled "Keeper of My Heart," where Christy and her friend Colleen used stories, skits, and teaching to communicate the trustworthiness of God to keep these girls' hearts while He wrote their love stories. It influenced the people in the large audiences and small gatherings where the story was repeated. It influenced my friend Carol, who encouraged me to write it. Maybe it will influence you to know that God cares about the deepest desires of your heart.

But most of all, the piano story influenced Christy to trust a faithful God with everything in her life. She now serves on a challenging mission field with her husband, Joey, and her two precious children. And she teaches piano to her daughter, Claire. Her story goes on, but I will let her write her own book—about her ministries, her love story, her missionary adventures, and more—God stories that hinge on a faithful, loving God!

MINDSET

What's a mindset? "Driving five miles over the speed limit is *not* speeding." "Valentine candy has *no* calories." "Five or ten minutes late is *not* late." "As parents, we aren't perfect; our kids aren't perfect either; but our grandchildren are *practically perfect*!" You can probably add your own examples to these common mindsets.

Mindset became my focus when I studied Proverbs 23:7: "For as [a man] thinks within himself, so he is." Or, to interpret this verse for myself and my daughters, friends, and the women I speak to, "What a woman thinks about, she becomes." The fact that we become what we think about captivates me! If the thoughts running through our minds when we're reflecting on truth, daydreaming, driving, or lying in bed have a direct effect on our actions, then selecting the best mindsets is critical for our lives and influence.

My definition of *mindset* is "an intentional and determined made-up mind." "Mindset" was included in my messages long before I could google the word and add to my definition "an inclination, a habit, a fixed mental attitude." Bob adds "a predisposition to think a certain way; a determined progression of thought."

Since our mindsets impact our thought lives, which impact our actions, we need to evaluate them carefully. If our goal is to have life-impacting influence on those in our spheres, we must choose mindsets that will make us the most influential. Influence is not accidental; it results from making deliberate, determined, and repeated choices, beginning in the mind and then acted out day by day. Choices empowered by God and His Word.

The four mindsets I talk about in these next chapters—loving like Jesus, serving others, encouraging others through our words, and living with eternity in mind—are my priorities. As you read and consider these, I encourage you to think through your priorities in life and establish your own biblical mindsets. And by God's grace, strive to live out those mindsets in a way that has a lasting impact on the people in your sphere of influence.

For as a woman thinks within herself,
so she is.

SEE PROVERBS 23:7

Chapter 10

LOVE LIKE
OUR MASTER

Writing only one chapter on love is challenging. Love is the subject that I knew least about when I met my Master but that I could write the most about now. It's not because I'm an expert or love perfectly. In fact, even though the Bible teaches that "love never fails" (1 Corinthians 13:8), I often fail to love. Until I was an adult, I encountered very few examples of genuine love. But I didn't want that to be the case for my husband, children, friends, neighbors, or anyone I hoped to influence. Even before I finally grasped, after years of doubt, that God really loves me, I was motivated to learn all I could about loving well. To quote my husband, "Love is the strongest force in all the world." And love, I believe, is our greatest personal platform to impact the world of people in our spheres.

JESUS LOVES ME, THIS I KNOW

Do you comprehend God's love for you? Growing up, I assumed that my heavenly Father's love was just like that of my earthly father. My dad, an army colonel, fought in World War II and the Korean War, and he was on high alert during the Cuban missile crisis and in the years to follow. As a result, he wasn't around for much of my youth. When he was home, he was preoccupied. I rarely had his attention unless I elevated myself in his view. His job demanded that he judge people based on their merit, and that carried over to his personal life. He showed more interest in me when a "cut above" accomplishment made him proud of me. He bragged about me and treated me differently when I made the honor roll or received an award than when I made less-than-perfect grades or was not the star of the show. When I didn't meet his expectations and high standards for success, his disappointment was obvious.

You may think God's love for you is based on your performance, just as I did. That was my mindset. Even after years of walking with the Lord, I didn't have a handle on God's unconditional love. I sang, "Jesus loves me, this I know," but the truth of those words didn't resonate with me. When bad things happened in my life, I assumed it meant God didn't really love me. How could He? You may believe as I did that illness, mishaps, and other challenges in life blow our way without warning like tornadoes, wreaking havoc on our lives, because we don't measure up to God's standards. It seems obvious by the circumstances we are in. God gives us what we deserve. Right?

I'm so thankful to respond, "Wrong!" As I work on this chapter, I'm flying home from ministering in a country where the majority of citizens believe that statement is true. The god most of them worship is not loving. He puts everyone in categories based on their merits. Since people are assumed to get what they deserve, there is no compassion for the sick, disadvantaged, helpless, and hurting. There is no hope, no joy, no security! You and I may be too sophisticated to believe in such a god, but the enemy's subtle lies still weave their way into our minds and hearts, like a snake slithering through the grass.

Through the years, Bob regularly taught various groups on the love of God. Finally, after I heard the life-impacting truth for the umpteenth time, I began to resist the same old deceptive messages from the enemy. You know the ones he whispers in your ear: "God doesn't really love you because . . ." "You promised you weren't going to lose your temper anymore, but you did." "You think you're a good mom, but think again." "You'll never conquer that bad habit." "No one would love you if they knew your secret thoughts." "You didn't deserve the promotion anyway." I fell for a few of those lies. Maybe you believe some of them too.

As a mother, I didn't want my children to trust the circulating rumors that God's love is based on our performance. Even when I still struggled with that perception, I determined to halt the negative ripple effects on the precious lives over whom I had the most influence. I cried happy tears when my oldest daughter called to tell me this story.

Christy wanted to teach her little three-year-old son about God's unconditional love. When she put him to sleep at night, she would sing, "I love you when you sleep . . . I love you when you wake up . . . I love you when you disobey me . . . I love you when you fight with your sister . . . I love you when you hug me." And so forth. You get the idea—and so did he.

When a family with a baby stayed overnight in their home, Joe taught the baby what he had been learning. Christy found him with his little guitar singing to the baby in the crib: "I love you when you cry . . . I love you when you smile . . . I love you when you make a mess in your diapers." What a blessing at Joe's young age that he is secure in his mother's love and God's. My daughter had life-impacting influence on her little boy!

FOR THE BIBLE TELLS ME SO

Our grandson learned the truth about God's love much sooner than I did. But thankfully the Bible verses I meditated on began to change my thinking about His love for me. Romans 5:8 says, "God demonstrates His own love toward us, in that while we were yet sinners, Christ died for us." He loves us so much that He sent His only Son, Jesus, to die for me and for you—when we were in the midst of opposing Him with our words, thoughts, and actions, unaware of our need for Him. I wouldn't give up one of my sons to save another person. But God did. What love! I finally started to get it: God loves me. He really loves me. God's love isn't based on my performance! God doesn't love me "if" or "because"; He loves me "anyway."

I'm still vulnerable, so the "belt of truth" became an essential piece of my wardrobe (see Ephesians 6:14). I need to know what the Bible says about God's love. Each time I'm tempted to think, *God doesn't really love me*, I counteract that lie with Scripture like Romans 8:38-39: "I am convinced that neither death, nor life, nor angels, nor principalities, nor things present, nor things to come, nor powers, nor height, nor depth, nor any other created thing, will be able to separate us from the love of God, which is in Christ Jesus our Lord." God loves us, and nothing we do will ever stop Him from loving us. The truth about God's love from His Manual shouts much louder than the enemy's whisper. Please don't wait as long as I did to nail it down.

Over time, believing God loves me transformed me, enabling me to respond to His love and become secure in my relationship with Him. I'd had eternal security since I trusted in Jesus at age twelve, but when I really comprehended that I was also secure in His love, my overwhelming gratitude caused me to respond by loving Him back. I'll never get over God's incredible love for you and me. When people in our spheres fail to love us, God still loves us. When we blow it, God still loves us. When our worlds fall apart, God still loves us. "Jesus loves me, this I know, for the Bible tells me so."

LOVING OTHERS

When we finally catch on to God's love for us, loving others is a by-product. First John 4:11 says, "Beloved, if God so loved us, we also ought to love one another." Jesus explained our mandate for love to a lawyer who questioned Him about the greatest commandment: "'You shall love the LORD your God with all your heart, and with all your soul, and with all your mind.' This is the great and foremost commandment. The second is like it, 'You shall love your neighbor as yourself'" (Matthew 22:37-39). Or as Bob often reminds our family, "Love God and love people." Both kinds of love are in response to God's love for us.

We have countless opportunities to love people. About fifteen years ago, I had the privilege to speak to a group of mostly unchurched, high-achieving high school girls. I journaled my thoughts:

> *I knew going in that this situation was beyond me. The group of adorable high school girls would probably be intimidated. Little did they know that I was too. In fact, I felt more comfortable speaking to girls in one of the foreign countries where we minister than to this challenging audience. Thankfully, I had time to prepare what I would say when we met. But my preparation had to involve more than words. Their discerning eyes would see right through me. I couldn't fake it. I begged the Lord to give me a love for them that paid no attention to their reputation, makeup, hairstyle, dress, or whatever. A love that didn't judge. Genuine enough to break down barriers.*

Bob encourages me and every person who goes on his mission trips that the most important priority for speakers, teachers, mentors, and parents is to love their audience. His definition of *love* is "choosing the best interest of others and acting on their behalf." It was in the best interest of these high school girls for me to love them unconditionally, and that became my goal as I spoke to this impressive young group. I was well aware of my inadequacy for the task, because I have blown it before—too many times. I've often halted the transfer of God's unconditional love through me to others. Just as I assumed God put conditions on His love for me, I put conditions on my love for my husband, my children, my friends, and people I met and instantly judged. I know better now. My earthly father's love was conditional; God's love is not! I don't have to earn it, and I will never lose it. Believing God loves me unconditionally doesn't just set me straight about me; it equips me with the ability to copy Him. When I'm secure in God's love, I am freed up to love others. As Paul wrote in 2 Corinthians 3:5, "Not that we are adequate in ourselves to consider anything as coming from ourselves, but our adequacy is from God."

When I went to the speaking event, I was so conscious of God loving the high school girls through me. How did the girls respond? By God's grace, and I mean that literally, they did respond. The wall of judgment that stood between us crumbled, replaced by love. Though we were years apart in age, I had no problem identifying with the main issue my young audience wrestled with: the longing for approval, recognition, and acceptance from their peers. Some responded when I shared about my Jesus and His unconditional love for us. Others formed a circle around me when I finished speaking, asking for advice on specific issues. We laughed and talked and hugged. I even had the sweet privilege to pray with one of the girls. I still keep up with some of the young women who attended that event. Over the years, I received graduation announcements,

Christmas cards, wedding invitations, and baby pictures. Ripple effects of God's love.

It took me so long to comprehend the depth of God's love. Please don't make the same mistake. Don't believe the enemy's lies. He is a schemer, prowling like a lion to devour unsuspecting prey (see 1 Peter 5:8). His priority is to prevent us from believing God loves us. And coming in a close second are his efforts to keep us from loving others. Loving people is hard, but next to loving God, it should be our number one priority. You may have someone in your sphere who is not especially lovable. A rebellious teenager. A demanding boss. A self-absorbed friend. An unpleasant neighbor. A critical husband. A needy acquaintance. But when people are at their worst, they need love the most.

"Thank you for taking the time to love me," a woman wrote me recently in a scribbled note. She had left her addiction behind but not her reputation, which seemed to stand between her

When people are at their worst, they need love the most.

and the love of others. The enemy tries to convince us to turn our backs on those who need our love. But when life is hard, people need love—God's and ours.

I have no idea what heavy burdens the women I speak to lug around. One woman might conceal the pain of a wayward child. Her friend might be consumed with a habit she can't break. Sitting beside her could be a lady eaten up by bitterness. The person in front might doubt her self-worth because her husband shows very little interest in her. Her friend might grieve over her parent's cancer diagnosis. All of these women are just like you and me. They need to be loved. God is the only One who ultimately meets that need, but we can be the catalysts to demonstrate what His love looks like by liberally loving the people in our spheres.

We have great influence when we demonstrate God's love through our love. That might be by listening with interest, meeting a physical or financial need, offering friendship, looking out for someone's well-being, volunteering for a ministry, praying for others, and much more. I certainly don't love perfectly, but I want to. Love changes everything and everyone. It changed me and it will change you. Love transforms the atmosphere in our homes, our workplaces, our schools, our churches, our communities, and our world. Allow God to love you, really love you, and then be the channel for God to love others through you. In 1 Corinthians 13, Paul shows us how much God values love: "And now abide faith, hope, love, these three; but the greatest of these is love" (verse 13, NKJV).

MY BEST PARENTING ADVICE

"What's the most important parenting advice you have for a mom?" shouted the cute blonde pushing a stroller as we passed on the street in San Francisco.

I only had a moment to respond. My hosts were rushing me to my position in the Walk for Life West Coast, but they were also sensitive to the mom's question, allowing me to pause long enough to answer. I don't always process quickly, but thankfully, I have been asked the same question many times. I have had years to think through my answer.

"Love your children unconditionally, just like God loves you," I almost shouted so I could be heard above the crowd gathered in the street for the parade.

She smiled in response, and her lips formed a silent "Thank you." A nice-looking young man, holding a child's hand, grabbed the mom's, and they disappeared through the crowd.

A few months later I was asked a variation of the same question. This time, I sat in the office of a doctor at Mayo Clinic. I had been in an accident and needed an exam. My regular doctor was on vacation, so I was seeing a "substitute" doctor, who was extremely professional and kind. As I was preparing to leave, he said, "Mrs. Tebow, can I ask you a question?"

"Of course," I responded.

"Can you tell me how my wife and I can raise our children to love Jesus?" he asked with sincerity.

What a privilege to answer such a question! I had the opportunity to influence a person of influence with the greatest form of influence. "Love your children unconditionally," I said, pausing for emphasis. This time, there was no parade to attend. I continued, "Just the way God loves you. Your unconditional love will demonstrate God's love for your children. That love will continually draw them to you and ultimately to the Lord."

The doctor nodded his head, and his eyes gleamed. It was obvious he understood. I bet he already loves his family like that.

I don't pretend to be a parenting expert, but this often-asked question has a life-impacting answer. If the "greatest of these is love" (1 Corinthians 13:13), then loving our children must be the most important thing we can do for them.

One of our children was speaking to a large group of his peers, and I went online to hear him. He shared that one time when he confessed something to us, my husband's response was "Son, I love you so much that I would lay down my life for you." Then our son added, "And my mother said that nothing I would ever do would stop her from loving me."

I've made many mistakes as a mother, but despite my wrong thinking about God's love for me, He somehow gave me the grace to love my children. I believe that loving them unconditionally is the most important influence I have ever had. A Mother's Day card I cherished and saved reads, "Mom, I never really did those things I threatened to do, because you loved me too much. Thanks for being my cheerleader. When no one else thought I would make it, you did. Your love made the difference!"

Love makes a difference! It made the difference for the person who taught me about the meaning of love. I interviewed him for the story below.

THE POWER OF LOVE

The wiggly little third-grade boy waited with anticipation for his name to be called. His teacher had already selected the kids, mostly girls, to be in the first reading group. Now she was calling out the names of his classmates for the second group. He watched as each child whose name was called hurried to secure a chair in the circle. He listened more intently now than he usually did when his teacher was speaking, but she did not call his name. Finally the remaining kids, mostly boys, were directed to the third arrangement of chairs. He should have expected this; it always happened to him.

From where he sat, he could hear the children in the other two groups taking turns reading from their books. He was a little envious as he listened. His brown eyes opened wide when the kid next to him slowly sounded out the words from his assigned page. Bobby's mind had been wandering, thinking about exploring in the woods near his home or hitting the baseball into the outfield, but now his heart raced as he focused on the grouping of letters on the page—because it was his turn to read out loud.

The words were short, but as hard as he tried, he couldn't decipher them. His plan was to guess, but guessing did not produce the reaction he hoped for. The teacher's assistant frowned and urged him to try again. He *was* trying. A few of the kids in his group made comments that he couldn't quite hear, but Bobby could imagine what they were saying. This was not the first time kids had made fun of him because he couldn't read.

Home at last, he thought later as he stepped off the school bus. He couldn't wait to ride his bike to one of his friends' houses or grab his wooden gun and head off to the nearby woods. After several hours of play, Bobby heard his mother call him to dinner. He was always hungry, but as he headed toward the house, he braced himself for his mother's reaction to his report card. She would know he got it today, because his sisters would be proudly showing her their grades. He was so happy he made an A in math. Maybe his mother would be happy about that.

Bobby went to bed earlier than usual that night because he didn't want his sisters to see him cry. He was real good at pretending, but he had pretended enough for one day. The sound of his mom and dad yelling at each other from the other room was not unusual, but tonight, he could hear his name a lot during their argument. He guessed that his parents were like his teacher: They were disappointed in him.

I didn't expect such a dramatic response to this story the first time I shared it at a large parenting conference. As I told a brief version of Bobby's struggles, women fought back tears as some escaped down their cheeks.

"I thought God made a mistake when He gave me a child who struggled to read" was the comment I heard over and over afterward. Others shared that they couldn't wait to go home and hug their little boy or girl, whose struggle was similar to Bobby's. Mothers lined up to share their stories with me, admitting that the child in the story could have been theirs. The little boy in the story *is* actually mine— my husband.

When my Bob was young, his parents were so frustrated with his inability to read, spell, and write that they had his IQ tested. Afterward they were even more upset with him, because the results indicated that not only was he capable of excelling, he should have been at the top of his class. All the while, however, he saw words and letters differently than most of his classmates. The disapproval of his parents and teachers led to deep insecurity and the belief that he was somehow unworthy of love because he didn't measure up to their expectations. He couldn't earn their love! His insecurities were enhanced by an unstable family; his parents were too consumed with their own problems to deal with his. Bobby had friends but was shy in group settings. He could never muster up the confidence to ask a girl to the prom. *Why would a girl go out with me?* he asked himself.

Like many boys his age, Bobby loved sports, but his parents never encouraged his efforts or attended his games. There was no one to applaud a home run or give a hug after a loss. And as a kid with obvious learning disabilities, he needed some reassurance and encouragement. It seemed pointless to believe in himself when no one else believed in him. Like every other child, teenager, or adult, his greatest need was for someone to love him.

Someone did. When Bob was sixteen, he begged his parents to let him go on a Young Life ski trip during Christmas vacation. The "cool" kids were going, and he was excited about skiing for the first time. But it was too warm for snow, so the first ski experience would have to wait. With no outdoor activities, Bobby had no excuse to avoid attending the last day's session. And that's when it happened: He experienced a more important "first" when he heard for the first time that someone loved him after all. God loved him, and He proved His love by sending His Son, Jesus, to die for him on the cross. Bob had been to church, but he had never heard about that kind of love before. He asked lots of questions of the speakers and the counselors. Although he didn't understand all the details, he got the love part. Bob returned to his room and talked to God about His love. He wanted in on it. No special prayer or wording—just the desire of a teenage boy to be loved by God.

As my husband tells the story, God's love made him somebody. He soaked in the truth that God loved him enough to pursue a relationship with him. Even if he struggled in school. Even if he didn't measure up to his parents' expectations. When I met my husband as a college student, I thought he was a little fanatical (or maybe a lot fanatical), but I had never witnessed anything like his zeal to tell others about the love of God. How was he transformed from a shy, insecure teenager to a passionate leader of the growing Christian group on our large campus? Someone loved him unconditionally— just the way he was.

People in our spheres may not have dyslexia, but they know if we love them. And they aren't fooled when we just pretend to love. Husbands, girlfriends, coworkers, neighbors, friends at church, people at the gym, and the cashier at the store all respond when we really care about what's best for them. And one of my favorite verses on love encourages me that when I genuinely love people I interact with on a daily basis, I'm imitating God: "Be imitators of God, as beloved children; and walk in love, just as Christ also loved you and gave Himself up for us, an offering and a sacrifice to God as a fragrant aroma" (Ephesians 5:1-2). When I am intentional about loving people in my sphere, it's as if I were offering a sweet-smelling sacrifice that ascends straight to the throne of God.

THE GREATEST OF THESE IS LOVE

As I travel and talk with women of all ages, I find that the desire to be loved is a common theme. The country song about "lookin' for love in all the wrong places" often rings true. Whether we admit it or not, we are all looking for love, but there is only one right place to find it. My husband found it. I found it. No matter the circumstances, you can find it too. And when we encounter God's love, we can love others. Love is powerful and life transforming. It supersedes every other motivating force in life.

Because love is the greatest need my husband, my children, and everyone I know has, I determined that love needed to be the subject I majored in. As a young wife and mother, I looked up each quality of love listed in 1 Corinthians 13 and specifically worked on each one: *Patient.* Love doesn't mind waiting—even for a long time. *Kind.* Love is tender, caring, unselfish. *Not jealous.* Love doesn't want what others have; instead, it's happy for them. *Does not brag. Isn't arrogant.* Love doesn't talk about itself. *Doesn't act unbecomingly. Doesn't seek its own.* It puts the needs of others first, expecting nothing in return. *Isn't provoked.* Love doesn't snap back and isn't touchy, getting its feelings hurt. *Doesn't take into account a wrong suffered. Doesn't rejoice in unrighteousness. Rejoices with the truth. Bears all things, believes all things, hopes all things, endures all things.* Love forgives everyone everything. It doesn't give up or throw away people, because it believes God transforms the people we love. *Never fails.* It doesn't quit. It took time to work on each quality, but what a good use of time. I wish I could tell you that I have loving down. I don't! I'm still studying.

Titus 2:3-4 instructs older women, of which I am one, to teach what is good, so that they may encourage the young women to love their husbands and their children. I realize that not everyone reading this book has a husband and children, some by choice and some not. My heart goes out to those who long to be married and become mothers. But I believe that all women mother someone. It's in our DNA to nurture and care for those God brings our way. I wrote the words below to encourage a large group of moms to clearly articulate their love to their children through their words. The response was overwhelming.

One of the most common and life-impacting ways we love is through words. I often plan precise words to say in order to meet the varying needs of each of my children. A mother usually knows when a child needs to be instructed, affirmed, or motivated. Our words can inspire our children to overcome obstacles and setbacks. . . .

Although I communicate my love to my children in other ways, there is no substitute for my carefully thought out words that clearly communicate my love. Moms, let's make a commitment: Let's not let our children go out the door, get out of the car, hang up on the phone, or go to sleep without saying, "I love you!" Let those three powerful words ring in their ears long after they leave our presence. If a child fails the test, forgets the recital piece, or loses the ball game, he will remember that Mom loves him. If a child is ill, discouraged, or angry, she will remember that Mom loves her. If a friend, a teacher, or a sibling hurts our child, he will remember that Mom loves him . . . because of her words that convey her love.

When we say these three words many times a day, day after day, year after year, our children will believe us. Love is the greatest need our children have, and we are the best equipped to meet that need by saying over and over again, "I love you."

I scribbled a silly poem the other day:

Life—
It goes so fast
And then it's past.
Life!

Work—
Must be done
Under the sun.
Work!

Love—
What we can give
While we live.
Love!

Although the poem isn't impressive, it makes a valid point: While we live, we can give our love. Love is a gift we receive from the Lord and then are privileged to give away at every opportunity. Our gift is priceless. No amount of treasure can purchase the love of God, made possible by the sacrifice of His only Son. I often sing to myself my favorite hymn, "When I Survey the Wondrous Cross" by Isaac Watts, and I pause at the line "Love so amazing, so divine, demands my soul, my life, my all." The only reasonable response to God's love is for us to willingly give away that love for as long as we live.

Love is a gift we receive from the Lord and then are privileged to give away at every opportunity.

Love has no parallel and no equal. It never fails. Love has more potential for life-impacting influence than anything else. The ripple effects of loving people with our words and actions are endless. Having a mindset of love is the ultimate miraculous motivating power!

Chapter 11

SERVING ISN'T FOR SISSIES

Hurricane Irma slammed into our community as an uninvited guest in 2017, leaving massive destruction in her path. She was the most powerful hurricane ever recorded in the Atlantic Ocean and the most anticipated one ever to hit Florida. Our area had not experienced a disaster of this magnitude in 150 years! During Irma's rainy, windy journey up the length of Florida, she swamped homes, toppled trees, flooded streets, snapped miles of power lines, and sent hundreds of residents to local shelters.

While thousands of Floridians evacuated, we elected to remain in our sturdy home, miles from water. We were exhausted from days of preparation, and even the roar of hurricane-force winds and thundering rain didn't prevent us from sleeping a few hours the night Irma blew through. Although we had thoroughly prepared for the expected onslaught, we were not ready for what we saw in the early morning light: A sea of water surrounded our home. It appeared as if our house, barn, and stables were three unusual boats floating in the middle of the ocean, with no land in sight. As the sun peeked through the clouds, floodwater trickled through the front doors. We gasped that our "houseboat" was leaking.

Irma exited just as suddenly as she arrived, wreaking more havoc as she traveled north. After the worst was over, we expected many days of cleanup. We did not, however, expect the multiple texts, calls, and e-mails from friends, neighbors, and even casual acquaintances who cared and were willing to help. We were so encouraged by the multiple offers to serve. We experienced concern. Compassion. Kindness. Prayers. Assistance. Generosity. Acts of service were the bright spot in the aftermath of a devastating storm.

When the power returned, we paused from cleanup to watch the news, which highlighted numerous examples of people serving those who needed help. Help with power outages, downed trees, flooding, and, in some cases, overwhelming loss. Finding ways to serve was a common theme throughout the state. Our son Timmy and his friends visited shelters and thanked first responders. Our church fed the hungry. Our neighbors used their chain saws to remove trees that had toppled onto homes and fences. Friends shared water and food and assisted with efforts to return order to lives and property. Countless acts of service.

THE GREATEST AMONG US— AND THE NOT SO GREAT

Reaching out to help others during challenging circumstances is more than just doing the right thing; it's our God-given privilege and responsibility. The focus in the previous chapter was on love, which should be the primary mindset of a Christian. When God's love rules in our hearts, they are enlarged with the capacity to serve. We act as His ambassadors when we work to meet the needs of others. And serving provides incredible opportunities for lasting influence!

I can't remember the first time I thought about serving. The subject wasn't discussed in my home growing up, it wasn't the topic of my early Bible studies in college, and it wasn't the focus of any conversation I recall. I don't ever remember encountering a genuine servant . . . until I met Teresa.

When God's love rules in our hearts, they are enlarged with the capacity to serve.

The cook in our sorority house sang hymns as she prepared and served breakfast. She rarely talked, perhaps because she felt her grammar did not match that of all of us college girls, but we were no match for her radiant smile, contagious joy, and sweet spirit. I can still picture her flipping pancakes when I came down for breakfast. She probably wasn't paid much or thanked often. But cooking for a bunch of self-centered sorority girls wasn't just a job for her; it was a ministry.

Even back then I was a morning person, and I would often be the first one to breakfast. When I began my sophomore year, I was a mess. There was a war going on inside me, and somehow Teresa knew. I kept my struggles to myself, yet she sensed when my tank was empty. She would wrap her arms around me and just love me. She prayed for me, and I think she was the only person who cared about my spiritual life. That's the year I relinquished control of my life to the Lord. When I married Bob a few years later, Teresa was at our wedding. I heard that her sons became successful NFL players. I am not surprised. I'm sure she served them, too.

Until I met Teresa, I didn't know what a servant looked like. To me, she looked so much like Jesus. Her quiet influence was powerful, and I know her reward in heaven will be great. Teresa is an exception in a world dominated by selfish pursuits. We are continually told by the media, "Have it your way," "You deserve this or that," and "Look out for number one." I received a flyer once with my phone bill that claimed, "Life is all about you!" But is life really about me—or you? I eventually realized that in order to be influential, I couldn't buy into that self-absorbed philosophy and focus only on myself.

Even in the secular world, serving has a positive impact on those who serve. A 2010 survey of 4,500 American adults revealed that of those who volunteered an average of one hundred hours a year, 68 percent reported that volunteering had made them feel physically healthier, 73 percent said it lowered their stress levels, and 89 percent said it improved their sense of well-being.[1]

The Bible is replete with life-impacting motivation to serve. We're instructed to have the mindset of Christ, who gave up all the glories of heaven to serve us so that we can know His Father. In order to be like Him, we have to turn our eyes away from ourselves and focus them on others.

A few years ago, I suggested to a recently married young woman that she could bring lunch to her husband. "Why should I serve him, when he is perfectly capable of getting it himself?" she asked. Several families had gathered at a large home for a football game. It was past lunchtime, and the men were busy with a project in another room. As a kindness, the wives were bringing lunch to their husbands, but this young woman was not interested. I was hesitant to meddle, but the woman's observant friend pleaded with me to encourage the newlywed. Although I love to influence women, my efforts in this instance fell on pretty pierced ears that were indifferent to biblical truth. This young wife was influenced, instead, by our culture's negative connotation of serving, which is often thought of as demeaning, inferior, or connected with lowly tasks.

Years ago I was also a clueless newlywed. At the time, there weren't many books available on my new role. Bob and I were married right after college and immediately moved far away from family for grad school. I had lots of girlfriends, but they didn't know any more about being a wife than I did. Besides Teresa, there were no obvious servants in my life. I needed an example to follow, a person to shadow. And I found one! He was there all along, serving me and meeting my needs. In fact, He met my biggest need when He gave up His physical life so I could have eternal life. Mark 10:45 tells us, "Even the Son of Man did not come to be served, but to serve, and to give His life a ransom for many." I'm overcome with gratitude! Christ's sacrifice influences me to serve others.

Although the concept of serving my husband was still new, the opportunity I'd had to serve the girls in my college Bible study remained my favorite life experience. I reasoned that I needed to apply that same concept to my marriage. Talk about a challenge! Serving Bob involved giving up rights I didn't want to relinquish. But a Bible sat on my nightstand, the Holy Spirit lived in my heart, and the God of heaven had a plan to transform me to look more like Him. Reading verses like the one above caused my comfort zone to be uncomfortable—especially when I had to apply them.

My brilliant but dyslexic husband needed my service in typing his papers. As he was attending grad-school classes, studying, and writing papers, I was rewriting papers and learning some of what he was learning. I took night classes offered especially for seminary wives and learned more. My day job provided an income as well as a course in working with difficult people, and I learned even more. More about giving up rights. More about serving. I'd give up a right one day, only to take it back the next. That happens to all of us because we have a sin nature that wars with our new nature in Christ. Whichever one we feed the most wins the battle, and the war won't be over until we go to heaven.

My first real job allowed me to take advantage of my public relations training, but I failed to take advantage of the opportunity to serve. During my first week of work, an employee I'd just met informed me that she didn't like me. I never responded, but her obvious animosity added drama to my workday. Even though I fulfilled my job requirements and my bosses were pleased, I didn't go to work every day with the purpose of making my employer and my coworkers successful—especially the coworker who disliked me. In other words, it never occurred to me to serve them. It's humbling to admit, and I wish I could have a do-over. The testimony I hoped to have with my coworkers would have been more effective if I had demonstrated a servant's heart.

A working environment can be challenging to serve in. You probably identify. We may count the minutes until five o'clock or the years until retirement, but if influence is our goal, our job becomes an opportunity for an impact on those we work with. Thankfully, over time, I began to learn more biblical principles of serving and apply them to my many nonpaying jobs.

SERVING AT HOME

This concept of serving began to change my perspective on being a wife and mother. I realized that in the context of serving my family, I could have great influence. A servant is focused on making those in her sphere successful. When a wife serves her husband, she enables him to be the man God intends him to be. She reminds him of his potential. Believes in him. Encourages him. Supports him. Wives have a choice: We can ignore our opportunities to serve, or we can choose to serve, despite the requirements of effort, endurance, and sacrifice. The rewards are worth much more than a paycheck!

Only a handful of people believed in my husband when we left for the mission field. I was one of them. Thirty-four years later, thousands (even millions, which is really not an exaggeration) of Filipinos have come to Christ, hundreds of Americans have joined his mission trips, and nearly sixty national staff preach and plant churches throughout the Philippines. In 1991, Bob used his inheritance to purchase land for an orphanage, which has served as home to orphans ever since. In another semi-closed country, he was surprised by the opportunity to rescue girls caught up in human trafficking, which led to establishing a safe house. And there's much more. I continue to serve my husband as he serves others, by believing in him, encouraging him, and helping him with aspects of the ministry that are not his strengths.

Serving our children requires even more time and effort for a season. Mothers so look forward to holding our precious babies, often without giving much thought to the hours we will serve before our children leave our homes. Yet the privilege of rearing children is one I will never take for granted. Investing in my five was worth every second of service—teaching, doing laundry, cooking, hugging, praying, and shuttling them where they needed to go.

As a young mom, I spent a season in Philippians 2:5-8: "Have this attitude in yourselves which was also in Christ Jesus, who, although He existed in the form of God, did not regard equality with God a thing to be grasped, but emptied Himself, taking the form of a bond-servant. . . . He humbled Himself by becoming obedient to the point of death, even death on a cross." I never emptied myself of all the selfishness, and I never gave up my life for a child, although it was close with child number five. But my Savior's ultimate sacrifice to serve me motivates me to keep on serving people in my sphere.

We taught our children that they would be great, not because they were athletic, had impressive résumés, made lots of money, or did anything else that the world deems valuable. They would be great if they served. This echoes Matthew 23:11-12: "The greatest among you shall be your servant. Whoever exalts himself shall be humbled; and whoever humbles himself shall be exalted." I put these essential verses to a tune, and we sang it often. I wanted the passage to be in their young minds and take up residence in their hearts.

Bob and I desired that all of our children learn to serve from an early age. And the Lord provided the perfect opportunity—right next door. After Bob graduated with two seminary degrees, we moved back to Florida for his job—area director for the Fellowship of Christian Athletes—and we bought our first home. Our neighbor, an accountant, had polio as a child and walked with a slight limp. Because of his health issues and his willingness to care for his elderly parents, he never married and had a family. He had lived all his life in Louisville, Kentucky, until his company transferred him to our city. Looking back, we know it was God's wonderful plan for Dick's life and ours to be forever transformed by the ripple effects of serving one another.

Our two-year-old daughter Christy and I often visited Dick's elderly mother while he was at work and offered to help if needed. The relationship grew as I had our second child the next year, the third three years later, and the fourth three years after that. Meanwhile, "Uncle Dick," as my children affectionately called him, and his mom became like family and were included in special dinners, birthdays, and holidays. We taught the kids about empathy when Dick's mother died. And they experienced firsthand that serving sometimes involves menial tasks like scrubbing toilets and washing dishes, which was more fun to do for Uncle Dick than for Mom.

Even at young ages, our children learned that serving is a win-win. We bless the ones we serve, and God blesses us for serving. The kids helped Dick do things he couldn't do, and they were rewarded with small bottles of soda (which they didn't get at home) and special time with him they will cherish all their lives. After Dick retired, the children spent hours playing games with him. The boys watched old Westerns and played ball with him in the yard. He always had time for our children. Because both my father and Bob's had died, Uncle Dick became the only "grandfather" for our kids. If you ask any of our five children, they would agree that Uncle Dick's life enriched theirs in countless ways. Only heaven will reveal the resulting ripples from God's weaving our lives together.

When Bob planted a new church, the first official meeting was in our house. Dick only had to walk next door to participate. That first Sunday, Bob shared the gospel, and Dick invited Jesus to live in his heart. Our small church family embraced Dick and loved him almost as much as we did. Dick involved himself in every aspect of our church and served the congregation as he served our kids. When God called us to the mission field, Dick volunteered with our ministry, meticulously overseeing the finances. He concluded that he had not done much up until that point to impact eternity, but he determined to finish strong. His greatest joy, next to meeting his Savior, was when we called him from the hospital in the Philippines to tell him we had named our youngest son Timothy "Richard" after him. We hoped that our son would have a legacy of serving like Uncle Dick. That legacy is already being fulfilled through Timmy's personal life and his foundation, whose purpose is "To bring Faith, Hope and Love to those needing a brighter day in their darkest hour of need."

Only hours before Dick went to heaven, I sat on the edge of his hospital bed and fed him ice cream, his favorite. Serving Dick, the servant of all, was one of the highlights of all of our lives.

When Dick died, we were surprised that he had left a large amount of money to our ministry. We didn't know he had saved any money. He dressed in well-worn clothes and drove an old car, because he chose to invest his resources in eternal things. The money he left helped to purchase the dorms for our orphanage, which Bob renamed "Uncle Dick's Home." I'm certain Dick is pleased, and so is his heavenly Father. Our family will always value Dick as the "greatest among us."

SOME SPECIAL SERVANTS

Snapshots of some of our other favorite servants are featured below. None of them seek recognition, which is typical of servants. I hope their brief stories inspire you who already serve to remember that God values you greatly!

I'm writing this chapter in my daughter Katie's home, where I visited for Mother's Day. I have a real-life visual of the countless ways a working mom serves. The people and responsibilities she juggles. The sacrifices she makes that go unnoticed. Her limited free time. Yet her love and service for her three daughters are reflected in their lives. Her eleven-year-old, Abby, held a car wash to earn money to treat her mom and me to a scavenger hunt leading to flowers, gifts, and a homemade breakfast, and later to a lovely lunch after church. What a clear example of the ripple effects of serving!

My oldest daughter, Christy, and her husband have multiple degrees and have authored books, but they chose to move far from fanfare and serve on a difficult mission field. Why? Because God has called them to serve a people who need to know their God. My favorite picture is of my daughter and our granddaughter Claire washing a woman's feet, which in their country demonstrates respect. My little granddaughter is looking lovingly into the face of a worn and wrinkled old woman who is not valued by her husband or others. Yet on that day, she felt valued.

In an effort to serve other young women in her sphere, my lovely daughter-in-law Casey formed a book club. Working women gathered in her home once a week to discuss a specific Christian book. When Casey had her first child, she invited other young moms to a Bible study in her home. Casey graciously uses her home as a means of influencing women, who greatly benefit from edifying friendships and encouragement in their walk with the Lord.

Maryanne is still as beautiful as when we first met years ago, and she is still serving with grace and compassion. When Bob and I flew to her northern city a couple of years ago to speak in the church her husband pastors, we were invited to their home for lunch between the morning and afternoon services. I offered to set the table or help in some way. Maryanne responded apologetically that she wouldn't be able to serve our meal in a formal setting. I later learned she had willingly turned her dining room into a bedroom for her husband's mother, who had dementia and could no longer care for herself. Maryanne selflessly gave up social engagements, church services, and time to do what she wanted to do, in order to meet the increasing needs of her mother-in-law.

Maryanne influenced me! I left her home aware of how often I fall short in this challenging area of serving. I couldn't begin to imagine the sacrifices my longtime friend made to serve. And she faithfully served someone who no longer had the mental capacity to thank her.

You may not be asked to transform your dining room. But have you had to transform your mindset because of an obvious call to serve someone in your sphere? Maybe it's a child with special needs, an elderly neighbor, or a friend in need. When we plan a wedding or get a positive pregnancy test, the thought of serving may not cross our minds—at least it didn't cross mine the first time. But the second, third, fourth, and fifth times the test was positive, I already had an idea that more serving opportunities awaited me. As I shared with a large group I spoke to recently, I realized early on that it was in the context of serving my husband and children that I had the greatest influence. After the event, I was encouraged beyond words when the event planner shared a comment from a successful businessman in the audience. He told her he now realized that the most significant influence he would ever have in life was the investment of time with his young son. He got it! Because our most significant influence often involves serving, it's worth rearranging priorities, schedules, and dining rooms to do it.

I have two special friends named Sue who are servants. One lovely friend of many years volunteers weekly at a rescue mission, serving those who walk in off the streets, hopeless and addicted. She quietly fills prescriptions written by another dear friend, Karen, who takes time from her medical practice to treat the women physically and also spiritually with a Bible study. Most of the women they faithfully serve find their hope in Jesus, who enables them to live differently when they leave the mission.

My other friend Sue has difficulty turning down opportunities to serve. She tutors dyslexic kids, including my youngest son, who struggled to read in elementary school. But he not only won the Heisman Trophy for the best college football player, he also won the "Academic Heisman" for the best scholar-athlete—twice! He is so grateful for Sue's efforts on his behalf. She has taught elementary Sunday school for forty years, and her greatest joy is when a child prays with her to be saved. She mentors moms, sings in the choir, and goes on mission trips. But Sue also was willing to give up service that is occasionally applauded (if there is such a thing) to quietly and sacrificially serve the needs of her extended family. I am one of only a few who know the extent of her service. I am blessed to call her my friend. The ripple effects of her service have greatly impacted my family and countless others.

My friend Brenda is a testimony to the fact that one person who is willing to give up personal rights in order to serve others can make a huge difference in the world. She certainly had an impact on our world. Brenda's husband, Craig, wrote the home education legislation that is still in effect in Florida. Soon after, Craig passed away with cancer, and Brenda became a lobbyist to safeguard the freedoms of homeschoolers, living by faith on their sporadic donations. She trained herself to decode laws and work wisely with those who made them. Then, against all odds, she wrote and helped to pass the extracurricular law allowing homeschoolers to participate in sports and other extracurricular activities through the state athletic association. Our son Robby thought the Lord and Brenda passed the law specifically for him—just in time for him to play three sports in high school and earn a football scholarship to college. States that pass a similar law now refer to it as the "Tim Tebow" rule. Timmy was young when it passed in Florida, but he is one of the first homeschoolers to play football at a major university.

Brenda is dedicated to a fault, rarely taking a day off, and is one of the most courageous women I know. But above all, she is a servant.

In our self-absorbed world, someone like Brenda is so rare, because she is a living example of Philippians 2:3-4: "Do nothing from selfishness or empty conceit, but with humility of mind regard one another as more important than yourselves; do not merely look out for your own personal interests, but also for the interests of others." She is not well paid and is rarely thanked for the sacrifices she makes on behalf of others. Thank you, Brenda!

This year, I was privileged to attend my husband's annual national staff conference in the Philippines. The fifty-seven Filipino staff, along with special speakers from the United States, gathered for a week of training and encouragement. The men are educated, trained, and committed to preaching the gospel in the areas where they are assigned, with the goal of reaching everyone in their country for Christ. They preach at film showings and follow up with new believers, connecting them to the local churches we work with. I've never been in a group of so many servants. They willingly make sacrifices for the gospel, often preaching in hostile environments. I had the privilege of thanking them for serving.

A WORD, A GIFT, A HUG

But what if nobody thanks you for serving? Maybe those you serve don't even notice your efforts. Your children take you for granted. Your coworker is wrapped up in herself. Your grandchildren are busy with school and activities. Your neighbor is oblivious. You don't promote yourself, and no one else does either. Your husband's job is too stressful and consuming. Your friends would get it, because you are certain they feel just as you do, but you hate to admit your unspiritual thoughts. Should you keep serving? If you quit, would anyone notice? What's the point? Who sees all you do?

God does. He sees everything and everyone. He sees you serving faithfully when no one else notices. When there is no gratitude. When you are overlooked and underpaid. When another takes credit. When you are left to clean up the mess.

He sees the diapers you changed. The meal you brought to the new mom. The invitation you declined in order to care for your elderly parent. The vacation time you spent going on a mission trip. Your volunteer efforts at a crisis pregnancy center. The times you checked on your sick neighbor. The way you care for babies in the church nursery or tutor a struggling student. Your sacrificial efforts on behalf of a child with special needs. The list is endless. We are most like our Master when we serve the least of these, people who cannot reciprocate. What you do for the least of these, you do for the Lord. You will be rewarded for even a cup of cold water you give in His name (see Matthew 10:42).

We are most like our Master when we serve the least of these, people who cannot reciprocate.

Most women serve in some capacity but are rarely thanked. When I speak at women's events, I love to thank the servants in the group. And at almost every event, I meet women who didn't realize God valued them. I still remember a lady in Texas who, with tears in her eyes, commented that she had been volunteering in a crisis pregnancy center for twenty years and never realized that God values servants. What a joy to commend her for her faithful service that has ripple effects for the cause of life.

Spread the word to your friends that serving the people in our spheres of influence is worth it. Women sit up straighter, hold their heads higher, wake up motivated, go to sleep fulfilled, and keep on keeping on, no matter what the world around them thinks, when they comprehend that the One whose opinion counts the most considers them *great*!

To God, servants stand out from all the rest because they are the greatest among us. You may not be voted "most likely to succeed," "most popular," or any other typical "most." But you, faithful servant, are the "most like Jesus." Talk about influence! Demonstrating what Jesus is like is a goal of influence. You may have to wait until heaven to get your prize, but it will be worth waiting for.

During my recent two-night stay at a hotel, the maid was noticeably pleasant, seemed to put an extra effort into cleaning, and didn't mind trading the decaf coffee packets for the real ones. I had a speaking event in the area and was preparing when she cleaned my room the first day. I asked about her family, and she responded with such eagerness, glad that I'd shown interest in her. She hugged me as she left the room. The next morning, I left a tip, a little note, and my favorite gospel tract. When I returned later that evening, I found a sincere note of gratitude in broken English. I tip more now than I once did, probably because I know what it's like to serve without recognition. You do too! The smallest acknowledgment of your service is an encouragement to keep serving. We can encourage those who serve us with a tip, a small gift, a thank-you verbalized or written, or an occasional hug.

I was fighting tears when I arrived at our airport's curbside check-in a few weeks ago. Moments before, I'd learned that my sincere, time-consuming efforts to serve in a significant situation were disregarded. My heart ached! Bob and I always tip the hardworking, kind men who weigh our bags and converse about our trips. This time, even though I handed my favorite guy a tip, I was too overcome with the unresolved heartache to talk. Instead of my serving him, he served me. He put his big arms around me with a hug I really needed at that moment. He whispered with heartfelt compassion, "Mrs. Tebow, whatever it is, you know God's got it." His hug was a tangible reminder of that truth. God always has it! All you servants, God does have it, and He sees all your efforts that others fail to notice. He keeps account of even the smallest ways you serve in His name. Your hug may be delayed, but God will reward you for every act of service you do because of your love for Jesus.

When the opportunity presents itself, thank the servants in your life. Perhaps you will be the one person who doesn't take them for granted. Your gratitude could be the influential encouragement they need to continue serving. I entitled this chapter "Serving Isn't for Sissies" for good reason. Serving is hard. It was hard for Jesus. Serving forces us to bite our tongues, to humble ourselves, and to surrender our rights, our time, and sometimes our reputations and our treasure. But serving is worth it, even when we have to wait for our reward.

Developing a mindset of serving is one of the most powerful ways we can impact others and show them what Jesus is really like. On the night before He was crucified, Jesus demonstrated to His disciples what it means to serve when He washed their feet. He taught them, "If I then, the Lord and the Teacher, washed your feet, you also ought to wash one another's feet. For I gave you an example that you also should do as I did to you" (John 13:14-15). When we put someone else's needs before our own, we are becoming more like Jesus.

Chapter 12

THE POWER
OF WORDS

Strikingly pretty, the college coed had dark curly hair and large hazel eyes. She left the office of her music professor with a smile, and for good reason. He had raved about her lovely alto voice and perfect pitch. And, to her amazement, he congratulated her for being selected to sing in the school's girls' trio—a dream come true.

But as she entered her next class, she sat in the back of the room, desperately hoping the professor wouldn't call on her to answer any questions. History was such a challenge for her. As hard as she tried to memorize the material, she just couldn't do it. She looked down at the floor to avoid the teacher's eyes, but he called on her anyway. And, like all the other times, she stammered and stumbled. When she was unable to come up with the right answer, the professor chided her for being unprepared for class.

They were right, she thought to herself as she quickly exited the class, embarrassed and discouraged. *I will never amount to anything.*

They told me I'm stupid, and I am. "They" were her parents and an older sister who, instead of encouraging and supporting her as she headed off to college, predicted she would never succeed. As a child, she had suffered head trauma from a fall, resulting in an inability to memorize. As hard as she tried, she couldn't retain history facts.

After several more weeks of struggling in class, she gave up and decided to quit school. The dean of students tried to talk her out of it. "After all," she said, "the story you submitted for the school newspaper was excellent, and your English teacher commented on the beautiful poems you wrote for class. And what about your vocal opportunities?" she asked. "Don't you want to develop your talents?"

"I don't have any talent," the insecure teenager responded, and she left the dean's office—and the college.

When I heard that story, it broke my heart. The teenager wasn't just any kid who became discouraged and dropped out of college. She was my mother, and she lived most of her life influenced by the critical words of her family—words that shaped her view of who she was and what she was capable of achieving. When I was in high school, my mother showed me the poems and stories she wrote when she was younger. They were lovely, brimming with potential. But she quit writing, convinced by her family's words that she had no ability to do anything well. She expected to fail at whatever she attempted, because that's what she was told by the people whose opinions mattered most to her. What a sad legacy of the power of negative words!

Fortunately, my mother did not pass on that negativity to me. In one of the small ironies of life, I probably would not be writing this book were it not for my mother's encouragement when I was younger. She used the power of words to give me the confidence to submit my poems and stories for selection into the Fine Arts Club. Her affirming words continued as I went to college. I majored in journalism because my mother convinced me I could write. As I look back, I realize that my efforts were actually magnified by the impact of my mother's encouraging words. Words have influence! They have the power to build us up and fill us with confidence, and they also have the power to destroy the potential for greatness that every person has.

STICKS AND STONES—AND FIRES

We live in a world where criticism, put-downs, and insults seem to be the norm. Negative words are dominant in our society and sometimes even in our families. They rest on the lips of children as soon as they begin to talk. Uncomplimentary names like *dummy* and *stupid* are as commonplace on the playground as swings and slides.

When our children were young, they responded to such name-calling with a popular singsong comeback: "Sticks and stones may break my bones, but words will never hurt me." But our kids soon discovered what we adults already know: Words do hurt us.

> *Words have influence! They have the power to build us up and fill us with confidence, and they also have the power to destroy.*

Negative words are like permanent markers indelibly etching our hearts with enduring pain. If my mother, an intelligent and gifted woman, gave up on her dream because of words, just imagine what these familiar statements can do to a child's tender spirit: "Why can't you be like your brother?" "Can't you do anything right?" "I can't wait until you go back to school."

Adults are just as susceptible to the blows of hurtful words. We've probably all snapped at our husbands, "I told you so!" or said something impatient to the cashier at the grocery store, made fun of a coworker because she didn't read the memo, or gossiped about one neighbor to another. Just a few hastily spoken words can cause more long-term damage than sticks and stones breaking bones.

The damaging effect of our words is dealt with throughout the

Bible, and I have to believe that God allowed a shift in the wind to help Bob and me teach our kids about one of these passages: "See how great a forest is set aflame by such a small fire! And the tongue is a fire" (James 3:5-6).

Shortly after we moved to the property we live on now, my husband decided to use a controlled fire to burn the weeds on the pasture adjacent to our home. He was having some success when a sudden wind picked up a spark. In seconds, the whole pasture was on fire. The entire family ran out with rakes and shovels, trying to put out the flames that were racing toward the woods. Even five-year-old Timmy and eight-year-old Peter slammed shovels, as big as they were, on the flaming grass. After what seemed like hours, the fire consumed the whole pasture and part of another, stopping just short of the woods. Hot, dirty, and exhausted, we made our way to the house, where my husband wisely turned our experience into a life lesson.

"Wouldn't we be sad if our woods caught on fire?" Bob asked, as I passed out glasses of water to our thirsty children. "Think of all the pretty trees and plants and the different animals that would be destroyed. Just one little spark of fire blazed out of control, and then suddenly the pastures were engulfed in flames."

The kids nodded their ash-smudged heads as they listened carefully to their dad. "It sure took all of us a long time to put the fire out," Bob continued. "We nearly lost our beautiful woods to that fire." After a slight pause, he continued. "Our tongues are just like that spark; they can cause great damage when they are not controlled. The book of James says, 'See how great a forest is set aflame by such a small fire! And the tongue is a fire.'" Then we had a lively family discussion comparing the small spark to the tongue. We wanted our children to comprehend the seriousness of calling their brothers, sisters, and friends hurtful names and using unkind labels.

"Words," we warned them, "hurt worse when they are spoken by someone we care about." Such words can, indeed, cause more serious damage than sticks and stones. Although our family tried so hard to reverse the impact on my mother's self-image, the crushing words from her childhood haunted her for her entire life. By God's grace, we were able to avert a similar experience in our family.

I still remember how excited my daughter was when I dropped her off for the first meeting of her church youth group. "This year is going to be so great!" she exclaimed as she opened the car door. "I love you, Mom. See you in a couple of hours." She looked adorable in her new outfit and was full of energy and enthusiasm as she joined her friends.

When I returned a few minutes early to pick her up, she was uncharacteristically waiting for me outside. Usually the last to leave an event like this, she was standing alone, with her head lowered to hide the fact that she'd been crying.

"Honey, what's wrong?" I asked as she quickly slid into the front seat.

"My teacher doesn't like me at all, Mom," she responded as she wiped the tears.

"What makes you say that?" I questioned.

"Because I am not my sister," she continued. "I don't want to go to any more church activities."

I learned later that this woman had approached my daughter and asked her why she couldn't be more like her sister. My daughter's heart was broken, and my heart ached for her. The woman who spoke those hurtful words is not a bad person. She just made the same mistake we all make when we forget how powerful our words are. King Solomon, the wisest man who ever lived, wrote, "Death and life are in the power of the tongue" (Proverbs 18:21). To my daughter, the words of her youth worker brought death to her self-image, optimism, and desire to belong.

As an important side note, it is always wrong to compare one person to another! Kids—especially during the teenage years—already have a problem comparing themselves with others. They don't need assistance in that area. God created each of our children with unique abilities and personalities, but when we compare them to one of their siblings, it feeds their insecurity, creates jealousy, and is like a dagger in their hearts. How many of us, in a tense moment, throw out a comparison in order to validate the point we are trying to make? The damage caused by such words is nearly irreversible, especially when they're spoken by people entrusted with the responsibility to "train up a child in the way he should go" (Proverbs 22:6).

How do we counteract the negative words shot like arrows into the hearts of people we love? I am not usually an "interfering mother," but in this case, I had to protect my tenderhearted little girl from the possibility of hearing more hurtful words and unfair comparisons. At certain ages and in specific situations, a mother senses when a child is more fragile and needs to be "handled with care." Our church youth group organized the kids into Bible fellowship classes, and I chose to move my daughter to a different one with a new teacher. I'm so glad I did.

I watched from the back of the room as the new teacher introduced my daughter to the other students, saying, "We are so blessed to have you join our class!" This teacher clearly understood the power of encouraging words. "You are just so precious" was a phrase she used liberally and sincerely. During the next few years, my daughter thrived with such positive words from her youth leader. She rarely missed class, and neither did the other girls, because their teacher was constantly building them up. Her words brought healing, as in Proverbs 12:18: "There is one who speaks rashly like the thrusts of a sword, but the tongue of the wise brings healing."

How many hurting people do you encounter on a daily basis whom you could influence by offering a kind, healing word? I'm often too busy to notice people around me who are hurting, but I'll never forget the lady in the grocery store one day. She was trying to reach an item on the top shelf, and I offered to help. I smiled after I handed her the can and said something trite like "Have a nice day." But she seemed to be struggling with more than groceries. A few minutes later, I encountered her again in another aisle. Without a cart, she was juggling several items that tumbled and rolled. I stopped to pick them up. This time, I thought about my words in an attempt to calm her. She was in need of kindness. We talked for a few minutes, and I brought her a cart. I gave her a hug, hesitant to leave. And then she said four words I will never forget: "Are you an angel?"

Oh, Lord, I prayed while checking out, *please let me have more "angel" moments, times when I represent You well.*

TAMING THE TONGUE

Second Samuel 22:26 is a verse I adapted and camped on with my kids: "With the kind God shows Himself kind." I reminded my three boys (over and over), "What is desirable in a man is his kindness" (Proverbs 19:22). The world is in need of kindness. I regret the times I bypassed those who were in as much need of a kind word as the lady in the grocery store. The family raising a child with special needs. The elderly neighbor who is lonely. The visitor at church. People believe God is real when He sends real people to communicate with words His love for them.

Most of Proverbs 31 is devoted to describing an excellent or virtuous woman. Verse 26 is a verse about kindness, written especially for us! Because our opportunity for life-impacting influence is at stake, I pray daily to open my mouth in wisdom, with the teaching of kindness on my tongue (see Proverbs 31:26). And we women do open our mouths a lot! In fact, for her master's degree, my daughter Christy researched speech patterns and found sources suggesting that men speak about six thousand words a day and women twenty thousand. So in the multitude of words we speak every day, we need an intentional mindset of choosing those that build up and encourage rather than tear down and hurt.

Unfortunately, I have wounded people I love with my words. It's natural to speak quickly, without thinking; but a hasty word can't be taken back or erased from memory, even when we ask for forgiveness.

"Isn't that the third time today you spilled your milk?" I snapped at a child. The first and second time it happened, I just cleaned up the mess and reminded him to be more careful. But when he spilled the third time, I reacted with sharp words and then immediately regretted them as I looked into his sad little eyes. I realized he was just having a clumsy day, and my harsh words made it worse for him. I had no intention of crushing my son's spirit with my outburst. I was exhausted, a normal condition for young mothers, and frustrated, engaging my mouth before I engaged my mind. That's when we often say things we later regret.

Lord, will I ever be able to change? I prayed as I cried over my angry, hurtful words. Until I became a parent, I didn't realize I was even capable of uttering words I didn't mean to say. *Please help me!* I pleaded to the Lord, not once but over and over again through the years. I am so very thankful that God did, indeed, help me. I am far from where I want to be, but so far from where I was.

Our words hold the power of life and death (see Proverbs 18:21) and mark the lives of the people in our spheres. We speak life when we teach, encourage, love, reprove, evangelize, or disciple. We speak death when we discourage, gossip, grumble, manipulate, nag, argue, or ridicule. I've heard that children need to hear ten positive words to counteract the effects of just one negative word.

What exactly are positive words? In Ephesians 4:29, Paul contrasted positive and negative words: "Let no unwholesome word proceed from your mouth, but only such a word as is good for edification according to the need of the moment, so that it will give grace to those who hear." *THE MESSAGE* version reads, "Watch the way you talk. Let nothing foul or dirty come out of your mouth. Say only what helps, each word a gift." Positive words are not unwholesome, foul, or dirty. In contrast, they edify, build up, encourage, instruct, and help the recipient—just when it's needed most. Positive words are a gift of grace. But how do we wrap up positive, loving words and give them as gifts on a regular basis?

I certainly don't have the complete answer to that question, nor do I always say what I should say when I need to say it. It's humbling, because as hard as I try, I can't change myself. The power of positive thinking doesn't work. I can determine to speak positive words, but when I am tired, frustrated, overwhelmed, angry, or discouraged, I still say things I don't mean to say. So once again, my inability to do anything in my own strength results in my turning to God, who is "greater than our heart and knows all things" (1 John 3:20). Since He knows all things, He also knows how to help us progress in this area of speech. Improvement in our speech, and in every area of life, requires God's grace and our effort. We can count on God to come through on His end because He is faithful, but what about our part?

"I will never be able to write in cursive," exclaimed one of my three left-handed children. "I keep trying, and I can't do it. I don't want to practice anymore. Cursive is too hard, so I just want to print."

"But this writing guide I found is especially for left-handers like you," I explained. "It will take some effort on your part, but you can eventually learn to write in cursive if you practice."

"But I don't want to practice," my child continued. "Cursive writing takes too much time to learn, and it's just too hard!"

When it comes to changing our speech habits, some of us are like that child. The promise of transformed speech is just outside our reach, but we decide the process is too hard and we settle for the way we are. We aren't willing to make the necessary effort. One close relative excused her blunt, often hurtful words with "I can't help it; it's just the way I am!" But I am convinced that we *can* help it.

If our goal is to have a positive influence on the lives of those we speak to, we need to find a way to halt the negative words before they leave our lips. The consequences of speaking hasty, negative words should be implanted in our minds with a huge red octagonal sign that tells us to **STOP** and carefully consider what we say. Personal memories can serve as fuel to drive us toward the goal of positive speech habits. You may have a memory from childhood that could serve as a reminder of the long-term damage of negative words: when a classmate made fun of you, a teacher embarrassed you, or a parent crushed you with an angry phrase. I remember their long-term effect on my mother, the spilled milk incident that hurt my son, and a more recent illustration of derogatory words.

As I was writing this section on words, a lady in a store I occasionally shop in stopped me to talk. Her friend had told her I was writing a book, and she commented, "Of course, you have someone writing it for you." Then she moved on to another subject. I didn't bother to respond, but my pride had been wounded by her words. When I exited the store, I laughed out loud. She meant no harm, and I moved on quickly, but there have been times when it was hard to move on.

I'm sure you can identify times in your life when words hurt you. None of us can stop the flow of offensive words, but we can choose how we respond. Release your hurt to the Lord, and ask Him to help you forgive, as you want others to forgive you when you say something you shouldn't. We can use memories of negative words to remind us to "stop and think" before we speak, because our influence on others is at stake. Even more effective is to ask the Lord to enable us to be quick to hear, slow to speak, and slow to anger (see James 1:19).

GOD'S WORDS IMPACT OURS

The impact of the Word of God on my speech has been undeniable. I can quote 2 Timothy 3:16-17 concerning the Scripture's supernatural ability to teach, reprove, correct, and train in order to equip me for good works, but to see it worked out in this area of my life, over the course of many years, is astounding.

Because of the eternal impact of my words on the lives of people I interact with, I have made it a habit to memorize key Bible verses that deal with the area of speech. Many mornings, I review the verses and ask the Lord to enable me to apply them.

You might have just skimmed the preceding sentences without giving them too much thought, but my life and the lives of people I communicate with are forever changed by the transforming truth of what I just wrote. I encourage you to engraft verses on speech any way you can. The left-handed child never did put forth the effort to learn cursive writing, but we *must*, if our goal is positive influence, make the commitment to do what it takes for our speech to be transformed.

One of the speech-impacting verses I learned is "Set a guard, O Lord, over my mouth; keep watch over the door of my lips" (Psalm 141:3). I've often been in the middle of a sentence and stopped abruptly, because what I am about to say will not edify, or build up, the person I am talking to. It is as if the Lord is literally setting a guard over my mouth.

Can you imagine God Himself keeping watch over the doors of our lips? Our lips are the doors to our mouths, and whatever I am thinking about can be verbalized when I open mine. I have flung that door open wide too many times when I really needed to keep it shut. I still remember reading for the first time that I will be held accountable for "every careless word" that I speak (Matthew 12:36). Keeping the door closed prevents those careless words from getting out and wreaking havoc.

An even more striking visual image about controlling my speech is found in Psalm 39:1. I need to be as determined as this writer: "I said, 'I will guard my ways that I may not sin with my tongue;

I will guard my mouth as with a muzzle.'" The visual image of a muzzle on my mouth has prevented me from speaking countless times and has proved especially effective at ball games, which for some reason seem to bring out the worst in a person. I've had so many kids playing so many kinds of ball that there have been numerous opportunities to practice the advice I'm passing on. It's much easier for us to do what comes naturally: loudly express indignation when a referee or an umpire makes a questionable call, or whisper words of disdain for a coach's choice of plays. Not only can such words hurt others, they don't edify anyone or set a good example.

This invisible muzzle also prevents us from wounding impressionable children, sensitive husbands, thin-skinned coworkers, and friends who need to be encouraged rather than discouraged by our careless words. I'm reminded to think about what I say before I say it, questioning how my words will impact the listener: Am I speaking out of frustration, anger, or impatience? Am I so tired that I may need to save this conversation for the next day? Is the listener in the right frame of mind, or would my words make a greater impact another time?

Making a habit of engrafting specific verses on speech, like the ones above, has helped to transform the way I talk to my husband, my children, friends, salespeople, and others I meet along the way. The guard stationed in front of the door of my lips and the muzzle over my mouth have the power to prevent me from saying words that will spark a forest fire that's impossible to extinguish.

I'd much rather focus on positive words: "Let your speech always be with grace, as though seasoned with salt, so that you will know how you should respond to each person" (Colossians 4:6). This verse implies that my speech needs to be sprinkled with love, in a conversation that is especially suited to each person I talk with.

Our words can inspire people in our spheres to overcome obstacles and setbacks. I wait for an appropriate opportunity to speak positive words to those who are facing challenges. And as my children grow older and establish their own homes and families, they still need to hear positive words from me that will ring in their ears when they doubt their abilities, are tempted to give up on a dream, or sense pressure to compromise in a competitive world. As long as they will listen, I hope to exercise wisdom and grace to sprinkle positive, loving words into our conversation as I once sprinkled salt on the food I served them.

Transformation in the way we talk requires humility to admit our need. I came to the place where I would rather humble myself than be humbled by harmful words that I can't take back. Transformation also involves time, commitment, and practice. And it occurs slowly, as I daily come to the Lord, ask Him for help in this area, learn truths about speech as I read in the Bible, and engraft applicable verses to form a grid I can sift my words through. If there were a shortcut to being transformed, we would all gladly take it. But then we would miss out on developing a relationship with the God who desires to renew our minds through his powerful Word, which in time transforms our hearts and our speech.

> *Transformation in the way we talk requires humility to admit our need.*

Two years ago, Bob was diagnosed with Parkinson's, a neurological disease for which there is no known cause and no known cure. Many people, at least those who read *People* magazine, are aware of his diagnosis because our son Timmy's picture was on the cover with the headline "My Father's Brave Parkinson's Battle." Bob doesn't mind if people know about his condition, but he does mind when he drops things and inadvertently makes messes. Earlier in our marriage my response might have been unkind, but now he says, "I've never seen you so patient as you are now with my Parkinson's. When I drop, spill, or break something, you just say, 'That's okay, it doesn't matter.' It's the most patient you've ever been with me."

I can respond with patient words because, as I remind him, what's important is not that his hand shakes, but that he still leads his ministry and family with love and passion. And the ripple effects of both impact eternity!

I'm thankful (and so is my husband) that I no longer react with impatient words as I did years ago. The credit and praise belong to our mighty God, who alone has the power to transform our speech and so much more. The ripple effect of a changed life brings glory to the One who changed it!

OUR WORDS CAN BRING BLESSING

Most families have traditions, and incorporating positive words into them adds to their value. Occasions like Thanksgiving can provide the opportunity to share what we are thankful for about every family member. Birthdays can be times to let the celebrants know why they are special. And spiritual birthdays provide a chance to focus on spiritual growth.

When we tried a new tradition a few years ago, everyone said that it was the best Christmas ever. It was my husband's idea. That year, when our family gathered to celebrate Jesus' birth, we also made time to encourage one another. Every person took turns expressing three things he or she appreciated about each family member present.

This practice served as a showcase for positive words. Some of the character qualities identified were generosity, humility, perseverance, kindness, diligence, and compassion. Some family members were commended for their work ethic, wisdom, enthusiasm, and passion, while others were praised for their success in the workplace, in the classroom, on the athletic field, and on the mission field. Still others were appreciated for their service, their sacrifices, and their wise choices.

The response to the words of affirmation included laughter,

smiles, and many tears. All of our tanks were full to overflowing. When we parted the next day, we were better equipped to face our multiple responsibilities and challenging lives—because of the power of positive words. "Like apples of gold in settings of silver is a word spoken in right circumstances" (Proverbs 25:11).

Words are a gift from God to be used for good. With words, parents pass on their value systems to their children. With words, we express our belief in the people we love. With words, we communicate the truths of our faith. With words, we can alter the course of a life that is in our charge. When we develop the mindset that our words have impact, the ripple effects of our positive words will echo into eternity.

Chapter 13

HAPPY ENDINGS AND HEAVENLY REWARDS

We long for a happy ending—but it's not here yet!

Since I was a little girl, I've loved happy endings. A "happily ever after" is an added enticement to watch a movie or read a book. I'm not sure the writer of Proverbs had movies in mind when he highlighted the woman who "smiles at the future" (31:25), but perhaps she loves happy endings too!

Do you smile at the future? Most of us are so busy navigating the present, with all its twists and turns, on our jog through a busy day and a busy life, that we don't give much thought to next week, let alone eternity. We have appointments, jobs, to-do lists, chores. Eternity seems a long way off. And then—

"BALLISTIC MISSILE THREAT INBOUND TO HAWAII. SEEK IMMEDIATE SHELTER. THIS IS NOT A DRILL."

The text flashed on our phones early Saturday morning while we were in Hawaii to celebrate Bob's milestone birthday with our adult kids. For thirty-eight terrifying minutes, a million and a half residents and tourists believed the government-issued text. Was January 13, 2018, the day we would take our last breath? Stunned, our kids called their kids back at home to express their love. Then they knocked frantically on our door in the hotel. We prayed together. Our concern was for those we would leave behind, but we were secure that when the missile struck, we would meet Jesus face-to-face.

How would you respond? Most of us aren't focused on whatever is next; our norm is "here and now." Until you receive a text like that. Until you receive the lab report. Until the truck in the lane next to you swerves. Until your loved one collapses with a massive heart attack.

After thirty-eight minutes, another text flashed on all our phones: "THERE IS NO MISSILE THREAT OF DANGER TO THE STATE OF HAWAII. REPEAT. FALSE ALARM." Overcome with relief and gratitude, we made more phone calls home.

Looking up is not our "go to," but maybe it should be. On 9/11, Todd Beamer was ready to face eternity. He became known as an American hero for shouting "Let's roll" and inspiring a planeload of people to fight back against their terrorist hijackers. As a result, their plane crashed into an empty Pennsylvania field rather than the Capitol building where it appeared to be headed. Months later, his father spoke in our city, saying, "We all have difficulties in life. I know that as a Christian you can survive the worst day of your life because there is not only something better ahead, but the best is yet ahead."

Do you believe the best is ahead? Solomon wrote that God has set eternity in our hearts (see Ecclesiastes 3:11), and most of us seem to have an inborn curiosity about eternal things. One of the "happy ending" movies I enjoy is *Miracle on 34th Street*, set in New York City in the 1940s. In an effort to protect her daughter from disillusionment and disappointment, a young girl's mother stresses logic: Only believe what you can see. Her approach is challenged when the two befriend a man who goes by the name Kris Kringle and calls himself the real Santa Claus. They're struck by his kindness and his focus on the spirit of Christmas. In the movie's climax, with only a glimpse of evidence that their friend could be Santa, both mother and daughter proclaim, "I believe, I believe."

Some people view heaven the way they view Santa—as purely fictional. Others, if they think of it at all, imagine heaven as a place where residents dress in white, play harps, and float on clouds. Santa is pretend, but heaven is real! We can't see heaven in its entirety now, but we see glimpses. We see it with the eyes of faith, the same way we believe in an invisible God we can't see. We read about the reality of heaven in the Manual. The book of Revelation talks about it in detail as a beautiful physical place where we will rejoice because we're in the presence of God (see Revelation 21 and 22). And the apostle Paul reminds us that heaven is actually more real than what we see on earth: "We look not at the things which are seen, but at the things which are not seen; for the things which are seen are temporal, but the things which are not seen are eternal" (2 Corinthians 4:18).

HOME SWEET HOME

The seemingly illogical concept of heaven may be a first for you. I didn't grow up with that perspective or anything close. I can't remember when I first heard about eternal things, but I'm sure the concept veered off on a few side roads while on the highway from my ears to my brain.

The impact of our Manual's ability to replace misconceptions with truth can't be overstated. When our children were young, Bob attempted to teach them about the truth we can't see—that our eternal home is in heaven, not in Florida, or America, or even Earth! He read the first verse in the first chapter in the book of 1 Peter. (Lots of firsts!) Thankful for my husband's willingness to simplify hard-to-understand truth for our young children, I held two-and-a-half-year-old Robby on my lap while his sisters sat beside me, attempting to curb their wiggles. As Bob explained that Peter was writing to "those who reside as aliens" (1 Peter 1:1), Robby jumped off my lap, held his little Bible upside down, and shouted, "Obey God, you aliens!" I'm not sure he understood the concept yet! But it would not be the last time we discussed eternal things.

Eternity is always on Bob's mind. His eternal focus infuses him with purpose and determination, and the perspective he lives out has influenced our family and countless others. He envisions a wing of heaven filled with Filipinos led to Christ through his ministry. That vision drives him, filling him with a sense of urgency. I'm one of the many people he has inspired to trade in an earthly passport for a heavenly one. With the speed of a turtle, over the course of years I transferred my allegiance to the God of heaven.

Bob and the apostle Paul remind us to "set [our minds] on the things above, not on the things that are on earth" (Colossians 3:2). What's above? Heaven, where we will spend eternity if we know Jesus Christ personally. Just as he taught our family, my husband teaches those he preaches to and takes on mission trips about the things that last forever: God, our Master; His Word, our Manual; people; and rewards. He's personally fired up about eternal rewards, the ones we receive in heaven for what God has called and equipped us to do. Rewards are mentioned more than seventy-five times in Scripture and are a legitimate motivation to work hard for a goal. And you don't have to be as intensely competitive as some of my family members to be motivated by the concept of rewards. What about a promotion and a raise at work? An A on your term paper? A scholarship to college? Or a crown, medal, trophy, ribbon, or ring?

Bob has been known to flash his national championship ring, a generous gift from Timmy, in order to contrast rewards here with rewards in heaven. Like the rest of us, my husband and son don't mind a significant earthly reward. Years of training and effort are represented in that ring, and it was worth the sacrifice required to earn it. We encourage and commend efforts to work hard, train, and compete. And when those efforts are recognized and rewarded, they often provide a platform that God can use for great influence!

Earthly rewards are valuable for the present, but ribbons will eventually fade and medals will tarnish. Both Bob and Timmy are quick to point out that much more valuable rewards are waiting in heaven, rewards that last forever. God has a different value system. And aren't we grateful, since most of us don't have a room full of trophies!

A TREASURE MAP

Just as earthly rewards are an incentive in the secular world, eternal rewards motivate us to invest in eternal things. In Matthew 6:19-21, Jesus told us, "Do not store up for yourselves treasures on earth, where moth and rust destroy, and where thieves break in and steal. But store up for yourselves treasures in heaven, where neither moth nor rust destroys, and where thieves do not break in or steal; for where your treasure is, there your heart will be also." Our hearts follow our treasure. Like my purse stolen by the robber when we first moved to the Philippines and our house in Florida nibbled by termites shortly after we moved in, earthly treasure is susceptible to any number of setbacks, but that's not true of heavenly treasure.

It took me a while to comprehend these verses, and I'm still learning. It's mind-boggling to think that you and I store up treasure in heaven for ourselves by wisely investing whatever resources we have now. That truth motivates me! Nothing can diminish our treasure in heaven. No down economy. No stock market crash. No hurricane! It is safe, waiting for us when we get there.

Bob and I choose carefully where we invest our financial resources. We want our dollars, like our lives, to have an eternal impact. When

I was younger, I gave money to worthy causes out of obedience. Learning to be a cheerful giver has been a process. But as a result of my doing what I knew to be right, God began to tag team my efforts with enthusiasm and joy. When we invest our earthly treasure in eternal things, we reap eternal treasure. Over time, that truth invades our minds and takes up residence in our hearts. And the reality is that we only have a brief window to make our life-impacting investments.

My good friend Pec opened my eyes to that perspective when she opened the door to her "organization" room, the envy of people like me who dream of organizing the world, or at least our little corners of it. Perfectly placed plastic containers lined built-in shelves. When I inquired about their contents, Pec explained that each container held the earthly treasures of a deceased relative. Everything of value each person accumulated on earth was put in one box. Pec and I lamented that we are guilty of putting more emphasis than is warranted on hanging on to such things, but it's hard to toss the remains of someone's life. Pec and her husband are blessed, however, that many of their relatives also invested in eternal treasures, which they are presently enjoying in heaven while their boxes sit on shelves.

When we invest our earthly treasure in eternal things, we reap eternal treasure.

Unlike the boxes packed with the temporal, it's obvious that Pec and her husband fill their lives with eternal priorities. The couple regularly entertains young families new to their community. Drawn to the kindness and generosity of my friends, many of these couples come to know their Savior, and then join the Bible study Pec's husband gears to their season of life.

HEADING HOME

Pec's husband and mine share an eternal perspective and passion for the gospel. When Timmy was in high school, Bob took him to the hospital to visit an eleven-year-old with leukemia. The girl's father worked for Bob's friend, and Bob had visited her before, but he wanted to give our son the opportunity to share his faith in Jesus. After they talked for a while, Timmy asked the young girl if he could tell her about the most important thing in his life. She said yes. He went through the simple plan of salvation, and she prayed with him to ask Jesus to be her Savior. Bob read a passage from John to the family.

Excited about the decision she had just made, the new believer asked to be wheeled all over the hospital to tell everyone who would listen—doctors, nurses, orderlies, the other kids in nearby rooms— that she knew she was going to heaven. She died a few days later.

Her parents struggled with the Lord for taking their daughter from them. After a few months passed, the father wrote this note to my husband: "Bob, you left us with a passage from John, and I was very upset that you chose those verses. I did not want to consider my daughter not being here with us, but as it turns out—it was that passage that gave me comfort in the end. The thought that Jesus was waiting in a place the Father had prepared for her gave me so much hope. Thank you."

The words that Bob shared with the precious girl's family are words that Jesus said to His disciples before His death:

"Do not let your heart be troubled; believe in God, believe
also in Me. In My Father's house are many dwelling places;
if it were not so, I would have told you; for I go to prepare
a place for you. If I go and prepare a place for you, I will
come again and receive you to Myself, that where I am, there
you may be also. And you know the way where I am going."
Thomas said to Him, "Lord, we do not know where You are
going, how do we know the way?" Jesus said to him, "I am

the way, and the truth, and the life; no one comes to the
Father but through Me."

JOHN 14:1-6

Although the girl was only eleven, she grasped the reality of
spending eternity with her Savior in a place He prepared just for her.
Our young friend knew for certain where she was going.

A few years ago, an old friend was desperate to know where her
twin sister was going. The twins were my first friends when I moved
to a new city in middle school. We went through high school together
and shared common friends and activities until we graduated and
went different ways. In those days, we didn't have cell phones or
e-mail to keep in touch, and we probably only saw each other once
at a high school reunion—until a few years ago, when I met them at
a restaurant for a long catch-up lunch.

Our conversation turned from trivial to our deepest concerns,
which included family, health, and eternity. One of the twins had
been diagnosed with cancer. Although she put up a courageous fight,
cancer was winning. She had regrets, but we all do. She longed for
hope—hope for herself and for the family members she loved so
much. There were tears as we talked, because of the depth of her
love and concern.

We met again months later in Mayo Clinic, as my sweet friend
lay dying. Her sister, who had been radically saved by a loving Savior
some years before, was determined to make certain of her beloved
twin's eternal destination. We both sensed her time was close. On
the day we'd had lunch, the three of us had talked about a relationship with Jesus, who secures our eternity, but the sick sister thought
she had more time. Our conversation that day in the hospital was
more serious and one-sided. My friend could barely talk, but she
listened. I sensed the power of God's love as her sister and I shared
how much He loved her. His great love sent His Son, Jesus, to die

for her. Simply, the Bible teaches that we must believe in the Lord Jesus Christ and we'll be saved. I stood beside her bed and prayed for her, incorporating an opportunity for her to pray along with me. She listened, and her breathing suddenly changed. She nodded slightly, indicating that she understood, and a supernatural peace seemed to envelop her.

I can't explain it, but her sister and I believe that the Prince of Peace wrapped His arms around her and gave her the assurance that she would soon be in His presence. That she would leave her frail, cancer-ridden body behind and, in the twinkling of an eye, put on a new, perfect body in heaven, where she will spend eternity. Her sister invited me to say a few words at her funeral. Although I didn't know her family, I briefly shared that if my friend could return, she would convey her love and hope that they would trust Jesus and join her someday in heaven.

WITH ETERNITY IN MIND

My friend Dee understands an eternal focus! I first met Dee at a college football game, when my alma mater played her favorite team. While only one of our teams won that day, we both won, because a lifelong friendship began. The next spring, Dee invited me to speak at a women's event at her church. I soon learned that Dee has an administrative gift that yields results, as every detail of the weekend was planned with precision and prayer.

Our son Timmy's foundation sponsors Night to Shine, where churches all over the world host proms for people with special needs. When Dee heard about it, she knew she'd found her calling, and she set about convincing her church to host a prom. It's a daunting task to persuade a church staff, recruit volunteers, involve the community in a myriad of details, and everything else necessary to put on an event of this magnitude, but Dee felt it was worth it if the goal was to influence people in her sphere to recognize that those with special needs are valuable and worth celebrating. And it was worth it to demonstrate in a very tangible way to all the honored guests that they are worthy of being crowned kings and queens! Although the Tim Tebow Foundation offers personal and financial assistance for those hosting Night to Shine, overseeing every detail of a big event, with the potential to eternally impact many lives, is no small feat.

Bob and I attended the Night to Shine prom Dee hosted, and it was magical. We had the privilege of cheering as each guest walked (or ran, or was wheeled) down the red carpet with his or her buddy. What a night! After the packed house of people enjoyed an incredible evening of cheering, dancing, eating, karaoke, and more, Dee planned a memorable finale. A gifted vocalist sang a special version of "This Little Light of Mine," and each special guest held a little light and sang along. Bob was honored to present a brief, simple gospel message, and then he prayed, giving guests the opportunity to pray along with him if they wanted to ask Jesus to be their Savior. I'll never forget hearing many of the special guests pray aloud with childlike faith to be saved. For me, very few moments compare to that one.

Dee is already planning her fourth Night to Shine, which will involve inviting other churches to get in on the fun. Her church ran out of room—a challenge, but a welcome one. After the first prom, Dee shared with great enthusiasm, "No matter how much is required, I'm going to do it! I want everything I do to affect eternity. That's why I'm here—to impact lives for eternity."

Because God loves us, He pursues us. He pursued me, and the girl with cancer, the twin sister, the kids with special needs—and you.

Even if you have ignored past opportunities to meet the Lord, it isn't too late. He is pursuing you right now and will continue to pursue you until you breathe your last breath. But don't wait until then to begin a relationship with Him. You don't want to miss out on the blessings God has planned for your life! And you don't want to miss out on the joy of eternal life with Him. Luke 10:20 encourages us to "rejoice that [our] names are recorded in heaven."

You can begin now and focus on eternity. When our oldest daughter, Christy, was in high school, she wrote, "When we live for a purpose outside of ourselves and something that will last forever, it gives us the courage to delay instant gratification, to embrace trials, to make difficult decisions, and to not live as if the best life is now." Her family does not serve on the mission field because they can't do anything else. They are focused on eternity!

Bob's passion about eternal things overflows to our family. Not all of us are gifted evangelists, but everyone can share the simple plan of salvation with friends, loved ones, coworkers, neighbors, and people we meet along the way. Leading a person to Christ has a ripple effect of staggering proportions. No other single decision a person makes has as much significance, because coming to Christ moves us from the domain of darkness to the Kingdom of God's beloved Son (see Colossians 1:13).

Every person will live forever somewhere. That should motivate us to go to great lengths to get the gospel to people who have never heard it even once. Although the Bible clearly teaches this truth, our enemy, Satan, deceives us to believe that a loving God is more like a vending machine that dispenses good things to anyone who asks. But the Bible is clear that God is both merciful and just, holding us accountable for our actions, and Jesus is given the authority by His Father to be the judge of where each person will spend eternity (see John 5:22-23).

According to John's account in Revelation, someday all people will be divided into two groups. Those who don't know Jesus will face Him at the great white throne (see 20:11-13). They will be judged according to their deeds and whether or not their names are written in the Book of Life. John's comment about their destiny is sobering:

"If anyone's name was not found written in the book of life, he was thrown into the lake of fire" (Revelation 20:15).

Those who do know Christ have eternal security. Nothing will take God's love away from us, but we will also face accountability at the bema seat (judgment seat of Christ). Second Corinthians 5:10 says, "We must all appear before the judgment seat of Christ, so that each one may be recompensed for his deeds in the body, according to what he has done, whether good or bad." This judgment seat of Christ is not about sin; that was judged at the Cross. It's about service. Bob calls this "résumé day." When we write our résumés for a job, we might try to embellish them in an effort to look more impressive to prospective employers. But when we stand before Jesus, He will be the One to evaluate us. Jesus alone knows the intentions of our hearts, our motives, and all of our service. He knows what no one else knows and what we don't even remember. He takes note of every cup of cold water we give in His name (see Matthew 10:42).

Paul wrote, "Each will receive his own reward according to his own labor" (1 Corinthians 3:8). Your reward is personal. No one else's failure will penalize you, and the good your friend does cannot be shared with you. Paul explained that our service will be tested by fire to reveal the quality of our work. If the fire burns up our work, we suffer loss. If our work remains, we receive a reward (see 1 Corinthians 3:13-15).

HEAVENLY REWARDS

Those who know Jesus will receive rewards based on their service, and these will be worth more than anything imaginable. Your choices today make a difference tomorrow (see John 5:21-27). It's worth whatever is required to live for eternity!

Jesus said, "I am coming quickly, and My reward is with Me, to render to every man according to what he has done" (Revelation

22:12). Many rewards are mentioned in the New Testament. One of all my guys' favorites is praise from our Master.

When Timmy talks to groups about standing in front of Jesus at the end of time, he compares it to running to the sidelines after winning the national championship. The coach greeted him with a big hug and affirming words. We all like an "attaboy." But how much greater will it be when we see Jesus and He hugs us and praises us with His words? We women want a hug from our Master too, and an "Attagirl; I'm so proud of you!"

The ripple effects of our eternal influence not only yield ongoing blessings for those we touch, but they bring blessings to us, too. We are the beneficiaries of the ripples we initiate. I can hardly wrap my mind around that truth. But my heart is to encourage you, because biblical rewards have encouraged me to keep on keeping on when life is hard and I'm tempted to revert to "life is all about me." I believe we'll be blessed beyond our wildest dreams when we live our lives focused on eternity. "Let us not lose heart in doing good, for in due time we will reap if we do not grow weary" (Galatians 6:9).

A variety of eternal rewards are noted in various Scripture passages. If you enjoy being in charge, ruling a country, state, or city in the new heaven is the reward that will motivate you (see 2 Timothy 2:12)! My favorite rewards mentioned in Scripture are praise from my Master (see Matthew 25:21), joy unlike anything we've ever known (see Isaiah 35:10), and the winner: attire in heaven that's sewn and sown by the deeds we do on earth (see Revelation 19:8). Just try to fathom that the good works we do now are weaving the fabric for our eternal wardrobe! Most of us cannot afford the latest fashion on earth, but the visual of being well-dressed for all eternity is awe-inspiring.

All of the rewards motivate me to love, give, serve, and do it all over and over again. There is Someone watching who keeps a perfect accounting of our lives. One day, a day no one knows, the God who created us and loves us enough to offer the greatest sacrifice of all will bestow on us eternal rewards. Our finite minds can't grasp eternal things, but I believe with all my heart that the most beautiful woman on earth is the one who steadily makes herself ready to meet her Savior face-to-face.

HAPPY ENDINGS!

One of my favorite speaking topics is "Hope." A decade ago, as I was preparing to speak on "High Hopes for a Woman's Heart," my daughter called to remind me, "Mom, don't forget to tell them about the happy ending!" The promise of my eternal destination gives me hope. And that sure hope, as Bob says, is the battery in our lives that charges us with resolve and keeps us going.

The apostle Peter wrote the book we studied when our children were young. Peter was transformed by his hope in Jesus, the One he denied three times earlier in his life. Mary Magdalene was once filled with seven devils, but her life was transformed when she met Jesus. He delivered her and saved her, and she had the great joy of being the first one to see the risen Christ.

We can have the sure hope that everything we've encountered here works together in the end for our good and God's glory.

Your perspective on eternity can be altered by that same transforming power when you "fix your hope completely on the grace to be brought to you at the revelation of Jesus Christ" (1 Peter 1:13). We'll never experience heaven on earth. Heaven is yet to come. Though we are wounded from our trials and battles in this life, we can have the sure hope that everything we've encountered here works together in the end for our good and God's glory. And when we have the mindset of investing our present lives in eternal things, our future life will be rich with rewards. Our past doesn't have to define our future. We can't go back to a new beginning, but we can begin now to make a new ending—a happy ending!

MISSION

Mission is the fifth component of the miraculous motivating power of influence. God, our Master, has a perfect plan for each of us, which includes good works He intends for us to accomplish. He created each of us special and unique. My strengths complement my husband's, and your strengths are different from mine. Together, with our similarities and our differences, we make up the body of Christ. And as only God can do, He planned missions for us that perfectly match our abilities and season in life.

Knowing our Master and spending time in the Manual and in prayer enable us to discover the missions God has for us. He won't try to hide them. And our missions may change during the course of our lives. Mothers have the obvious mission of parenting, but they will have more time for other missions as children grow up. Women often have multiple missions, such as training up children, teaching a class at church, and assisting an elderly neighbor with chores, or serving an employer during the week and volunteering twice a month for a nonprofit. As a young person, while you train for a profession, you may lead a Bible study in your dorm and go on a summer mission trip. The options are endless.

We are to fulfill our missions with godly passion, which ultimately draws others to the mission and brings honor to the Lord. And our creative God orchestrates our lives in such a way that when we fulfill our God-given missions, we will have purpose, fulfillment, significance, and the ripple effects of life-impacting influence.

> We are His workmanship, created in Christ Jesus for good works, which God prepared beforehand so that we would walk in them.
> EPHESIANS 2:10

Chapter 14

CREATED FOR GOOD WORKS

Has it ever occurred to you that you were created by God for a specific mission in life? Ephesians 2:10 tells us, "We are His workmanship, created in Christ Jesus for good works, which God prepared beforehand so that we would walk in them." The word *workmanship* is taken from the Greek word that's also used for *poem*. I like to think about it this way: Before the foundation of the world, before you were ever born, God wrote a poem about you, which contains good works that He planned just for you.

A POEM ABOUT YOU

God's poem for you includes a specific purpose, plan, and agenda. He has created a unique mission for you that incorporates your talents, spiritual gifts, abilities, personality, sphere of influence, energy, opportunities, resources, and life experiences. It's not your job, your social status, your looks, or your résumé that gives you purpose, fulfillment, significance, and influence—it's your mission. God has created an incredible opportunity for you to bless those in your sphere and, in the process, be blessed beyond your imagination. You don't want to miss it! We might make five- and ten-year plans for our lives, but no matter how well thought out we believe they are, our preconceived ideas of the perfect plan fall far short of the one God has for us.

God creates perfect plans for imperfect people.

The good news is we don't need to have it all together to accomplish our God-given missions. God creates perfect plans for imperfect people. As my daughter Christy says, "God likes to shine His light through cracked pots." I know I'm a cracked pot; yet the God who wrote a story for the world created a plan to use me—and you—in that story and to give us influence through the good works He planned for us to do.

Ephesians 2:8-9, which precedes the verse I quoted earlier about our being God's masterpiece, provides the context and tone for our good works: "By grace you have been saved through faith; and that not of yourselves, it is the gift of God; not as a result of works, so that no one may boast." We can't brag about our salvation, because we didn't work for it or do anything to deserve it. Jesus died to pay for our sins, and our faith in Christ is what saves us. But after we're saved, we are privileged to participate in the good works God planned for us. And because it's God's plan, we can't boast about our plans, any more than we can boast about our salvation. Our gratitude for God's love should motivate us to bring Him glory by living out the plan He created out of His love and grace.

Since it doesn't snow often in Florida, we were delighted years ago with the opportunity to take our young family skiing. Bob was quick to take advantage of the snow to point out that each snowflake was unique, different from every other snowflake. He taught our kids that although all five have the same set of parents, they all have different genes, eye patterns, fingerprints, motivations, bents, and types of intelligences. God, the Master craftsman, is into the details. We had a lively family discussion about our individual strengths and skills, which are suited for a variety of missions. Even at their young ages, we desired for our kids to comprehend their potential for influence as they lived out their God-given missions.

Because our missions are created for us by the Lord, we need Him to energize us for the works in front of us each day. According to Ephesians 2:10, our missions are "good" and involve "work." But as you already know from experience, nearly everything worthwhile in life requires effort: marriage, parenting, careers, ministry, friendship, influence. God created us for fulfilling, meaningful, profitable work, but He doesn't force us to participate in the missions He created for us. We make daily choices about how to spend our time and resources. God's plan is not for the lazy, but we have a gracious Poet who gives us the choice to jump into the poem for a few lines or push "delete" and leave our poem unlived.

God's plan for us is that we be known for our good works. Although two chapters on the Manual are included in this book, a library full of books couldn't contain the illustrations of how God's Word impacts our missions in life. "All Scripture is inspired by God and profitable for teaching, for reproof, for correction, for training in righteousness; so that the man of God may be adequate, equipped for *every good work*" (2 Timothy 3:16-17, emphasis added). In other words, God equips us for the good works He intends for us to do through His Word, our Manual for life.

THE MOMMY MISSION

There are certain missions that only I can accomplish: I'm the daughter to my parents, the wife to my husband, and the mother to my children. I'm also a witness to my neighbor, and I enjoy opportunities as an employee, friend, and more. God's plan for us may encompass multiple missions that we fulfill in our varied life roles. Wives are given a unique and important mission to respect their husbands and encourage them to become men of God. Employees have a mission to serve their employers with integrity and a good work ethic. Children are to obey their parents when they live at home and to honor them throughout their lives.

Sometimes our missions are directly in front of us, especially during certain seasons of life. As a mother, whether I work outside my home or not, my main mission is my children, because the window to impact their lives is open for a relatively short time. Maybe you are in that season. Often, the world's value system deceives us to think that our roles as mothers are less important than more recognized missions. But if you are blessed with children living at home, then they are your primary mission.

When my five kids were at home, I didn't need to look around to find a mission. And once I began to homeschool, I couldn't hand them over to a teacher during the day. The responsibility to prepare my children for life sat squarely on my shoulders. When Bob was around, his broad shoulders were very involved too as we shared the mission to pass our value system on to our kids. Of course, we first needed to think through what we believed.

Over time, I began to develop my own "mission statement," derived from Psalm 127: *To love and train my children as the gifts and rewards that God intends them to be and aim them toward the target of an influential life that honors God and impacts their world.* I had no sense of a mission when I was growing up, so I was highly motivated to provide a framework for purpose and influence through the unique missions God created for my children. To paraphrase Psalm 78, my role was to tell the generations to come the praises of God, His strength, and the wonderful things that He has done, so their confidence would be in God. One generation influences the next when we convey God's wondrous works. Tell your God stories to influence those in your sphere to ask Him to write amazing God stories just for them.

I wasn't very far into mothering when I realized that the most effective way to teach my kids was from an overflow of my life. That put pressure on me—pressure I needed to change my focus from me to the lives in my charge. I was forced to take intangibles and make them tangible. I couldn't lead my children any further than where I had gone myself, which forced me to grow in countless areas.

Mothering illustrations abound on the pages of this book. That's because my responsibility to teach truth to my children was the catalyst for me to first engraft truth into my own life. Bob usually presented the big picture, and I painted the details day by day into my children's unique frames. Learning about Ephesians 2:10 provided the framework, as I began to internalize the fact that the Lord wrote a special "poem" for me and for each child, and He had specific good works planned for each of us. Bob and I prayed for wisdom as we exposed our children to various missions, knowing it was worth the time and energy involved to help them discover the missions God created them for. Our efforts are multiplied when they live out their missions to impact their world for good.

PASSING ON VALUES

Character is the combination of virtues embroidered on the moral fabric of a person's life, and developing it in our children was the mission Bob and I shared. As impressive as that sounds, pulling it off is another story. Early on, it was clear that everyone in our family struggled with pride. *Me first! I want it my way! I won't share! I'm stronger than he is! I'm better at math! I won!* And so it went. But pride really reared its cocky head when we played board games. Let's just say it's better not to play Monopoly or Risk with our family. And then the boys began to play competitive ball. Even when the younger kids on the T-ball team only played for the snow cones, our little baseball players really wanted to win. A participation trophy was never the goal. Surely they got those tendencies from their dad! What's a mom going to do? Well, of course there's a verse for that.

Since no one in our family takes losing well, I had to figure out a way to teach my competitive children how to win and lose graciously. Winning is more fun, but it breeds pride and cockiness. Realizing I wouldn't be in charge when they were twenty, I began "humility lessons" when the boys were five and six. I found a great verse: "Let another praise you, and not your own mouth; a stranger, and not your own lips" (Proverbs 27:2), and I put it to a simple tune to stick in little minds and hopefully stay stuck throughout their lives. When a child hit a home run or scored a touchdown, he wasn't allowed to brag about it. If someone asked him how he did in a game, he had permission, with a dose of humility, to share the details.

After a Saturday game, athletic little boys were bursting to tell their accomplishments to whoever would listen at church the next day. We alerted a few close friends about our efforts, and they loved being the ones to ask, "How did your game go yesterday?" An excited little boy would blurt, "I hit a double and drove in the winning run," "I shot six points, and we won," or "We lost, but I scored a touchdown." But they were not allowed to boast, and over the years, that verse became the huge red stop sign in their minds preventing arrogant words from leaving their lips. Robby, who played college football and was a high school all-American in baseball, set a great example for his brothers by heeding the admonition to let others praise him instead of himself. But as much effort as I put into preparation, I couldn't have predicted the future.

And the Winner Is

On December 8, 2007, our entire family gathered in a New York hotel room. We were overwhelmed at the circumstances surrounding our reunion and were unspeakably grateful to our mighty God, who providentially brought us all together for the Heisman Trophy ceremony.

Three days earlier, we'd received the official invitation to come to New York. Two days earlier, by the grace of God and the generosity of Uncle Bill, our oldest daughter, her husband, Joey, and baby Claire began their thirty-two-hour journey from their remote mission field to join us. They got the last two seats on the plane, one of only three flights a week from their city. One day earlier, both Bob and I kept our speaking obligations scheduled months before. Minutes earlier, all eleven of us—Bob and me, our five kids, two sons-in-law, and the two grandchildren we had at the time—reunited for the first time in six months. Words can't describe the joy of being together, completely surprised by God's plan.

As we sat with our arms wrapped around each other, we were excited, nervous, and energized by being together. We bowed our heads, smiling at our two precious, wiggly blonde granddaughters. Bob prayed that God would use our family to draw others to Himself, and that we would have a great impact with the platform we had been given.

A few hours later, our youngest son, Timmy, became the first sophomore to win the Heisman Trophy. I was grateful for his humility as he began his acceptance speech with "I would just like to first start off by thanking my Lord and Savior, Jesus Christ, who gave me the ability to play football and gave me a great family . . ."

OPEN YOUR GIFT!

Sometimes our missions are right in front of us. That's true if we have children. Other times, we need to look for them. But God doesn't make them difficult to find. Some of the clues He gives us are in our interests, our talents, and especially our spiritual gifts.

Gifts aren't just for Christmas or birthdays! The instant you enter into a personal relationship with Jesus, you receive a special gift just for you. There's no fancy gift wrap or cute little bow, but there's an accompanying card: "Welcome to the family of God. With love, the Holy Spirit."

I remember the first time I studied spiritual gifts. I was a newly-wed. Not only was my marriage new, but so was the concept of spiritual gifts. In a study with other young wives, I heard defini-tions for some of the gifts, including service, teaching, leadership, giving, mercy, hospitality, evangelism, and more. When the gift of encouragement was mentioned, I silently prayed, *Lord, it might be that one. But it's too much to hope for. Of all the gifts, that's the one I would pick. I don't want to assume, but I really want to know for sure. So could You please, please somehow confirm it this week?*

I wasn't overly confident about my timid prayer, but I under-estimated how much God loves me and desired for me to unwrap my special present—so I could use it! That week, as only God would arrange, three different people mentioned that I had encour-aged them. It's so like God to confirm my gift of encouragement through not just one or two but three people who were not privy to my prayer.

I regularly meet some Christian women who have no idea they have spiritual gifts, and others who know they have gifts but haven't identified them. Still others think it's prideful to assume they have spiritual gifts. I disagree. My husband gave me a beautiful bracelet for our fortieth anniversary, and I'm reminded of his love when I wear it. What if I kept the bracelet in my jewelry box because I didn't feel worthy to wear such a beautiful piece of jewelry? Unlike my bracelet, our spiritual gifts are for the benefit of others, and we need to unwrap them and put them to use!

Spiritual gifts are listed in the Bible (see Romans 12 and 1 Corinthians 12, in particular), and you can reference numerous books and Bible studies to help you determine your gift or gifts. I'm not an expert, but I believe God will use the gifts He has chosen for us to afford us great influence. We can't take credit for or brag about our gifts, because we didn't earn them, ask for them, or deserve them. We have spiritual gifts to *use*, not keep to ourselves. The purpose of spiritual gifts is to build up the body of Christ—in other words, people. We can use our good works to influence the people in our spheres.

Our spiritual gifts are for the benefit of others, and we need to unwrap them and put them to use!

I'd like to share examples of some of my special friends who have great influence because they use their spiritual gifts to edify people and glorify God.

My friend Anne has the gift of leadership. Through the years, I've observed her lead everything from her children's school booster club to a variety of local Christian ministries. She works hard and is rarely recognized, but she steps up to lead when there is a need, and others follow.

Another, younger Anne is an organizer who works behind the scenes to make others successful. Countless people enjoy the results of her gift. She handles life's details for a person with great influence. She's not the star, but without her, the star would not shine as bright.

My dear friend Nancy has the gift of mercy. Nancy and my daughter Katie are the people I want to talk to when I have a physical, spiritual, or emotional challenge. Their compassion is uplifting. Nancy's mission is influential as she serves women in crisis pregnancies.

My daughter Christy has the gift of teaching, which was obvious even when she was a little girl. Her siblings, however, often refused to be her students. My husband and I encouraged Christy to pursue advanced degrees to enhance her spiritual gift. She has taught Bible studies through a variety of seasons and now teaches devalued and abused women in the country where she serves. She also has a heart for physical and spiritual life lived out on the mission field.

Katye is a gifted administrator, exactly what we need in our ministry office. What a blessing she is to people who need her gift, especially my husband. Her gifts have ripple effects on all those impacted by Bob's evangelistic association.

Sarah has a heart to serve, joyfully using her gift to serve orphans in the Ukraine and children in America, including my sweet granddaughters. Sarah overcame setbacks in her youth to represent her Lord well as she uses her gifts to bless others.

Georgiana works a day or two a week as a nurse in the neonatal unit. Although her husband is retired, she continues working, motivated by her gift of service to love and care for babies and their families.

Judy's influence grew from her passion to share God's Word and impact others to do the same. Both as a hairstylist and as a women's ministry leader in her church, she uses her gift of teaching to show women the importance of studying God's "love letter" to them.

Tina's lovely home showcases her gift of hospitality. She has also blessed our family and others through the years with her incredible generosity.

Janet retired from her job but not from ministering to her large, active family. Her gift is service, and she regularly serves her working daughters-in-law and her grandchildren with fun and creative playdates.

Kitty is a generous leader who has a heart to draw women to the Savior. She organizes a Christmas luncheon in her community with an evangelistic speaker, a prayer chain for those in her husband's company, and impactful activities in her local church.

Josie has the gift of encouragement. Her heart to encourage young moms evolved into a wonderful curriculum entitled *It's 4 uMom.*

My sweet friend Kelly loves teaching the Word of God, and she inspires other women to love it too when they attend her Bible study. Kelly also has a special gift of prayer, incorporating the powerful Word of God in her prayers for the family of believers scattered throughout the world.

Natalie couldn't have envisioned God's plan when her eight-year-old son brought three friends home from school, boys lacking dads and hope for their future. Years later, her son is playing college football, while Natalie and her husband, Jeff, run Power Cross, a ministry impacting the lives of more than three hundred at-risk boys a year. God has used Natalie's gift of serving to influence hundreds of boys to meet Jesus and to develop discipline for their studies, athletics, character, and influence.

Terry Ann is a visionary with five children who encourages and motivates others to stand for truth through speaking, writing, and loving people. When her children transferred from a Christian school to a public one, God gave her a plan to organize and write curriculum for Students Standing Strong, a legal, on-campus, student-led organization that influences thousands of students in their faith through high school.

Julie, my daughter's close friend, is a pastor's wife and mother of four, who has gifts in teaching and encouragement. Well aware of the challenges that sleep-deprived, kid-consumed, network-lacking moms like her are dealing with, Julie began to interact with other women who shared her season in life. She made connections in church, the grocery store, the cleaners, and various stops along the way, inviting women to join her at a mom's group she now calls Mom to Mom. Fifty-plus moms gather, with retirees providing babysitting for their kids, to converse with other adults, explore their options to make life fun, and thrive as moms. Julie also draws them to their Savior through her energetic, relatable teaching from God's Word. (In case any of you are in that season, find Julie's website at silverlinings4moms.com.)

I have known Judy since I was eighteen, and she is still as attractive as she was then. Kids are drawn to her because it is obvious that she loves them. For more than thirty-five years, she has used her gift of teaching to reach the hearts and minds of the children entrusted to her. I have heard some say that such efforts on behalf of children are a waste of time and talent. Judy, however, has never wavered in her belief that serving children matters. She has the incredible privilege of influencing young lives for eternity.

These women are different in age, personality, education, and economic status, and yet each one is using her gifting in a unique way to impact the world around her. You can too! It's teamwork. God uses people He gifts to impact the world with those gifts, and then He gets the glory. The team is not complete if you fail to use or develop your gift. In fact, Scripture reminds us not to neglect our spiritual gifts (see 1 Timothy 4:14). When we use the gifts God gives us in the mission He created for us, our joy, fulfillment, and influence are unparalleled.

USING MY GIFT

Because I have the gift of encouragement, God leads me to do some tasks that others may deem unnecessary, such as encouraging someone with words, a call, an e-mail, a text, or a handwritten note or card. My efforts may not always be valued, but I must use the gift God blessed me with for the people He leads me to.

I mentioned above that the Tebows are a very competitive family. It made sense, then, that Family Olympics was the theme of our family vacation a couple of years ago. I'm not revealing who came up with the idea, but our family and special friends were all in.

In the first game on the first day, we played a version of beach basketball. Like the rest of my crew, I was ready to sacrifice for the team. Or so I thought, until I actually did sacrifice. The goal was to grab the ball from the opponent and be the first to make a basket, then get back in line. In my uncoordinated effort, running barefoot on the sand, I slipped and hurt my foot. I made the basket and kept playing. My team won.

My kids don't have much sympathy for wimps, so of course Mom cannot be one. After a few "shake it off" remarks, I continued playing games for the rest of the day. "You probably just twisted it a little," "You'll be okay," and "Take one for the team" were some of the compassionate comments I received.

My foot began to turn the color of the sky during a solar eclipse. "Should I have a doctor check it out?" I asked.

"It is just bruised," "It couldn't be broken," "You can sit out some games," they responded.

I could barely walk, so I resorted to the sit-down games. There was only one. I sat on the sidelines, enjoyed the grandkids, and cheered for my team.

"In all my years of practice, I have never seen anyone walk on a foot that badly broken! How have you been walking all week?" my longtime podiatrist exclaimed as he looked at the X-ray. He called the foot surgeon and immediately put me in a boot.

For months of travel to speaking events, I was wheeled through airports. Early on, I had to thank the Lord by faith and see what new influence there would be from my rolling chair. Tip money, a smile, and an interest in my "drivers" resulted in great conversations and witnessing opportunities. I met a variety of interesting airport personnel as I passed through different cities.

One special memory took place in a large airport in the city where I had a speaking event later in the evening. My wheelchair pusher inquired about my message for the event. I told her a little about my pro-life story; then she told me hers. She became pregnant at fifteen, and her grandmother took her to what she thought was an abortion clinic. But it was really a pregnancy center, and the kind ladies who worked there shared with her about her option for life. She cried when she spoke of her wonderful thirty-year-old son. She had never shared her story before, but I'm often privileged to be the first person to hear such stories. I sensed God using my gift as I encouraged her to think of how she could influence others to choose life.

I arrived early at my event and met the woman in charge, who was new to her event-planning job. She seemed a little upset, and I asked if I could help. She told me that the two people expected to give their testimonies that night had both canceled at the last minute, leaving her in a difficult position. When I told her about my new friend who had a great story, I asked if she wanted to take a chance on inviting this woman to participate. She perked up, excited about the possibility, and so I got out my phone and set the wheels in motion.

As dinner was being served, my new friend joined us. She had dressed up and was a little nervous but so excited. She spoke right before I did. As she shared her story, her voice quivered, but her face lit up and her smile broadened. Tears filled her eyes, as well as the eyes of many in the audience, when she related her happy ending—her son.

After the event, interested new friends gathered around to thank her for her courage and comment on her story. That night she found her calling, her purpose, her opportunity for influence. She was radiant and energized. The ladies from the pregnancy center invited her to be part of their team, and she eagerly accepted. Their ministry was new and they needed help. My friend needed to help. I marveled at how God put them together as only He could do. I loved being the middleman—or woman. What a privilege to influence others with the gift God gave me! What an amazing God!

How can you discover your mission, the good works God has created for you to do? Take time to pray, asking God to reveal His plans for you. Read the Scripture passages that deal with spiritual gifts and check out resources to try to identify your gifts. Look around you and see what areas in your life energize you. Ask your close friends and family what they think are your gifts. Do what I did, and ask the Lord to confirm a specific gift you think He gave you. Consider the people and the needs around you and where you might have an impact. And then begin. Don't worry about getting it perfect. Keep communicating with the Lord, and believe that He will direct you to the people and places where you can do good works and have godly influence.

NAPKINS OF INFLUENCE

Sometimes when I'm traveling, a flight attendant will recognize me or read my name on the passenger list but not want to bother me. That's when I get a note scribbled on an airplane napkin—not a bad substitute for notepaper when your options are limited. My collection of napkins is growing. I received another one last week from a flight attendant who thanked me for raising a son who serves as a role model for her son. I never tire of receiving such notes, because they remind me of the amazing things God has done in my life. The only napkins I received in the early days were ones I picked up after meals. I was a tired, overwhelmed mom, learning to homeschool, adapting to missionary life, figuring out my place in the world. But I knew God had given me a mission. At the beginning of our poems, we can't see how they end.

What would happen if you decided that when you put this book down, you would influence people on purpose through the mission God has created for you? God designed you for influence. Your role is to seek Him by faith, day by day, for grace to live out the perfect plan He has for you. God's part is to accomplish more than we could ask or think according to the power, the miraculous motivating power, that works within us (see Ephesians 3:20). And heaven will reveal the ripple effects when we fulfill our God-created missions.

PASSION

The last component of the miraculous motivating power of influence is passion. Positive influence is driven by a relentless passion with a specific aim. When we are passionate about loving the people in our spheres and making a positive impact on our world, others take notice and are motivated to follow our example. My sons admire the courageous life of William Wallace of *Braveheart* fame. Because of his passion for Scotland, he led a whole country to fight for freedom.

Although some portraits of Jesus paint Him as tranquil and soft-spoken, the Gospels are replete with stories of Jesus' passion that leads to true freedom. Angry that the money changers were doing business in the Temple, Jesus threw them out with a whip. He called the disciples to make the radical choice to follow Him, informing them in advance that most of them would give up their lives for the sake of the gospel. From His prayers in the garden until He cried out, "It is finished" and gave up His spirit, no greater example of passion exists than the last hours of Jesus' life.

We should follow Jesus' example and fulfill our missions with passion, enthusiasm, and joy. Passion demonstrates that we care. Our passion reflects our priorities and fuels us to keep going when we encounter challenges—and not to give up on our efforts to influence others for good. The first letters of the word *enthusiasm* are "en thus," which are close to the Greek words for "in God." I'm enthusiastic about my family and the incredible opportunities God gives us to positively influence others. And passion that springs from our joy in the Lord can powerfully motivate those with whom we share it. Ordinary women like you and me who display godly passion have the privilege of initiating extraordinary ripples of life-impacting influence.

> "You shall love the Lord your God with
> all your heart, and with all your soul,
> and with all your mind, and with all
> your strength." The second is this, "You
> shall love your neighbor as yourself."
> There is no other commandment
> greater than these.
>
> MARK 12:30-31

Chapter 15

LIVING WITH PASSION

Seconds after leading his team to a miraculous win over the Miami Dolphins, my youngest son spontaneously dropped to his knees in gratitude to God. His passion was contagious, affecting the other Denver Broncos players and those who watched from all over the world. His gesture became known as "Tebowing," and the term was trademarked and even added to some dictionaries.

Timmy is passionate about football and now baseball, but he's also passionate about his mission to share the gospel of Christ with as many people as possible and to fight on behalf of kids worldwide who cannot fight for themselves. We should all fulfill our missions with passion, which can be defined as deeply felt emotion or intense enthusiasm that comes from God. Passion fuels us, energizing us to act in support of a person or cause. Without passion, we won't be able to positively influence others.

WHEN WE LACK PASSION

Recently I spoke at a well-attended fund-raiser for a ministry. The more I learned about the significant impact of this nonprofit, the more excited I was to share specifics with the assembled guests. My role was to draw the crowd and share my life-affirming story. I preferred, however, to intertwine my story with valid points about the featured ministry, even though my responsibility didn't include persuading the audience to pledge support. I tried to build up to a climax for the director of the ministry, who followed me to offer closing remarks. Like the other guests, I was eager to hear what she had to say.

My bubble of enthusiasm began to leak as she spoke. With a solemn expression and a monotone voice, she made several points I can't remember. Another person with a ho-hum spirit thanked people for coming and sat down. Then the bubble burst for me, and I could only imagine what others were thinking. We all have options for investing our time and money. Why should we choose a particular ministry if those who are involved are not enthusiastic about the people they are helping and the way God is working through their organization?

What was missing? *Passion!* For the few minutes allotted me, I could be a passionate spokesperson. When I passed the baton, however, it was dropped. This isn't about having a certain personality; people can exhibit passion in different ways. It's really about being deeply invested in something. When we believe strongly in a cause, a natural response should be to exhibit passion. Passion shows we care.

PASSION FOR THE TEAM!

No one who knew my mom would doubt her passionate love for her grandchildren. Her friends knew she adored them; she looked forward to every phone call and visit and read their cards and letters over and over. At her funeral, every one of her seven grandchildren stood, faced the many people who attended the service, and proudly proclaimed, "Grandma loved me the most!" Mom's passion for her grandchildren demonstrated that they were her most prized possessions. They knew beyond a doubt that she loved them. I hope I can follow her lead.

My mother was also passionate about her favorite college team. It was the university my dad attended, where my husband and I graduated along with several of our kids, and where our son played football and won two national championships. The team fight song was the first song I remember singing as a child. Our kids grew up sleeping under bedspreads showcasing the team colors and logo, and those college colors are obvious on our walls and in our closets. When passion is referenced, sports is often the subject. Our mental image of passion is an energetic athlete, a fired-up coach, or a boisterous fan. But if we can be passionate about a football or soccer team, can't we display that same passion for passing on what matters most to us? And in sports, a victory this week doesn't ensure a victory next week, so passion can rise and fall with wins and losses. Should our passion for what really matters vary that much?

Not for my husband. His passion is consistent, especially when it comes to his family team—me, his children, and his grandchildren— and the gospel. Everyone in our family is secure because Bob's passion for us is clearly demonstrated. We know he loves us! When our family gathered recently, one of the kids spoke for the group: "Dad, none of your children ever had to wonder if you believed in them." I'm so thankful for a husband who is passionate about our children— and their children, and me! Bob and I hope to demonstrate to the onlookers that it's possible to remain passionate about a marriage of many years. Our kids like to see us hold hands and enjoy being together. Passion doesn't have to diminish in time, but it may develop a grayish tint!

PASSION FOR THE GOSPEL

It's impossible to estimate the ripple effects from my husband's passion for the Good News. His passion draws people to Jesus, the One who transforms lives for eternity. More than a million lives a year indicate a decision to trust Christ through the preaching of Bob and his American and Filipino staff, as well as the hundreds of people who join his mission trips. His nearly sixty Filipino staff are passionate and driven like their leader. Everyone in our family has been influenced by my husband's all-consuming passion for the gospel, as you'll see in the stories below.

After our oldest son, Robby, graduated from college, he worked as an area director for the Fellowship of Christian Athletes, exactly thirty years after his father held the same job as the first director in the city where we live. Robby mirrored his dad's passion to impact student athletes and coaches with the gospel. My husband always thinks big—I mean *really* big. Robby has Bob's passion and optimism, and he came up with a plan to use the influence of his job to impact the families in our community with the gospel through a big event. He talked well-known celebrities such as ESPN personalities, singers, and athletes into participating—without pay, of course. He persuaded a hotel to provide rooms for out-of-town celebrities and restaurants to donate food. Anything that was needed, Robby somehow got donated. His large event committee consisted of everyone from politicians, ministers, students, and businesspeople to local church volunteers, friends, and family. The coliseum was rented at way below market price for Night of Champions, which was billed as a family event. There were plenty of detractors who voiced their concerns: "Nothing like this has ever been done before." "The costs for this kind of event are prohibitive." "No one will show up." They hadn't counted on passion—Robby's as well as that of everyone else associated with the event—fueling their hard work.

I sat in the audience with more than eight thousand people who showed up. The crowd was entertained and inspired. The music and speakers were first-class. At the conclusion of the event, Robby introduced his brother Timmy, who shared the gospel. Then Bob invited those who wanted to ask Jesus to be their Savior to pray with him. I wiped away tears, because I didn't want to miss one second of the stream of people coming forward to talk to the many "counselors" from local churches. It was, indeed, a Night of Champions—champions who planned, prayed, worked tirelessly on details, counseled, spoke, and attended. What influence resulted from a passion for the gospel!

Several years later, I was at a football game when a woman approached me. "Mrs. Tebow, my life will never be the same because I attended your family's Night of Champions. I was lost without a reason to keep going. I was so moved by the whole evening, and I gave my life to Christ that night. Words cannot express my gratitude."

It happened again last year. A cute twentysomething girl tapped me on the shoulder at Night to Shine, the prom for kids with special needs that our son's foundation hosts. "Mrs. Tebow, ten years ago tonight I attended Night of Champions because I wanted to see your son and the other celebrities. I saw them, but I also met Jesus. My life changed that night."

Amazing! My husband's passion has influenced our family to love the gospel message in a way I cannot put on paper. It has marked our lives and the lives of those we share it with—like these two women I met by chance on earth but will see again in heaven.

Our daughter Katie received an e-mail a few years ago from a girl she barely remembers from her college days. She wrote to thank Katie for inviting her to a Christian event on campus. That night, she heard the gospel for the first time, and a short while later, she prayed to ask Jesus to be her Savior. She wrote that it was because of Katie's passion that she decided to go to the event and see what all the excitement was about. Katie's passion is sweeter and softer than my husband's but still irresistible.

Passion may look a little different on each person, but there is no denying its influential power! What does your passion look like? It might not be loud, insistent, or bubbly. It may be that in a quiet way you let others know what is most important to you, and you invite them to be a part of it.

The day before the 2008 national championship game against Oklahoma, Timmy agonized about whether to change the Scripture reference he wore on his eye black. His coaches and teammates were superstitious and begged him to keep the same verse he had used in the games leading up to this one, but God prompted him to use something different. After an exciting victory to win the national championship, reporters asked about his new verse. Timmy explained that he wanted to use the very large stage to passionately proclaim what he believes to be the basis of his faith: John 3:16, "For God so loved the world, that He gave His only begotten Son, that whoever believes in Him shall not perish, but have eternal life." The night of the game and for the next few days, John 3:16 was the most googled topic in the world. More than 94 million people googled John 3:16.

I couldn't understand what motivated my husband when I first met him, but his passion for the gospel was impossible to ignore. I had never seen anyone with that drive. His passion was contagious, impacting the lives of countless students like me. He still receives letters from people he doesn't remember whose lives were changed during those college years by his passion for Jesus.

MY PASSIONS

Bob is also passionate about life in the womb. But it became my passion when God used our story about my pregnancy with Timmy to impact lives. The first time it was told on national television when

Timmy won the Heisman, I received e-mails and letters about babies who were saved because of our story. A few years later, Focus on the Family approached Timmy and me about doing a Super Bowl commercial. Even though we knew there was a possibility our passion for life could cost my son sponsors, we both agreed to do a sweet and funny thirty-second commercial. The commercial contained nothing remotely controversial, but because of the noisy opponents and the media attention, the pro-life message still got out. In fact, Barna did a survey afterward and found that our simple commercial resulted in more than 5.5 million people "having cause to rethink their stand on abortion."[1]

Bob and I met one of the people represented in that staggering number when we spoke together at the Easter sunrise service at SeaWorld. Who knew that seven thousand people would wake up before dawn to sit around Shamu's tank and listen to me tell a few stories and Bob preach the gospel? Following the service, we agreed to meet with the people who had lined up to shake our hands. The very last person in line was a young lady who had watched our commercial. She pulled out her phone and, with tears in her eyes, showed us a picture of her little girl, saved because of our commercial. Only God could orchestrate such influence.

Our passions are often linked to our spiritual gifts, just as our missions are. It's true for Bob; his gift of evangelism and his passion for the gospel are woven together in a knot that's impossible to pull apart. They both fuel his mission, which is to share the gospel with as many people as possible, especially those who have never once heard it.

Even before I pinpointed my spiritual gift, my passion has always been to intentionally encourage those in my sphere. I love Hebrews 3:13, which says, "Encourage one another day after day, as long as it is still called 'Today.'" Over the years, the Lord graciously made me aware of ways to live out my passion. I began simply. My passion for encouragement can be illustrated in something as simple as a smile. I once asked my mother why I seemed to smile without thinking about it. She explained that it was because she intentionally smiled at me from the day I was born. Her words stuck in my mind, and whether I smiled at my children as a result of her example or because of a natural inclination, they are all "smilers" too. I highly recommend this influential practice. Smiling becomes a habit, a way of life. It sets us apart and demonstrates that we care about people. My goal as I walk through a store or an airport is to smile at those I pass. It's not always easy when I'm exhausted or in a city where nobody smiles, but when we're friendly, we represent Jesus. Smiling doesn't take anything from us, but it gives something to the recipient. When we recount specific blessings, our spirits become grateful, and joy bubbles up from the inside, causing us to smile. I picture Jesus as often smiling, drawing people to Himself.

Joy is not the same as happiness because it's not based on circumstance. Rather, it's a gift from God and the fruit of a right relationship with Him. To quote Bob, "Joy is an inner delight and excitement of the spirit that involves our hope in the present and future goodness and blessing of God." We can give joy away through our words or countenance. We can feel crummy or stressed to the max and still radiate joy, because it springs from our inner life. Joy can powerfully influence those with whom we share it as we transfer the focus from ourselves to people we encounter throughout our day. When we're filled with the joy of the Lord, our countenance should reflect that love and passion. I want my life to be characterized by an external smile and an internal joy. My prayer is that God will use the combination to encourage and influence the people in my sphere.

I stopped in a store one day to purchase something minor. I can't remember what, but I do remember the cashier. I asked her how she was and listened as she told me. I lingered, although in those days

I was always in a hurry. When I offered some encouraging words, she looked at me and said, "No one has ever been interested in me before." I was stunned. I was hesitant to give her a hug, but I found out she hadn't had one in a long time. I didn't do much, but it had an impact. There have been many days when I ran in and out of a situation and never looked up or around. I'm glad I did that day.

Lord, I whispered afterward, *please help me not to overlook an opportunity to encourage someone who needs it.* Isaiah 35:3-4 reminds us to "encourage the exhausted, and strengthen the feeble. Say to those with anxious heart, 'Take courage, fear not.'"

Is your passion connected with a mission—a specific way you can use your spiritual gifts to impact those around you? Mine is influencing people on purpose for eternity. You don't need to have it all together to impact lives with your passion. I'm a broken woman in a broken world. I fall short every day, but my passion drives me to keep on. When I don't feel good or when I'm worn out from the challenges of life, health issues, responsibilities, deadlines, and difficult people, I feel disqualified, unequipped, or unworthy. There's always a reason to quit, but there's a better reason to keep going. Passion provides the determination to keep on keeping on, trusting that our work is worthwhile and that God is faithful, even when we don't see results yet. Don't quit!

Nearly every chapter is this book includes illustrations of my passion to share God stories. Stories of faith stir up faith, and our passion for the God who wrote those stories stirs up passion. And I love to share stories of putting applicable verses to tunes to help me remember them during important moments. My passion resulted from my great need. As the Lord met that need through His Spirit and His Word, I became passionate about passing on the truth about engrafting Scripture that God used to impact my life.

But I don't always sing my Scriptures. Sometimes I hang them on the wall.

THE WRITING ON THE WALL

There's no biblical command to choose a life verse, but I was pregnant with our fourth child and needed all the help I could get. Actually, it seemed more like the verse chose me: "I have set the LORD continually before me; because He is at my right hand, I will not be shaken" (Psalm 16:8). Twenty years later, to honor a milestone birthday, a close friend sent a beautiful calligraphy version of "my" verse. Another friend adhered the verse tastefully to my kitchen wall.

On the day of an important high school playoff game, I tried to teach my youngest son this principle of setting the Lord continually before him, or in other words, "pursuing God." As he was preparing for his game, he asked me for a marker and scribbled something on his hand. Since he plays quarterback, I assumed he was writing a play, which was not uncommon. He is left-handed, so he wrote on his right hand. When I hugged him after the come-from-behind win, he showed me his hand. In big, bold, black letters, he had written "GOD." It was smudged and barely readable, but I was thrilled that he got the point: He literally set the Lord on his right hand. Although I haven't written God's name on my hand, my goal each day is to set the Lord continually before me as my Master and my God.

Just this year, I was overcome by the discovery of an amazing verse: "As for me, You uphold me in my integrity, and set me before Your face forever" (Psalm 41:12, NKJV). The encouraging truth is that even when we fail to set the Lord before us, He is faithful to set me and you before Him and will hold us in front of His face—forever! God loves me even when I fail to put Him first, when I take charge of my day, when I choose to be my own master. I picture Him gently turning my face toward Him, reminding me of His love, restoring my soul (see Psalm 23:3). How can I not pass on my passion for a God like my God!

SMALL INFLUENCE, BIG IMPACT

Over time, my growing passion to encourage people in my sphere that God and His Word are trustworthy yielded ripples of influence that bring Him glory. The truth that God created me for His glory (see Isaiah 43:7) lit a fire of passion that the setbacks of life couldn't quench. God uses even our smallest influence for His purposes and His glory.

"What beautiful trees you have on your property," my friend exclaimed on her first visit to our home. Huge, flowing oak trees, flowering crape myrtles, gum trees, maples, mulberry trees, and more serve as home to squirrels, a variety of birds, lizards, and who knows what else. One tree still has a frayed rope that held a tire, the target for countless footballs. Another has branches just the right size for a little girl to sit on while she wrote her stories and poems.

God uses even our smallest influence for His purposes and His glory.

Quite a contrast to the comment another friend's husband made after we first purchased our property at a government auction twenty-six years ago: "Why would you live here, without one tree?" Those words stung at first. But even without one tree, our family was beyond excited about our new home because we believed the Lord had given us a gift—a beautiful house and property that was far beyond what we had paid for and prayed for.

When we returned from the mission field in 1991, we trusted the Lord to provide a home, and we tried to be patient while we waited on God's provision. At a government auction the next year, we came prepared to make a bid for a four-year-old home on forty-four acres of land, left vacant when the previous owner went to prison for insurance fraud. My husband prayed that if God wanted us to live in that place, He would deliver it to us just as He delivered the giant Goliath to David. Bob's dream for our three sons was to live in a place where they could learn responsibility and develop a strong work ethic. They would later work side by side with their dad to put up fences, learn firsthand the laws of the harvest, care for a variety of animals, and play lots of ball.

Bob pictured a place of ministry where we could have life-impacting influence through bonfires for families and friends, church parties, homeschool gatherings, mission meetings, and so much more. We polled the gang on their specific requests, and the home we were bidding on met even the small desires of all seven of our hearts. The auctioneer dragged out the bidding process on other properties that were being auctioned, and we wondered if "our" property would end up out of our price range. When he got to the home we wanted, we put in a bid. Then, in what seemed like a snap of his fingers, he shouted, "Going, going, gone!" before anyone could outbid us. The large audience was stunned. Our family and friends who accompanied us to the upscale auction knew God was involved. One family member would later come to know Christ because she could think of no other explanation for what she witnessed that day.

We were beyond grateful and happily committed our home to the Lord, pleading with Him to make it a place where everyone who set foot on our property would be impacted. Chapters could be written about twenty-six years of ministry from our home base, and very few days go by that I do not thank the Lord for His gift to us. Even if there were no trees when we first moved in.

We often judge too soon! Property is assessed before trees are planted; children are judged before they grow; dreams are evaluated before they materialize; marriages may start out rocky but then flourish through God's grace. We don't know what potential will be realized and how prayers will be answered. Influence is like that. A word of encouragement, a truth taught, an example lived, an unexpected gift, a teacher's belief, a friend's note, and a mother's hug can all have ripple effects we didn't anticipate. The list of small but impactful ways to influence is endless.

Trees start small too. Some begin when a bird drops a seed. Our desire was to have more trees on our property, and my mother contributed a small tree from her yard, which we planted with care in a special place. A larger tree was transplanted from the home we sold; the new owners understood our attachment to a tree we had planted there years before and let us take it. My sister-in-law bought fledgling trees to help the cause. Most of our trees were planted on purpose for shade or landscaping, spaced to accommodate a football field in the front and a batting cage in the back. But some just grew while we were busy with life. If only the friend who made the "no tree" comment could see our property now!

Just as trees started small but grew and transformed our property, so God can use tiny seeds of influence to transform lives. The God who grew the trees is also responsible for one of my favorite stories.

"What will you do this summer?" I asked the sweet, intelligent daughter of my close friend years ago. Our conversation was brief because church was over and people were scattering.

"Well," she exclaimed, "I plan to spend the whole summer deciding on my major."

"Did you know there is a great verse that I often apply when I need wisdom and direction?" I said.

"Really?" she responded, with obvious interest.

"It's Psalm 32:8," I told her. "'I will instruct you and teach you in the way which you should go; I will counsel you with My eye upon you.'"

We said good-bye, but the influence continued.

Near the end of the summer, our family and my young friend were at a wedding. "How was your summer?" I inquired.

"Wonderful," she replied with enthusiasm. "I quoted and prayed your verse all summer, and as a result, I decided on my major."

I could hardly wait for her next words.

"Biomedical engineering," she stated calmly, as if it were a common major.

Wow, I thought, laughing to myself, *I taught that same verse to my children, and none of them chose biomedical engineering.* (Just in case our son Peter reads this book, I need to insert a disclaimer: He has a degree in computer science engineering.)

Some years later, our families were together again at an event. Bubbling over with enthusiasm, my young friend rushed up to me, holding the hand of a nice-looking young man.

"Nathan, I want you to meet the lady who helped me choose my major," she said. "Mrs. Tebow, this is my fiancé, Nathan."

Influence! I shared one short verse with a high school girl. But God did something with that seed, enabling my young friend to find a field that she cares deeply about. Now, with a doctorate in biomedical engineering, my friend is researching the means to repair injured spinal cords.

We only plant seedlings, but over time, God grows trees that provide beauty, shade, and life. I love the God who weaves together our small efforts and His big plan. I also love the fact that God gives this priceless privilege of influence, no matter how small, to every woman. Like the Bible story about the small boy who offered his bread and fish to Jesus to feed a large crowd, God turns our small offerings into a huge banquet. It doesn't matter whether our spheres of influence are big or small. What matters is that we're faithful to offer what we have to the Lord and trust Him to make it grow.

God selects ordinary women to star in extraordinary God stories, ones that impact the people around them.

Live with an awareness that people in your sphere are watching to see what you really believe and who your God really is. They may make important decisions based on watching your stories. God selects ordinary women to star in extraordinary God stories, ones that impact the people around them.

Share your God stories with passion that shows how important they are to you. Our passion ties our influence with a bow and makes it a lovely gift for others.

When I walk down our half-mile road to get the mail, I pass a jasmine bush. I pause every time to smell the sweet fragrance. What a picture of our opportunity to influence others by the sweet fragrance of Jesus in our lives! Second Corinthians 2:14 says, "Thanks be to God, who always leads us in triumph in Christ, and manifests through us the sweet aroma of the knowledge of Him in every place."

Over the years we see our influence grow as we become committed to our Master and follow His lead for our lives. It keeps growing as we get to know Him and trust Him more through the study of His Manual and through prayer. It expands even further as we develop mindsets—of love, service, wisdom in our words, and eternal perspective—that make us more like Jesus. And our influence becomes the most effective when we follow God's lead to find our missions—the good works He has called us to do—and live them out with passion. All of these come together in miraculous motivating power. A favorite verse that I focus on to remind me of my power for passionate influence is 2 Corinthians 4:7: "We have this treasure in earthen vessels, so that the surpassing greatness of the power will be of God and not from ourselves." Our miraculous motivating power for ripples of influence is from God!

Every woman has the privilege to be called by the God of the universe to be part of something so much bigger than ourselves. What matters more than influencing lives for eternity?

Father, thank You for offering us lives of purpose and influence. Until we go to heaven, please give all of us the grace to be women of influence, with the ripple effects of our lives impacting the people in our spheres for all eternity.

ACKNOWLEDGMENTS

Thank you to the wonderful women at the Fedd Agency, especially Esther and Whitney, for believing in my heart to encourage women with their God-given ability for life-impacting influence.

Thank you to everyone at Tyndale, especially Jan, Sarah, and Karin, for enabling me to write the message on my heart.

Thank you to AJ Gregory for encouraging me throughout the writing process.

Thank you to my praying friends for your many faithful prayers on my behalf.

READERS' DISCUSSION GUIDE

1. In the introduction, Pam writes, "When we reflect God's character through the gifts and opportunities He gives us, we are like rocks tossed into a pond, producing ripple effects that inspire those in our spheres and beyond to think and act differently." Who has had "ripple effects" on your life? Share a story about someone who has had a strong influence on you, either negative or positive. In what ways did their influence impact your faith, your view of yourself and your future, or the direction of your life? Think about a ripple effect you can have that could positively impact the life of someone in your sphere.

2. In chapter 1, Pam tells the story of Timmy discovering, through a box of Cocoa Krispies, that little eyes were watching him and that he had the power of influence. In what ways does the idea that we all have influence inspire you, and in what ways does it intimidate you? Think about who might be watching as you go about your day. What do you think they see? What would you like them to see?

3. If you're comfortable doing so, share some of your faith story with the group. When did God become your "Master," and

how has that affected your life? In what areas do you struggle to allow Him to be the boss? Why is letting God be in control of our lives foundational to having positive influence on others?

4. In chapter 4, Pam talks about developing our "faith muscles." When we trust God once, it becomes easier to trust Him the next time. How have you seen this idea play out in your own life? Share a time when your faith muscles grew because of challenging circumstances. What is something you could trust God for today that would strengthen your faith in your big God?

5. Pam shares a number of "God stories" throughout the book that highlight how God has worked in her family over the years. Which one is your favorite? How do these stories encourage your own faith? All of us have God stories, even if they're not always dramatic. Talk about a time when you experienced an answer to prayer or saw evidence of God moving in your life.

6. Memorizing Scripture through song has been a powerful influence in Pam's life—and on those with whom she shares her favorite verses. What are some Scripture passages that have been meaningful to you? How can you increase your love for God's Word? Brainstorm some ways you could make memorizing and meditating on Scripture a more integral part of each day. What specific passage can you memorize this week?

7. In chapter 8, Pam shares, "Most women I know do not pray because they are supposed to. They pray because they have no other recourse. . . . When our burdens are the heaviest, we are driven to pray." How does your prayer life change when you are in a time of crisis? What role does prayer play in your life?

Share any approaches that have helped you learn to talk to God more frequently and intentionally.

8. How has God's love for you made a difference in your life? Think of someone you could have a positive impact on by showing him or her unconditional love: a spouse, child, friend, coworker, or neighbor. Then read the description of love in 1 Corinthians 13. What specific quality of love do you most need to work on?

9. In chapter 11, Pam writes, "A servant is focused on making those in her sphere successful." How might this description change the way you think about serving? You may already be busy serving, but is there another person or ministry who could be impacted by your service? Think of specific people who have served you. Can you think of a way to thank the special servants in your life?

10. Chapter 12 talks about the power of words. Can you think of a time when someone else's positive, encouraging words made a difference in your life? Share it with the group. How might the Scripture verses Pam includes on pages 196–198 help you consistently speak words of life to those around you?

11. Our priorities can come into sharp focus when we face a life-threatening crisis, as we see in Pam's story about Hawaii's false missile alert at the beginning of chapter 13. Why is it often difficult to remember what is most important? How can you better focus your mind on eternal things—the happy ending and heavenly rewards—and what might that change about your choices or priorities?

12. Do you feel you have a clear sense of your spiritual gifts and personal mission, as described in chapter 14? What do you

think God might have equipped you to do? What areas of ministry do you find yourself most excited about? As a group, take a few minutes to encourage each other by expressing the unique ways you see God working through each woman. Sometimes we see a gift in another woman before she sees it in herself.

13. As you look back over this book, what key ideas or stories stand out in your mind? What changes are you encouraged to make in your life to maximize the influence you can have on others? Remember, these don't have to be big. As Pam says, "God uses even our smallest influence for His purposes and His glory." Think of specific people God might be calling you to notice and impact in a new way, and pray for His direction as you seek to influence them for His Kingdom.

NOTES

CHAPTER 1: FINDING OUR PURPOSE

1. John Maxwell, *Becoming a Person of Influence: How to Positively Impact the Lives of Others* (Nashville: Thomas Nelson, 2006), 3.
2. Alexia Elejalde-Ruiz, "Employees Want Their Job to Matter, but Meaning at Work Can Be Hard to Find," *Chicago Tribune*, November 10, 2017, http://www.chicago tribune.com/business/careers/topworkplaces/ct-biz-top-workplaces-2017-main-story -meaningfulness-20170913-story.html, emphasis added.
3. Ibid.
4. The Mayflower Compact, quoted in Peter J. Marshall and David B. Manuel Jr., *The Light and the Glory* (Grand Rapids, MI: Revell, 1977, 2009), 154.

CHAPTER 2: A MASTER PLAN

1. Joey Allen, *Welcome to Heaven* (Dallas: EvanTell, 2009).

CHAPTER 3: FIRST THINGS FIRST

1. *Vine's Expository Dictionary of New Testament Words*, s. v. "lord, lordship," https:// studybible.info/vines/Lord,%20Lordship.
2. *Encyclopaedia Britannica Online*, s.v. "habit," accessed September 4, 2018, https:// www.britannica.com/topic/habit-behaviour.

CHAPTER 6: WHEN ALL ELSE FAILS (READ THE DIRECTIONS)

1. Tim Engle, "A Year of Living Wisely through Fortune Cookies," *Seattle Times*, January 24, 2011, https://www.seattletimes.com/life/lifestyle/a-year-of-living-wisely -through-fortune-cookies/; Matt Kelsey, "Welcome to My Daily Fortune!" *My Daily Fortune* (blog), February 1, 2012, http://mydailyfortune.blogspot.com/.

CHAPTER 8: A RUNNING CONVERSATION

1. Jim Cymbala, *Fresh Wind, Fresh Fire* (Grand Rapids: Zondervan, 2018), 52.
2. Ray C. Stedman, *Talking with My Father* (Grand Rapids: Discovery House Publishers, 1997), 66.

CHAPTER 11: SERVING ISN'T FOR SISSIES

1. UnitedHealthcare and VolunteerMatch, "Do Good Live Well Study: Reviewing the Benefits of Volunteering," March 2010, https://cdn.volunteermatch.org/www/about /UnitedHealthcare_VolunteerMatch_Do_Good_Live_Well_Study.pdf.

CHAPTER 15: LIVING WITH PASSION

1. "Super Bowl Ad Research: New Barna Study Examines Tebow/Focus Commercial," Barna, February 15, 2010, https://www.barna.com/research/super-bowl-ad-research -new-barna-study-examines-tebowfocus-commercial/.

ABOUT THE AUTHOR

PAM TEBOW travels and speaks across the country, encouraging audiences to use the incredible influence God has given them to eternally impact their world. Pam has appeared on *Good Morning America* and has won national awards for her ministry work, including Eagle Forum's Woman of the Year and Witness in the Public Square in 2012, Commission for Women's Inspiring Woman of the Year in 2013, Extraordinary Woman of the Year in 2014, and the National Pro-Life Recognition Award in 2017. Pam graduated with honors from the College of Journalism and Communications at the University of Florida. She and her husband, Bob, live in Florida and have five children and eight grandchildren.